D0001186

BOOKCELLAR
FREEBIE

The Incredible Bread Machine

The Incredible Bread Machine

A Study of Capitalism, Freedom, and the State

Second Edition

by R. W. Grant

Tom Smith drawings by Richard Stein

Fox & Wilkes
San Francisco

Copyright © 1999 by R. W. Grant
All rights reserved.

Published by
Fox & Wilkes
938 Howard Street, Ste. 202
San Francisco, CA 94103

ISBN 0-930073-31-2 (pb)
ISBN 0-930073-32-0 (hc)

Printed in the USA.

Contents

Part Four:
The Principles Applied—
Alternatives to Political Force

Part Five:
What Now?

Author's Foreword

In the early 1960s, as a young engineer in the Southern California aerospace industry, I had little interest in political philosophy. But I had a friend at work (Hughes Aircraft) named Davey Alders who was absolutely intense on the subject. (Our nickname for Davey was "Burning Spear.") He urged me to attend a lecture series created by a unique and prickly character named Andrew Galambos.

The portly Galambos, an astrophysicist by training, offered a popular series of courses on the theory of capitalism and property rights. This was heady stuff. My background was a sort-of Pangloss Republicanism: this is the best of all possible worlds, and there's no other way to run things anyway. Accordingly, I was intrigued when Al Lowi, one of the Galambos instructors, suggested that education should be a function of the marketplace rather than of government. Who could take such ideas seriously?

But by chance, a school board dispute had erupted in my community a year or so before, and the bullying tactics of the California Teachers Association had made a lasting impression. The seeds planted by Galambos and Lowi began to take root. One result can be seen in Chapter Eighteen, "Escape from Public Education."

I was also impressed at the time by the ideas of novelist/philosopher Ayn Rand. Her dissection of the morality of altruism was highly illuminating, and the effect can be seen in the discussions of Chapter Eight.

However, I was somewhat put off by Rand's antagonism to religion. I am not religious in any formal sense, but I appreciate the fact that the Judeo-Christian tradition seeks to uphold certain values which we abandon at our peril. As Richard Wheeler once put it, "Today we abhor lampshades made of human skin; but tomorrow, who knows? It is precisely those persons who are not anchored to a set of eternal values who hanker the most for novelties." (Chapter Seven). Still, Ayn Rand's philosophy has been immensely helpful to many—myself included.

The growing libertarian ferment of the 1960s was the reverse image of the more visible New Left radicalism of Tom Hayden, the "Weathermen," et al. While they were into Marx, Lenin, Marcuse and vandalism, we were into Hayek, von Mises, Rothbard and Bastiat. The fine libertarian magazine *Reason* had its genesis in this turbulent period.

Inspired by all these interesting new ideas (new to me, that is), and inspired as well by the anti-capitalist tantrums of the New Left, I began to compose a long satirical poem called *Tom Smith and His Incredible Bread Machine*. Tom was an inventor who devised an amazing machine which could produce bread for under a penny a loaf, and for the first time in history the world was well-fed. But in the end poor Tom was vilified by precisely those who benefitted from his productive genius:

> "What right had he to get so rich
> On other people's hunger?"

This was the story, of course, of that incredible bread machine, capitalism. Around 1963 the Galambos people put on a symposium for past graduates, of which there were now hundreds, and a reading of *Tom Smith* was the poem's first public presentation. Part I is given in the Appendix.

The ideas implicit in the poem appeared in prose form in 1966 in a text entitled *The Incredible Bread Machine*. The book addressed two questions which had bothered me from the start: What about the "robber barons"? And what about the Great Depression? Wasn't government intervention required to solve these two problems? (No.) The balance of the book dealt with the three principles of a free society and their application to contemporary problems. (I was greatly indebted to Dr. Murray Rothbard for his guidance on the business cycle and the Great Depression.)

However, no self-respecting publisher would touch these far-out ideas by a total unknown. Accordingly, the book was privately published by a libertarian friend, Richard Bray. To our great satisfaction, the book was kindly received in the libertarian circles of the day, and showed up in a couple of university courses.

By this time I had developed an active interest in politics, and was an enthusiastic supporter of Barry Goldwater. However, I had no use at all for Richard Nixon. He pretended to be a champion of the market economy, but was the first president in U.S. history to impose price and wage controls during peacetime. I remember a revealing story Bob LeFevre told me years later. He had been an aide to Nixon during one of his previous campaigns in California, and had expressed his concern about some statist utterance by the candidate. Nixon explained, "To accomplish anything, we have to win. I will do whatever it takes, and say whatever it takes to get elected."

Unfortunately, this win-at-all-costs mentality is not the exception among professional politicians, but the rule. As a result, principles are soon forgotten, pushed aside by the latest opinion poll. Because of Nixon I not only left the Republican party, I dropped out of politics entirely, and didn't vote for years. Today I am a registered Independent. Chapter Twenty-Four, "The Limits of Political Action," was written around that time, and reflects my jaundiced view of politics. The lesson here is still valid: politics can be useful as an educational effort or as a delaying action, but not as a "solution." Our problems will not be solved by political force, but only by private effort in a free society.

It was around this time that I joined Sy Leon in his tongue-in-cheek effort "The League of Non-Voters," whose goal was a line on the ballot declaring "None of the Above." The effort bore some modest fruit, and some of the ballots in Nevada now include this option.

Another co-founder of the League was our good friend, the ubiquitous Charles Estes. Over the years it was he who was constantly arranging the discussion groups, supper clubs, symposia, etc. which served to hold together the loose network of like-minded people in the Southern California area.

It was Estes who introduced me to the aforementioned Bob LeFevre, another influential teacher in those days. LeFevre was the proprietor of Rampart College, a free-market educational enterprise. An outstanding speaker, he conducted well-attended courses on the principles of human liberty. He leaned toward pacifism (as I saw it) which put me off a bit, but his ideas on crime and punishment were provocative, and emerge in Chapter Twenty-One.

As these new perspectives crystalized, I began to realize that the highly-regarded liberal arts university from which I had graduated (Wesleyan, in Middletown, Connecticut.) had offered little about the principles on which a free society is based. I recall my economics professor distributing campaign literature for leftist Henry Wallace in the 1948 election. Fortunately, I was a lousy student and didn't absorb much of what he had to offer. In later years, however, I became increasingly aware, with many others, of the leftward drift in higher education. This concern perhaps comes through in Chapter Twelve, "The Death of Diana."

In 1974 the *Incredible Bread Machine* received a boost when a San Diego think tank, World Research, distributed thousands of copies of their condensed version of the book to organizations and universities around the country. In addition, they created an entertaining animated film of the Tom Smith poem, which was also widely distributed.

In 1978 a revised version of the poem, illustrated by the talented Richard Stein, appeared in hardcover. I was especially grateful to Captain James Lovell, commander of *Apollo 13*, who offered the generous blurb that "*Tom Smith* should be a primer for all MBA students."

Over the years the Tom Smith parable continued to achieve some modest attention in libertarian and business circles. In 1988 Michael Milken, who evidently saw something of Tom Smith in his own troubles with the government, distributed several thousand copies at his final High Yield Bond Conference in Los Angeles. In 1998 the Competitive Enterprise Institute, a Washington think tank, reprinted Part I of the Tom Smith saga for use in its educational efforts regarding antitrust issues. Tom lives on.

As for the present text: A couple of years ago Andrea Millen Rich of Laissez Faire Books contacted me about an updated version of the *Incredible Bread Machine*. I was pleased to hear that her office still receives inquiries about the book, now out of print nearly thirty years, and was delighted to accept her proposal. However, it still took a year or so of patient nudging by Andrea before I finally got busy. I am indebted to Andrea, and to her associate David Brooks, for their interest, encouragement, and thoughtful suggestions.

Times change. Perhaps we don't fully realize how much public attitudes toward government have shifted over the past three decades. I remember writing a local TV station in 1970 asking for time to rebut a "public service" program produced by the National Education Association which extolled the virtues of public education—while urging more spending, of course. The program director replied that since my view was shared by "no significant body of qualified and reliable opinion," no rebuttal was called for. Today, of course, public education is in a death spiral and private alternatives proliferate to fill the void. In many other areas as well (as described here in the final chapter) people are moving away from the institutions of political force and toward the voluntary alternatives of the marketplace.

Times change. Liberty works. Principles matter.

And we are winning!

R. W. Grant
March, 1999

Part One:
Historical Notes—
The Laissez Faire Capitalism
That Never Was

1: The Robber Barons

The evils attributed to nineteenth century capitalism more often arose because of interference with it.

Nineteenth century American capitalism, we are told, was a savage and ruthless system of "dog-eat-dog." Grasping and unprincipled men—the "robber barons"—seized control of vital areas of the economy and thereupon exacted tribute from an entire nation. This was "laissez-faire capitalism," and it led to fraud, depredation, ruin and despair. It was not until an aroused public demanded government regulation that the economy began to serve the many rather than the few. The Interstate Commerce Act, the Sherman Antitrust Act, the Clayton Act—gradually government participation began to bring order out of chaos, and social justice out of economic tyranny. So we are told. This is the accepted version of history promoted in every grade school and high school in the country, and in most universities as well.

But is this version of history correct?

Is it possible that this nation never really had laissez-faire capitalism? The Constitution itself explicitly provides for a tariff—in itself a major abrogation of a genuinely free economy. From the start the economy was riddled with subsidies, franchises, special privileges, immunities and political favors bestowed upon this or that favored interest. And is it possible that the multitude of evils attributed to nineteenth century American capitalism arose not because of capitalism but because of this type of interference with it?

This is an unsettling thought to those whose constant cry is for still greater government control in order to "protect the public," or to "help make capitalism work." One such person, for example, was Matthew Josephson, who wrote in 1934 an influential anticapitalist book called *The Robber Barons*. In the foreword to the 1962 edition Josephson again spoke in terms of the "freebooting capitalists," and it was with apparent pique that he observed,

Of late years...a group of academic historians have constituted themselves what may be called a revisionist school, which reacts against the critical spirit of the 1930s. They reject the idea that our nineteenth-century barons-of-the-bags may have been inspired by the same motives animating the ancient barons-of-the-crags—who, by force of arms, instead of corporate combinations, monopolized strategic valley roads or mountain passes through which commerce flowed. ...

This business of rewriting our history—perhaps in conformity to current fashions in intellectual reaction—has unpleasant connotations to my mind, recalling the propaganda schemes used in authoritarian societies, and the "truth factories" in George Orwell's antiutopian novel *1984*.[1]

It was the theme of Josephson's book (and it remains the conventional wisdom to the present day) that capitalism caused and government cured the excesses of the nineteenth century. He is wrong on both counts, and it is not necessary to "rewrite history" to demonstrate that fact. One need only read Josephson's book, which describes not only the depredations of certain nineteenth century scoundrels but also the government intervention which made it all possible. It is the unintended lesson of Josephson's book that the real villain was not capitalism but government! Consider, for example, the famous fight in 1872 for control of the hapless Erie Railroad.

Jay Gould, Jim Fisk and old Daniel Drew were indeed scoundrels without peer; the victim was the Erie. Josephson writes,

The Erie was then a great trunk line, nearly 500 miles long, plying between the harbor of New York and the Great Lakes. It had been built at a cost of $15,000,000, partly through state subsidies....Its rickety, lamp-lit trains, its weak iron rails had brought disaster and scandal, such as clung to its whole career; and when Daniel Drew, by virtue of his loans to the company, became its treasurer and master after the panic of 1857, it was soon clear that the flinty master was not in the least interested in the Erie Railroad as a public utility or highway of traffic.

His strategic position gave him intimate knowledge of the large railroad's affairs which he used only to advance his private speculations. The very decrepitude of the rolling stock, the occurrence of horrendous accidents, were a financial "good" to the Speculative Director, who used even the treasury of his railroad to augment his short-selling of its own stock....[2]

Gould and Fisk were soon "insiders" who might know in advance when the Erie shares might rise or fall, and smiling times began for them. Only a single cloud disturbed the busy gentlemen of the Erie Ring; it was the ponderous encroachments of a berserk force in the railroad field, the aged Cornelius Vanderbilt, whose seemingly resistless advance menaced them all with extinction.[3]

In a free economy if a company is mismanaged, an opposition group of stockholders can mount a "hostile takeover." It was the redoubtable Commodore Vanderbilt who led the opposition to the Erie Ring.

(Vanderbilt was no mere "freebooter"; he was a builder. This remarkable man had already created an eleven-million-dollar shipping empire when, at 68, he fashioned from a conglomeration of lesser roads the famous New York Central, in its day the most extensive railroad system in the world. What Vanderbilt touched turned to gold, for he ran his properties well and profitably.)

Day after day Vanderbilt bought heavily of Erie stock, seeking a controlling interest. Yet, it seemed, the more he bought the more appeared on the market. Fresh, brand-new shares. The Erie Ring—now under the masterful direction of Jay Gould—was simply printing stock faster than Vanderbilt could buy it. Said Jim Fisk in public: "If this printing press don't break down, I'll be damned if I don't give the old hog all he wants of Erie!"[4]

This, of course, was simply a case of fraud, and Vanderbilt sought an injunction. Had the government of New York State performed its proper task of punishing force and fraud, Drew and Fisk and Gould would have been restrained. But it was Vanderbilt who was finally defeated. Not by the Erie Ring, however, but by the gentlemen of the New York State Legislature. Those selfless public servants, selling out to the highest bidder, passed the nation's first "anti-takeover" measure, a special law legalizing the ring's actions.

[T]he legislature...passed the measure substantially as Gould desired it, and Governor Fenton, also believed to have been "assiduously cultivated," signed the bill....[Gould's] actions were made legal; his rule of the 800-mile trunk line was unchallenged.[5]

One can sympathize with the victimized Erie stockholders. Had Vanderbilt's takeover effort been successful, their investment would have been saved and the Erie would have been turned into a profitable line; profitable for the stockholders and profitable for the public. As it was, the Erie had by now been so thoroughly looted that it was unable to pay another dividend for sixty-nine years. But Josephson makes no distinction between

Vanderbilt and the men of the Erie Ring. To Josephson all were "robber barons." Moreover, many people today cite such episodes as the Fight For the Erie as horrible examples of dog-eat-dog, laissez-faire capitalism. But it was not capitalism that delivered the coup-de-grace to the Erie; it was the New York State Legislature.

In spite of his ill-concealed hostility to capitalism, Josephson continues to provide example after example of just where the real trouble lay: not with capitalism, but with government. One of the more infamous frauds in U.S. history was the "Credit Mobilier," a sort of construction company owned by those who controlled the Union Pacific Railroad. Capitalism has received the blame for what happened, but what Josephson describes is surely not capitalism.

> In short order the Pacific Railroad bill was passed [1862], and the two companies which undertook the colossal affair were given federal charters. The Union Pacific, building westward from the Missouri River, was granted 12,000,000 acres of unknown land, in alternate sections ten miles deep, and also $27,000,000 in 6-percent, thirty-year government bonds as a first mortgage. The Central Pacific, building from the sea eastward to meet the Union Pacific, was similarly granted 9,000,000 acres of land and $24,000,000 in government bonds.[6]

This was how the Credit Mobilier promoters got their capital—not by private investment, but by government subsidy. Subsidies, franchises, land grants and associated government involvements are hardly characteristics of laissez-faire capitalism. And with booty like this at stake, the result was inevitable. The men who became involved were not interested in building a railroad—they were out to milk it. Through the Credit Mobilier they subcontracted to themselves the actual construction work, and costs to the railroad skyrocketed, while the profits to the Credit Mobilier were immense.

> For this work the directors of the Union Pacific had ingeniously subcontracted with themselves at prices which rose from $80,000 to $90,000 and $96,000 a mile, twice the maximum estimates of engineers; so that the total cost eventually was $94,000,000. In after years no authorities or technicians, neither engineers nor accountants would ever be able to explain satisfactorily why the railroad had cost more than $44,000,000 to build, some $50,000,000 being left forever unaccounted for.

Hence the jubilation of the Union Pacific Ring....The affair had received the political benediction of both parties, among them a Speaker of the House and future President Garfield, a future vice-president, Schuyler Colfax, and an assortment of cabinet officials, Senators and Congressmen....These men were the stockholders of the Credit Mobilier, or the underlying Union Pacific, purchasing for nothing or little, through Oakes Ames, himself a representative from Massachusetts, who felt that the ownership of such a vast, patriotic venture should be distributed "where it will do most good for us."[7]

The Credit Mobilier was one of the early triumphs of the "mixed" economy. The Union Pacific was financed not by voluntary private investment, but by money extracted from the economy by political force. We should not be surprised at the consequences. When the true nature of the vast swindle became known,

> the tale of appalling waste, of crime and turpitude shook the whole country like a mighty quake and set many a weak structure to rocking. In the bourses panic seethed; thousands lost their savings in Union Pacific's fall, while distress spread quickly to the grain-growing regions. From the rostrum the tribunes of the people...began to speak out, in tones soon to become familiar whenever such provocation arose, against *the giant corporations which overran the country.* [emphasis added][8]

But was it "giant corporations" that had caused the trouble? Or was it government involvement in the economy? In contrast to the government-financed Union Pacific were Vanderbilt's New York Central and J. J. Hill's Great Northern. Both of these roads were privately financed; both honestly run and both were profitable, not only to the stockholders but to the nation as well. Both were products of capitalism.

The Great John D. Not only is capitalism often condemned for its alleged shortcomings, it is often condemned for its accomplishments as well. In fact, Josephson and other anticapitalist intellectuals seem to reserve their bitterest criticism for precisely those industrialists who were the most able and the most productive, and from whose efforts the consumer most benefitted. Consider, for example, the historical treatment afforded John D. Rockefeller, the founder of Standard Oil, the nation's first "trust."

In the years prior to the Civil War those who could not afford the costly whale oil did without lamp light, for kerosene was still the fuel of the future; it was not until 1859 that Edwin L. Drake brought in his famous gusher at Titusville, Pennsylvania. In the early 1860s the oil industry which Rockefeller was soon to dominate was still tiny, disorganized and chaotic; production was low, crude prices fluctuated wildly and the refined product was scarce and expensive. When Rockefeller first took notice of this brawling industry, its ramshackle derricks and wild-eyed men, he advised his friends to stay away. Just two years later, however, he lent $5,000 to the talented Samuel Andrews for the construction of a new refinery.

> The affair flourished quickly, as demand widened for the new illuminant. Soon Rockefeller missed not a day from the refinery where Andrews manufactured a kerosene better, purer than his competitors', and Rockefeller kept the books, conducted the purchasing of crude oil in his sharp fashion, and saved old iron, waste oils, made his own barrels, watched, pared, squirmed, for the smallest bargains.[9]

By means of a superior product and superior organizational skill Rockefeller's enterprise steadily expanded.

> Within a year or two the firm of Rockefeller, Flagler & Andrews was the biggest refinery in Cleveland, producing 1,500 barrels a day, having its own warehouses, its export agency in New York, its own wooden tank cars, its own staff of chemists or experts who labored to improve or economize the manufacturing processes. The company moved steadily to the front of the field, surpassing its rivals in quality, and outselling them by a small, though not certain or decisive, margin. How was this done?[10]

The criticism most often leveled against Rockefeller concerned his ability to undersell the competition by demanding and getting secret rebates from the railroad. Josephson describes the practice thus:

> Rockefeller and Flagler approached the railroad which carried so many carloads of their oil toward the seaboard, and whose tariff figured heavily in the ultimate cost. They demanded from it concessions in freight rates that would enable them to meet the advantages of other refinery centers such as Pittsburgh, Philadelphia and New York. Their company was now large enough to force the hand of the railroad, in this case, a branch of Vanderbilt's New York Central System; and they were granted their demands: a secret reduction or

"rebate" on all their shipments of oil....As the Rockefeller company became the largest shipper of oil, its production rising in 1870 to 3000 barrels a day, and offered to guarantee regular daily shipments of as much as sixty carloads, the railroads were impelled to accept further proposals for rebates. It was to their interest to do so in view of savings of several hundred thousand dollars a month in handling.[11]

It was this procedure which was largely responsible for the passage in 1887 of the Interstate Commerce Act. Yet, why should the rebate be condemned? One of the achievements of capitalism is its capacity for mass production at lower costs, and one of the major elements of cost is transportation. If Rockefeller was able to win lower rates, it was ultimately the consumer who gained. In fact, prices of refined products were falling steadily, and at the peak of Standard Oil's alleged monopoly, toward the close of the century, they reached the lowest levels in the history of this industry.

Another criticism of Rockefeller is that he bribed legislators. He certainly did; sometimes entire legislatures. Today we call it "campaign contributions," but the motivations are essentially the same: either to seek special favors, or to get government out of the way of legitimate business activity. In either event (and this is the theme of this portion of *The Incredible Bread Machine*) the problem is not capitalism as such but the power of government to meddle with it. It took many centuries of turmoil to get the government out of religion; perhaps one day it can be separated from the economy as well.

Anyway, under Rockefeller's aggressive leadership Standard Oil doubled in size and then doubled again. With lower prices, superior organization and a superior product, Rockefeller absorbed or overwhelmed the competition. By 1872, Standard Oil accounted for about 80% of the annual production. Josephson continues,

> Thenceforth, though persecuted and pilloried, himself the most hated man of the age, Rockefeller would retain his lead, hang on like death to his great unifying idea, advancing anew after each momentary retreat, evading all attempts at regulation, until the Standard Oil, with its refineries, pipe lines, tank wagons, ships and foreign terminals, had become an industrial empire as far-spreading as the British Empire, until Babylon and Nineveh and Peiping were illuminated by Standard kerosene.[12]

One of our great misconceptions is that it was only the antitrust suit, initiated in 1906, which reined in these predations. In reality, the marketplace at the turn of the century was exploding with new competition: Associated Oil and Gas (1901), Texaco (1902), Gulf (1907). By 1908 there were at least 125 independent refineries in the U.S., including Sun Oil, Union Oil and Tidewater.

While Standard Oil production was increasing, its market share of oil production was now declining steadily, from 34% in 1898 to 11% in 1906. When the antitrust case against Standard was finally confirmed in 1911, Standard was already contained by vigorous, nationwide competition of every description. As Dominick Armentano notes,

> Thus to seriously maintain that Standard was increasingly monopolizing the petroleum industry at the turn of the century, or that the antitrust suit against Standard begun in 1906 was a legitimate response to almost complete monopolistic control, is patently absurd. The raw data of the period indicate *no* such increasing monopoly by Standard. Reasonable inferences, even from a neoclassical perspective, would be all the other way.[13]

Back in 1859 when Drake brought in his first well, kerosene was a laboratory curiosity. Yet a mere 15 years later, Josephson tells us, "Babylon and Nineveh and Peiping were illuminated by Standard kerosene." Rockefeller was the Tom Smith of his age who created single-handedly a new and vibrant industry. Standard Oil contributed immensely to the comfort and well-being of millions all over the world, yet Rockefeller was excoriated for his "greed" and is depicted even today as an exploiter!

Morgan the Magnificent. The imperious J. P. Morgan, the most powerful financier in the nation at the turn of the century, was not an easy man to approach. However, one presumptuous young whippersnapper gave it a try, requesting permission to view the Hudson River yacht races from the deck of Morgan's elegant black-hulled craft, the *Corsair*. Morgan wrote in response,

> Unfortunately, I have loaned the *Corsair* to my friend, Mr. Ledyard, for the yacht races. However, if you think you would care to go on the yacht of either Mr. Gould, Mr. Goelet, Colonel Astor, or any of the others that may be going down the bay, I will try to get an invitation for you; and will assure whoever may take you that they will

have the honor of entertaining the cheekiest man I ever heard from.[14]

This was the forbidding Morgan, with the ferocious eyebrows and penetrating stare, whom the public loved to hate. But he had another side, for he was also a devoted father and loyal friend. For all his gruff exterior he was effusively charitable, donating tens of millions to churches, schools, museums and hospitals. In New York's lower East-side he founded the renowned Lying-In Hospital, dedicated to the care of expectant mothers. Morgan was intensely devoted to his Episcopal church, donated heavily to its causes, and was a prominent lay official. At the same time he loved big, black cigars and fine wines, and had a long string of exotic and well-maintained mistresses.

Morgan, whose father was a successful banker, grew up in an atmosphere of money and high finance. He attended the university at Gottingen in Germany where his mathematics professor later lamented losing his prize pupil to the world of business.

Morgan joined his father's firm in London in 1856 where he quickly mastered the intricacies of foreign exchange. After further apprenticeships in New York City he opened his own firm in 1860 at age 23. He was the first in the city to install his own private telegraph line, and during the Civil War many prominent people of the day dropped in regularly to learn the latest news from the front. One of the stories told about Morgan at the time was that he had sold the government faulty rifles. Nothing ever came of these charges, and judging from his subsequent reputation for probity the stories were certainly false.

One of Morgan's earliest triumphs was a dramatic victory over the corrupt Erie Ring in 1869. The prize was one element of the Ring's holdings, the 142-mile Albany and Susquehanna Railroad, and the issue hung on the outcome of a shareholders' meeting in Albany.

Jim Fisk, rotund and flashy front man for the Erie Ring, imported a gang of Bowery hoodlums to break up the meeting. But Morgan got word of their approach, and he and a group of tough railroad men met the invaders toe-to-toe in the A&S offices. Fisk got thrown down a flight of stairs, and was then arrested and carted off to jail. But not by a policeman, it turned out, but by a Morgan man in a policeman's uniform. The enraged Fisk was not one to back down, and armed battles broke out for physical possession of the road. So violent were the clashes, including a head-on collision between opposing trains, that the governor of the state threatened to call out the militia. In the courts, Morgan and the Erie Ring hurled injunctions at each other like thunderbolts—22 in all. But the smart and determined Morgan was always one step ahead of his heavy-handed opponents, and in the end the Ring was vanquished. The marketplace quickly expressed its approval as the A&S stock soared from 18 to 120. Morgan's reputation as a no-nonsense defender of corporate value and shareholders' rights was firmly established. He was just 32 years old.

Morgan was a genius with "the numbers," but more than that he was a visionary with a clear view of how the scattered elements of a young and turbulent economy could be organized into a more efficient and more productive whole. For years, however, in spite of his earlier success with the A&S, his efforts to reorganize the chaotic railroads were rebuffed by complacent and often corrupt managements. But with the Panic of 1893, things finally had to change.

The country was close to anarchy, and for more than a week the railroads around Chicago were in the hands of the unions. Within months nearly 114 of the over-extended roads were in bankruptcy. But the House of Morgan was one of the principal vendors of railroad securities and J. P. was determined that it should "stick by its goods." As John Moody wrote,

> No single financial problem in the previous history of the world equaled in difficulty and magnitude this reorganization of the railroads of the United States. These crazy financial structures had been patched together by any possible method of cohesion. They were leased, interleased, subleased; bought in whole or in part; and securities of every degree of inflation represented questionable claims upon them.

Typical of this near-impossible task was the reorganization of 30 railroads in the South operated under a consortium called Richmond and West Point Terminal. This railway, if it could be called that, consisted of 9000 miles of run-down track operated by a bewildering maze of overlapping interests, all under the control of four holding companies. Even before the panic the operators had come to Morgan for help, but his demand for complete control had been indignantly rejected. After the panic, however, the same Draconian conditions were quickly—and gratefully—accepted.

Straightening out the paper tangle was a monumental task confounded by scores of competing interests tugging in different directions. But the strong-willed Morgan pushed, bullied and cajoled, and the new Southern

Railway, recapitalized with $375,000 in 5% bonds, was soon a reality. In its first year of operation the new company showed a profit of $3 million.

One after another the shattered, demoralized and bankrupt roads came to Morgan, and one after another he restructured them into financially solvent enterprises. Within five years of the panic more than a billion and a half dollars were invested in roads reorganized by Morgan, representing 33,000 miles, one-sixth of the nation's total.

The Panic of 1893 also led to the most dramatic of Morgan's feats, the rescue of the U.S. Treasury from the complications arising from the unlimited coinage of silver.

In accordance with the cheap-money battle cry of "Free and unlimited coinage of silver at the ratio of 16:1," Congress had passed the Silver Purchase Act of 1890 which obliged the Treasury to purchase nearly the entire silver production of the nation and to issue silver certificates based upon it. But the over-priced silver certificates were redeemable also in gold, and as a result gold was leaving the Treasury at an alarming rate. In April of 1893 a particularly ominous drop in the gold supply triggered the Panic of '93. The Silver Purchase Act was quickly repealed, but confidence in the Treasury remained low, and the gold drain continued.

In January of 1895 the gold supply was approaching the peril point, and Morgan visited President Cleveland to propose a private loan. But Cleveland, the determined democrat, was convinced that a public rather than private bond issue was the proper course, and Morgan's proposal was rejected.

Congress, however, was paralyzed as usual, and the Springer Bill, which would have authorized a popular issue of gold-backed bonds, was scuttled by silverites in the House. The Treasury gold supply continued to plummet, and by February 5 there was literally only a one day supply remaining.

Back in New York, when Morgan learned of the defeat of the Springer measure, he quickly summoned his closest aides. Brushing past reporters without a word (a Morgan custom), he set off again, uninvited, for Washington.

Again, Morgan was rebuffed. This time, however, when informed by the Secretary of War that Cleveland would not see him Morgan replied, "I am going to the Arlington Hotel. I shall wait there until the President is ready to see me."

By the next morning, with repudiation of the nation's currency only hours away, Cleveland had nowhere else to turn. He summoned Morgan. "Have you anything to suggest?"

A major obstacle to a private loan would have been Congressional approval, sure to be blocked by populists and silverites. However, Morgan pointed out an obscure Civil War law in the Revised Statutes which permitted the Secretary of the Treasury to purchase gold if needed, paying for it with government obligations. Morgan and his syndicate proposed to supply $65 million in gold over a six-month period for 4½% bonds. Cleveland accepted the proposal, and the crisis was over.

The government's credit was saved, but Cleveland was excoriated for "selling out to Wall Street," while Morgan's position as the despised Captain of Industry, growing rich at the expense of the nation, was assured. As was his custom, however, Morgan simply ignored the attacks. An observer at the time, Carl Harvey, noted that "Almost any other man would have spoken in his own defense.... The subject simply irritated him. He never thought of meeting the public half-way with an explanation."

The closing years of the century were notable for an unprecedented wave of corporate restructuring, especially in iron and steel, as scores of smaller companies were combined into larger, more powerful entities. Whatever the motives of the various promoters (and there were more than enough shady characters to go around) the centralizing trend was inevitable and necessary. The economy was expanding rapidly, the appetite for iron and steel products was insatiable, and the economies of size had to be realized. However, the path of economic growth was not a smooth one, and in 1907 the economy was racked once again by panic.

A major weakness in the financial structure was the proliferation of highly speculative trusts which typically kept only around 5% of their deposits on hand in cash. There were fifty such trusts in New York City alone. But the smart money was getting nervous, and over a period of weeks the stock market lost about $5 billion in value. By October a panic was in full flood, and nearly every trust company was besieged by angry, frightened customers. In a single week nine banks closed in greater New York alone. The National Bank of America failed. On Thursday, October 24, Wall Street was in a state of paralysis. All activity simply ceased, and interest rates went to 150%.

President Theodore Roosevelt's contribution was to charge that law-breaking millionaires were producing hard times in order to embarrass him politically. But while Roosevelt postured, it was once again the indomitable J. P. Morgan, at age 72, who stepped into the breach. During intense, all-night sessions, Morgan marshaled and organized the nation's financial resources, deploying them where most desperately needed. For a period of several weeks he was a virtual czar with even the U.S. Treasury doing his bidding by depositing its funds with those houses which merited support. Morgan exercised a rough triage: those enterprises which were fundamentally sound he supported; those based on air and fraud went to the wall. Morgan had always conducted his own affairs responsibly, and he had little sympathy for those who had done otherwise. "I can't go on being everybody's goat," he said. "I have got to stop somewhere." He established a pool of $25 million to be loaned at 10%—but under his own rigid supervision. Gradually, the panic subsided. The wreckage of badly-managed enterprises was swept aside and order returned.

For a while Morgan was extolled as a hero. But not for long, and within a few months he was relegated once again to his more familiar role as despised Exploiter of the Downtrodden. As usual, he did not deign to respond.

A failure to communicate plagued Morgan all his life. He was one of the most productive people of his age, yet to Teddy Roosevelt and most of the public he was simply a "malefactor of great wealth." Some of the blame was certainly Morgan's. Like Michael Milken a century later, he was a genius with "the numbers," but he couldn't be bothered explaining to the public what it was all about. Also like Milken, he spent little time philosophizing about the principles of the economic system of which he was a part. At a dinner with Kaiser Wilhelm II, when the Emperor asked him what he thought of socialism, Morgan replied, "I pay no attention to such theories."

Morgan had a firm set of values, but they were more cultural than intellectual, based on his religious convictions and upbringing. A hint of his ethical code emerged at the Pujo Committee hearing in 1912, just a few months before his death at age 76.

The Pujo Committee was looking into the money trusts which were supposedly dominating the economy. Subpoenas had been issued, but to the delight of the newspapers many business leaders suddenly discovered urgent business in Europe. William Vanderbilt went literally into hiding.

Morgan, however, for the first time in his life, was willing to discuss his affairs in public.

He defended himself with great tenacity, insisting that if a man abused his power he would soon lose it. The ability to gain credit, he said, was largely a matter of personal trust. A person he did not trust could not get money from him on "all the bonds in Christendom." On the other hand, "I have known a man come into my office and I have given him a check for a million dollars and I knew that he had not a cent in the world."

Q. There were not many of them?
A. Yes, a good many.
Q. Commercial credits are based upon the possession of money or property?
A. No, sir; the first thing is character.
Q. Before money or property?
A. Before money or anything else. Money cannot buy it.
Q. So that a man with character, without anything at all behind it, can get all the credit he wants and a man with the property cannot get it?
A. That is very often the case.
Q. But that is the rule of business?
A. That is the rule of business, sir.

Guided by his own rigid ethical code, Morgan always kept his word and always lived up to his commitments. To Morgan, this was simply the way Christian gentlemen did business, and this unwavering integrity was certainly a major factor in his immense influence. Others may have feared his displeasure or resented his power, but they never had reason to mistrust him. In any event, he had spent close to a half a century salvaging the wreckage left by those less prudent and less scrupulous than he.

It would be a mistake, of course, to insist that every nineteenth century businessman was an "architect of progress." Some, like the Erie Ring or the manipulators of the Credit Mobilier, were simply crooks, often enabled in one way or another by government. But other men, such as J. P. Morgan, Vanderbilt, Hill, Carnegie and Rockefeller, were genuine builders to whom the nation owes an immense debt. Although many today agree with Josephson that all of it was "fearful sabotage practiced by capital upon the energy and intelligence of human society," the fact remains that the millions these men earned would not compare to the value of what they left behind.

The goal of the "Progressive Era" which followed was supposedly to protect competition against the rapacity of capitalist businessmen. The actual result, however, was not to protect competition, but to protect established interests *from* competition, as we will see in the following chapter.

> "Capitalism?" my friend mused,
> "I've heard that once or twice.
> I don't recall the context—
> But it wasn't very nice!"
> —from *Tom Smith and His Incredible Bread Machine*

2: The Progressive Era and Antitrust

The regulatory efforts of the Progressive Era, such as antitrust, were designed from the start not to promote competition, but to restrain it.

The Progressive Era—Teddy Roosevelt through Woodrow Wilson—is revered as the Golden Age of business regulation, during which the economic system was at last "brought under control." In reality, however, nothing much changed. The efforts were far more subtle than in the riotous days of the Credit Mobilier or the Erie Ring, but the principle was essentially the same: widespread and systematic government intervention in behalf of favored economic interests. While "progressive" legislation was indeed supported by a wide assortment of reformers, the major thrust and guidance came from the business community itself—that segment which was already firmly entrenched and wanted to stay that way.

A major goal of business leaders at the turn of the century was elimination of what they regarded as "ruinous" competition. As the manager of U.S. Envelope Company put it in 1901, "Competition is industrial war. Ignorant, unrestricted competition, carried to its logical conclusion, means death to some of the combatants and injury for all. Even the victor does not soon recover from the wounds received in the conflict."[1]

The steel industry, for example, found the "unfettered" competition especially vexatious, but frequent attempts to control prices by one means or another were invariably fruitless. No sooner would a pricing pool be established than some member of it would grab an order by shaving the price somehow—and the whole plan would collapse. Mergers were equally ineffective in subverting a relatively free and highly competitive structure.

The great wave of industrial mergers peaked in 1899 and then dropped sharply as it became painfully apparent that mere size did not lead to assured profits after all. The most prominent disappointment in the merger trend was mammoth U.S. Steel, a combination of 138 companies representing 60% of the nation's steel-making capacity. There's big and there's *too* big. Burdened by its excessive size, the company often found itself at a competitive disadvantage to its more nimble competitors. Its common stock, which had reached a high of 55 in 1901, was selling at 9 in 1904!

The inability of the steel barons to regulate their own industry by any private means yet discovered called for the boldest leadership. In November of 1907, 49 steel leaders met in New York at the first of the so-called "Gary dinners." Elbert Gary of U.S. Steel stressed the need for industry cooperation and an end to the invasion of each others' markets. The group agreed not to cut prices without mutual consultation and a committee of five, including Gary, was elected to advise and to conciliate differences. In January of 1908 the steel leaders—now representing 90% of the nation's productive capacity—met again at the Waldorf. According to Gary, "every manufacturer present gave the opinion that no necessity or reason exists for the reduction of prices at the present time."[2] By May, however, cracks were already starting to appear in the "gentlemen's agreements," and by February the accords were a dead issue. *The Iron Age* concluded, "So large a part of the current business has been going to those who were either willing or compelled to make lower prices that the situation finally became unendurable."[3] If ever price-fixing should have been effective, considering the magnitude of the effort, this was the time—but the effort was a complete failure.

The collapse of the Gary agreements represented the final failure of steel leaders to control the industry by voluntary means. Pools failed, mergers failed, "gentlemen's agreements" failed. Moreover, the inability of industrial leaders to subvert the marketplace by private means was just as complete in other industries. Standard Oil, in the face of young and vigorous competition from the Southwest, was already on the relative wane long before the dissolution order of 1911. In 1902 AT&T had been faced by 9100 independent competitors—but by 1907 the number was up to 22,000, many of which were more innovative and more profitable than the AT&T giant. The once-dominant New York banks were faced by a dispersion of wealth to other parts of the country and to other industries. In meat packing, copper, automobiles, agricultural machinery and elsewhere the story was the same: vigorous competition prevailed in spite of the best efforts of the business community to subvert it.

At the turn of the century, then, business leaders were convinced of the good sense and inevitability of a "cooperative" economy (i.e., an economy free of vexatious competition) but were unable to achieve that end by any voluntary means whatever. So, business leaders turned in another direction. They turned to government. As Kolko puts it, "The dominant fact of

American political life at the beginning of this century was that big business led the struggle for the federal regulation of the economy."[4]

And why not? Federal regulation had ended the railroad rate wars (to the disadvantage of the consumer); might not it be equally beneficial to other segments of the business community? In 1907 the National Civic Federation, a group consisting largely of "socially conscious" businessmen, endorsed federal licensing of corporations. In 1908 a special committee of the National Association of Manufacturers also welcomed the idea, describing it as "a national blessing...[which would] protect one corporation from the oppression and rapacity of another."[5] Gary, frustrated in his own attempts to fix prices, called on government to do the job, explaining to a Congressional committee,

> I believe we must come to enforced publicity and governmental control, even as to prices, and, so far as I am concerned, speaking for our company, so far as I have the right, I would be very glad if we had some place where we could go, to a responsible governmental authority, and say to them, "Here are our facts and figures, here is our property, here our cost of production; now you tell us what we have the right to do and what prices we have the right to charge."[6]

A committee member asked Gary, "Your idea, then, is that cooperation is bound to take the place of competition and that cooperation requires strict governmental supervision?"

"That is a very good statement," Gary replied.

Woodrow Wilson was surprised and gratified at the warm cooperation he received from business interests during his term of office, especially in the area of banking. In 1913 he wrote his Attorney General, "I gain the impression more and more from week to week that the businessmen of the country are sincerely desirous of conforming with the law, and it is very gratifying indeed to show them that all that we desire is an opportunity to cooperate with them."[7]

The movement for creation of a Federal Trade Commission was now gathering momentum and, as always, business leaders were in the vanguard. Back in 1912 Wilson had perceptively observed, "If the government is to tell big businessmen how to run their business, then don't you see that big businessmen have to get closer to the government even than they are now?"[8] But Wilson was soon won over, and in 1913 the Clayton Act, and the

Federal Trade Commission which was to implement it, were both enacted into law.

That the FTC was designed exclusively to protect business interests was abundantly clear from the makeup of the Commission appointees. Even applicants for lower echelon jobs were asked to present "letters of endorsement from good, sound businessmen." Edward N. Hurley, who became Commission Chairman in 1916, was a manufacturer and president of the Illinois Manufacturing Association. In addressing the National Industrial Conference Board he declared,

> I am glad to meet with a body of businessmen like you gentlemen, and I will plead guilty on the start by saying that I do not know anything about the law, and that applies to the Clayton Act and to the Federal Trade Commission Act. In my position on the Federal Trade Commission I am there as a businessman...and I think that the businessmen of the country will bear me out when I say that I try to work wholly in the interest of business.[9]

Wilson and Hurley were both supporters of trade associations—the principal concern of which was the elimination of price cutting. Hurley once announced, "We are making an inquiry into the coal industry today with the hope that we can recommend to Congress some legislation that will allow them to combine and fix prices." Wilson was only half wrong when he declared in 1916 that the FTC "has transformed the Government of the United States from being an antagonist of business into being a friend of business."[10]

Indeed.

Today, a history test in a California public high school asks, "Why was federal regulation necessary to control the trusts?" Not *was* regulation necessary, but *why* was it necessary. This one-sided question is typical of today's vast misunderstanding of what really happened. As we have seen, regulation was designed from the start not to "protect the public" but to protect favored groups from the rigors of competition. The same process everywhere assaults our eyes today. Pay TV was hamstrung by political means for years largely because of intense pressure from the networks and from motion picture theaters. Taxi companies are protected by city franchise requirements from "cut-throat competition." Doctors, lawyers, dentists, labor unions, funeral homes, barbers, all continue to be shielded from competition in spite of a rising public awareness that the consumer pays the bill.

Antitrust

The original antitrust law was the Sherman Act, passed in 1890. It declared, in part, that "contracts, combinations, or conspiracies in restraint of trade or commerce among the several states or foreign nations is hereby declared illegal." Being no more explicit than this, however, the law was at that time largely unenforceable.

The next step was passage in 1914 of the Clayton Act which sought to define with greater precision what was legal and what was not. It stated in part, "It shall be unlawful to discriminate in price between different purchasers where the effect may be substantially to lessen competition or tend to create a monopoly in any line of commerce." However, discounts based on grade, quality, or quantity were excepted; for example, to sell an item to one person for ten cents while selling to someone else for "twelve for a dollar" was not illegal. Not yet, anyway.

The Robinson-Patman Act of 1936, however, sharply limited the conditions under which such discounts were to be permitted. Henceforth, they were legal only where it could be demonstrated that they represented "differences in the cost of manufacture, sale, or delivery resulting from differing methods or quantities." For example, a manufacturer who had sought to broaden his market by absorbing the cost of freight was found guilty of an "unfair trade practice" since the "discount" did not reflect a difference in the cost of manufacture, sale, or delivery.

While private parties can (and often do) initiate antitrust suits, the important action is at the hands of two government agencies: (1) the Antitrust Division of the Justice Department, and (2) the Federal Trade Commission (FTC), established in 1914. The Justice Department concerns itself primarily with "conspiracies," "monopolies" and the like, while the FTC directs its attention to so-called "unfair trade practices" in pricing, sales practices, etc.

These two antitrust organizations operate in a somewhat different fashion. The Justice Department cannot itself issue an order or impose a penalty. It must initiate a suit through the courts. The defendant may demand a jury trial. The FTC, however, is an autonomous administrative agency: it is complainant, judge, jury and prosecutor all in one, and can issue its own cease-and-desist orders. At no time is there a jury trial in an FTC procedure. In either type of antitrust action the defendant may appeal the verdict to higher courts, but in a case that may involve thousands upon thousands of pieces of evidence in the form of vouchers, receipts, purchase orders, etc., the courts tend increasingly to rely on "expert" government testimony as to what is "unfair" or "monopolistic." The Supreme Court in particular usually upholds the government case.

Primarily from these three acts, administered and enforced by these two antitrust agencies, have sprung such a flood of edicts, suits, precedents, decisions, regulations and decrees that there is barely a step that a businessman can take that could not in some way be deemed illegal. Fifty years ago Lowell Mason, maverick FTC Commissioner, declared at Marquette University,

> I openly defy the entire University to explain to any businessman what he can or cannot legally do when making up his next season's price policy. Can he absorb freight? Perhaps, if he only does it now and then, or if he is not too big, or if the amount of the freight is not too much. But who is to say? How often is "now and then"? What size is "too big"? And how much is "too much"?
>
> What a young law student needs most after a diploma and a shingle and a client is a good pair of eyebrows and broad shoulders. Then when his client asks him how to stay out of trouble with the government, he can raise the first and shrug the second.

If there is any consistency to be found in antitrust legislation, it is that the businessman is always wrong and the bureaucrat always right. In his book, *Ten Thousand Commandments*,[11] Harold Fleming described the fate of Alcoa (Aluminum Company of America). In 1888 Alcoa consisted of little more than a corrugated shed and dirt floor, and its total output was ten pounds a day, selling at $8.00 a pound. By the late thirties, however, the founders of Alcoa had increased production to 300 million pounds a year. Aluminum was not only replacing other materials, it was creating entirely new markets. The price had dropped to 20¢ a pound. Then, in 1937, the Antitrust Division of the Department of Justice sued Alcoa on 140 counts including charges of conspiracy, unfair treatment of competitors, excessive prices, etc. The trial began in 1938 and lasted nearly two years. The government lost its case by a score of 140 to nothing. Antitrust appealed, and the case went ultimately to the Second Circuit Court of Appeals in 1944. The lower court decision was reversed on the one count of monopolizing the market for virgin aluminum ingots. Judge Learned Hand wrote this incredible decision:

> [Alcoa] insists that it never excluded competitors; but we can think of no more effective exclusion than progressively to embrace each new opportunity as it opened, and to face every newcomer with new capacity already geared into a great organization, having the advantage of experience, trade connections and the elite of personnel.

In short, Alcoa was punished not for its vices, but for its virtues, for doing a superior job of providing the nation with a vital commodity. Why should it be a crime to "embrace each new opportunity"? Should a company be punished for developing over a period of fifty years an organization with "experience, trade connections, and the elite of personnel"? A nation's economic health, its standard of living, and ultimately its military strength as well, depend on its productivity; to punish those companies which excel is folly.

Success can bear a bitter fruit when exposed to the chill winds of antitrust. In 1925 the General Electric Company bought a patent for a cutting material called tungsten carbide. GE set up an independent company, Carboloy, Inc., to perfect and sell the new material. For eleven years GE lost money steadily on this uncertain new product. It was not until the late thirties that tungsten carbide finally began to catch on. Between 1938 and 1942 production was increased 44 times. Then, when the undertaking was at last a success, the Department of Justice sued GE, Carboloy, and the Carboloy officers under terms of the Sherman Act. The defendants were fined $5000 each.

If the antitrust lawyers were consistent (which they are not) they would punish any company which develops a new product, because that company would thereby have a monopoly. The more beneficial the product, the more vigorous, of course, should be the prosecution. This does indeed seem to be the principle by which du Pont was prosecuted with regard to cellophane. After spending millions in research and development, du Pont put cellophane on the market in 1926 at $2.65 a pound. Over the next two decades the price was cut again and again to 45¢ a pound. By the end of World War II, sales had grown to $100,000,000 a year, and du Pont prepared to increase capacity. Then, under terms of the Sherman Act, the Department of Justice sued du Pont for "monopolizing" cellophane.

From the start antitrust has been less concerned with the consumer than with the company which claims it has been "harmed" by vigorous competition. The Morton Salt Company was found to have violated the Robinson-Patman Act because it gave quantity discounts to its bigger customers. Said the Supreme Court,

> We think that the language of the Act, and the legislative history show that Congress meant…that in a case involving competitive injury between a seller's customers the Commission need only prove that a seller had charged one purchaser a higher price for like goods than he had charged one or more of the purchaser's competitors….[the law] does not require that the discriminations must in fact have harmed competition, but only that there is a reasonable possibility that they "may" have such an effect.[12]

According to the court's interpretation, then, it was not necessary to prove that a competitor was harmed by the discounts; only that a "reasonable possibility" of harm existed.

In the Cement Institute Case (1948), cement companies were forbidden from absorbing in their prices the cost of freight. Certain companies had adopted this practice in order to compete more effectively in distant markets. As a result of the court decision this competition was, of course, discouraged—to the ultimate disadvantage of consumers in those distant markets.

The A&P case of the 1940s received particular public attention due largely to that company's spirited public defense of its position. One of the antitrust charges against the A&P chain concerned its purchases of corn flakes. On the basis of its large volume A&P had sought a discount from its supplier, making it clear that it was quite willing to manufacture the product itself. A&P received the discount but to government lawyers this was "coercion," "blacklisting," and "boycott." Antitrust harassment of A&P was so blatantly contrary to the interests of the consumer that even John Kenneth Galbraith—who is surely no foe of government meddling—commented unfavorably, declaring, "No explanation, however elaborate, could quite conceal the fact that the effect of antitrust enforcement, in this case, was to the disadvantage of the public."[13]

Antitrust activity covers an incredibly wide area. Former Attorney General Robert Kennedy filed in 1964 a complaint against several Los Angeles grocery chains which, unsuccessful in their attempt not to use trading stamps, had "conspired" to use only the stamps of a company controlled by themselves. Why they should be compelled to use someone else's stamps was not explained. Antitrust plumbed the depths of trivia in its 1962 suit against a bubble gum manufacturer. At the urging of a rival company, Topps, Inc. was charged with an antitrust violation for signing up major league baseball players for exclusive use of their pictures with its product.[14]

Hundreds upon hundreds of legitimate business practices have been outlawed by antitrust caprice. Suppose you own a grocery store and an acquaintance owns a farm. Suppose you say to him, "If you will patronize my store, I will patronize your farm." Would you suppose that you had committed what is in principle an illegal act? Guess again. The Supreme Court has upheld the FTC in its claim that "reciprocity" is illegal. The court found that the Consolidated Food Corporation had indeed violated the antitrust laws by suggesting to its suppliers, "you buy from me and I'll buy from you."[15]

When its guilt or innocence is largely a matter of subjective bureaucratic whim as to what is "fair" or "unfair" or "too much" or "too little," few companies have the stomach for a long, expensive and rancorous court trial. In April of 1962, U.S. Steel raised its prices and several other steel companies followed suit, but the mere threat by President Kennedy of antitrust action was sufficient to force a retreat. Or, a company faced by antitrust charges, no matter how flimsy, may plead "no contest." This means that the company pays the penalty but does not admit guilt. There is a particularly compelling reason for companies to seek in this manner to avoid a court trial in an antitrust case: a guilty verdict could later be used as evidence by "wronged" customers in suing for triple damages. This was the expensive prospect faced by twenty-nine electrical equipment manufacturers in a highly publicized 1962 case.

Fashions in antitrust enforcement change with the seasons, but the one continuing concern has been that great hobgoblin "conspiracy to fix prices." When a number of paper box companies pleaded "no contest" to price fixing charges a while ago, the Justice Department advised the presiding judge that "clearly, this case involves the type of hard-core pricefixing for which jail is the appropriate penalty." In the end 47 executives were fined, 15 of them receiving in addition jail terms of up to 60 days.[16]

But contrary to antitrust demonology, price fixing is an entirely legitimate business measure. The businessman should seek to maximize his profits, and if this calls at times for cooperation rather than competition, so be it. Agreements on prices or markets can make good economic sense for all concerned including, in the long run, the consumer.

The consumer has no reason to fear voluntary (as opposed to government-enforced) price fixing. As long as the agreements are voluntarily arrived at and maintained they must ultimately conform to market realities no matter what the desires of the participants. For example, the massive steel industry accords described previously collapsed in a matter of weeks due simply to market forces. More recently, the electrical industries encountered the same market phenomenon during the period of that famous conspiracy. As one GE executive later testified,

> Basically the thing just wasn't working. In other words, everybody would come to the meeting, the figures would be settled, and they were only as good as the distance to the closest telephone before they were broken. In other words, the thing just wasn't working.[17]

But what is a company like General Electric supposed to do? Should it charge more than the competition in order to lose its customers? Or should it charge less and be prosecuted for "cutthroat competition"? These companies were punished for seeking to stabilize prices at reasonable levels—a practice which, it should be noted, is loudly applauded when indulged in by bureaucracy itself.

Thanks to antitrust it has become increasingly risky over the years for the businessman to make any decision regarding his own business. Today, it is no exaggeration to say that any business practice, no matter how reasonable, may suddenly be declared illegal (Consolidated Food Corp.). Any price a manufacturer might charge could be deemed illegal depending on the particular bias of the antitrust lawyers at the moment. If the price is deemed too high (Alcoa) there is the immediate suspicion of monopoly, and the company could be fined or ordered broken up. If, on the other hand, the manufacturer wants to charge *less* than the competition (A&P), the policy may be deemed "predatory" or "cutthroat" or "coercive." But suppose the businessman plays it safe and charges the *same* as the competition? This, of course, is "conscious parallelism of action," or "collusion," which is also illegal. The businessman may be subject not only to fine or imprisonment, but to retroactive claims of triple damages by "wronged" customers (the electrical industries case). The mere threat of antitrust action is a potent weapon of political and economic intimidation (the steel price conflict). Through it all, the surest targets of antitrust attention will be the most successful and the most innovative companies.

Small wonder that William Baxter, a former antitrust chief, once described much of prevailing antitrust theory as "wacko."[18]

When it comes to a mugger or a rapist or a murderer, the courts exercise commendable concern for the civil rights of the defendant. When it comes to the businessman charged with an antitrust violation, however, it is quite a different matter. Former FTC commissioner Mason wrote,

> If American bureaucracy turns its attention to you, you may be sure that you will have all of the trappings of democracy available for your defense. You will have an air-conditioned courtroom and be allowed full representation by counsel in which and with which to plead your case. But the men who sit in judgment on you will be the men who originally complained against you. Even if the heavy facts of life are on your side, rest assured that the light inferences of bureaucracy will be against you. And in the scales, one feather of government inference is worth a ton of a private citizen's facts. You may not be found guilty of doing anything wrong, but this does not mean that you may not be ordered to stop doing something which is right. Perhaps you will be saved the burden of defending yourself by being tried in absentia. In this event, the order entered against you will come as an unpleasant surprise. Perhaps you will be told what prices you must charge your customers while your uninhibited competitors take your business away from you. However, you may console yourself with the thought that the shame and the sham is so limited, so inconspicuous, so personal and particular, that only you and no one else will care. Of course, you may protest—this Constitutional guarantee of freedom of speech has not yet been reinterpreted. But your plight will diminish the effectiveness of your plea, for your voice will be that of a man already found guilty. Your cry will amount to nothing more than a discredited whisper. When your guilt is established, maybe it will be at a trial where all the witnesses testified in your favor, but, if so, the courts will nevertheless uphold your conviction on the grounds that the witnesses should have known better.[19]
>
> Down, down, down go the defendants—all in the public interest; and up, up, up go the precedents like coral polyps building a hidden reef to wreck our liberties.[20]

Antitrust is a bad idea gone wrong, perverse in theory and capricious in practice. But the basic objection is philosophical: the assumption that the businessman must serve the interests of "society" as determined by government. Much more on this later, but in a free society the individual is not forced to serve "others." That is the fate of slaves, not of free people.

As illustrated in these two chapters, the U.S. has never practiced laissez faire capitalism. From the start, government has intervened constantly, often in behalf of this-or-that favored interest. In the next chapter we will see another consequence of government intervention, the boom-and-bust business cycle.

> You're gouging on your prices
> If you charge more than the rest.
> But it's unfair competition
> If you think you can charge less!
> A second point that we would make,
> To help avoid confusion:
> Don't try to charge the same amount,
> For that would be collusion!
> —from *Tom Smith and His Incredible Bread Machine*

3: Boom and Bust

Political force does not solve problems—it causes them. Government control of the money supply has not brought economic stability but repeated dislocations.

The boom-and-bust cycles of the past have been a result not of too little government, but of too much. Explanations of the business cycle are as numerous as the economists ready to argue about it, but the most coherent theory—and the most consistent with historical fact—is that of renowned economist, the late Ludwig von Mises. The von Mises theory will be described briefly and will then be applied to a few of the major boom-and-bust cycles in U.S. history,[1] including the greatest government-induced disaster of all time, the Great Depression.

The von Mises Theory. A tendency toward instability is not an inherent characteristic of private capitalism. In fact, a money market free from government intervention provides the ideal economic stabilizer: the interest rate. The free-market interest rate provides the businessman with a true and undistorted picture of the economic realities. Low interest rates encourage business activity in the long-term capital goods areas, while high interest rates shift activity to the shorter-term consumer goods. The interest rate is a sign-post pointing out to the businessman the direction his investment effort should take.

What low interest rates indicate. If interest rates are low it is an indication that people are saving rather than spending; they are foregoing immediate consumption for the sake of future consumption. For example, an individual might forego the purchase of a new refrigerator today in order to save his money to build a house ten years from now. Accordingly, instead of spending his money on consumer goods, he puts it in the bank. This money now becomes available for loans to businessmen. If this consumer preference happens to be shared by tens of thousands of others, money for lending purposes will be abundant and interest rates will fall. Because interest rates are now low, businessmen will be encouraged to take out long-term loans with which to develop long-term capital goods such as steel mills, railroads, land, etc. These undertakings will not come to fruition for years, but when they do, a market will exist because those original savers are now ready to build those houses. And the developed land is ready and waiting, the steel mills can supply appropriate nails, and the railroads can haul the lumber. The low interest rates, then, have resulted in an economic structure appropriate to the long-term desires of the consuming public.

What high interest rates indicate. If, on the other hand, interest rates are high, it is an indication that money for lending is in short supply. Perhaps lending has already been excessive. Or perhaps people are reluctant to lend because of political instability. Or perhaps people have found it possible to build those homes today rather than ten years hence. Whatever the reason, the higher rates automatically discourage investment in the longer-term capital goods areas for which no secure market would exist.

The interest rate, then, acts as a road sign indicating to the businessman the direction his investment should take. If rates are low, investment in long-term capital goods is encouraged; if rates are high, investment in long-term capital goods is discouraged. But suppose the rates would have been high but are held at artificially low levels[2] by some kind of government intervention? The road signs have been switched. As a result, investment will be diverted toward the capital goods areas. This is not, then, "over investment" necessarily, but rather "malinvestment"; investment in the wrong things. An example of malinvestment might be the construction of a railroad to an area not yet sufficiently populated to provide a market for the railroad's service. Another example might be the construction of a steel mill before the complementary factors of production such as power and transportation have been developed. Or it might involve excessive speculation in land or heavy industry or in any such long-term capital goods area. In any event, the businessman has been misled by the artificially low rates, and sooner or later he will be forced to realize that he has on his hands an expensive white elephant. The day of reckoning can be postponed by further credit expansion, but it cannot be evaded permanently,[3] for businessmen have invested in things which cannot be successfully integrated with the rest of the economy. Accordingly, these ventures must finally cease operation. Workers will be laid off, and the effects will quickly percolate down to the consumer goods industries as well. The depression has begun. (The von Mises theory explains why in every depression it is the capital goods industries which are hit first and hardest.)

The credit structure, then, (in terms of the interest rate) constitutes the automatic sign post for economic activity, but time and again it has been tampered with by government. Artificial credit expansion might be caused by direct government control of credit, or by issuance of unsound currency. In any case the result of this monetary inflation will be an interest rate held (for a time) at artificially low levels, thus setting the stage for a boom-and-bust cycle. Some of the more severe cycles are described below.

Panic of 1837. President Jackson's second term was accompanied by a period of vast over-confidence in the nation's rapid growth. In particular, speculation in public land was intense. Land sales, which had amounted to less than two million dollars in 1830, jumped to $14 million in 1835, and then to $24 million in 1836. The land was being paid for in the unsound paper currency being issued by various western banks. However, by 1836 the federal treasury was bulging with this worthless money, and on July 11th Jackson issued his famous "specie circular" ordering the treasury to accept henceforth only gold or silver or bank notes based thereon as payment for the public lands. This was the needle that pricked the bubble. The state banks could not redeem their currency, and the great boom collapsed. Land sales plummeted, while building all but ceased. Railroad construction was halted. Soon, nearly every factory in the East was closed. Over 600 banks failed, including many in which the federal government had deposited its own money. For nearly five years the nation was in a depression exceeded in severity only by that which started nearly a century later in 1929.

What had happened? According to the von Mises theory a boom is generated by excessive credit expansion caused by some form of government intervention. Both the state governments and the federal government were responsible for the inflationary boom of the 1830s. The legislatures of the western states were remiss in encouraging the printing of worthless bank notes while the federal government was equally negligent in honoring these notes at face value, for this lent to them an aura of soundness they could not have earned in a market free from government involvement. People were misled by an apparent abundance of money; they invested and spent and borrowed and invested again. But the rosy prospects were only an illusion, and people were malinvesting in things for which no real demand yet existed. The result was economic disaster.

Panic of 1873. The boom which culminated in the Panic of 1873 had its origin in the inflation attending the Civil War. Taxes accounted for about $667 million of the expense of the Union effort, while about $2 billion was raised from the sale of bonds. In order to sell these bonds more readily, Secretary of the Treasury Chase created in 1863 a national bank system whereby any group of five men could be granted a bank charter by purchasing U.S. bonds and depositing them in Washington. The government then used the proceeds from these bond sales to finance the war. In the meanwhile, the newly-created banks were permitted to issue bank notes to the amount of 90% of the value of the bonds. As a result, where one dollar had been in circulation previously, now $1.90 was in circulation. The result, of course, was highly inflationary. An even more drastic inflationary expedient was the issuance of $450 million in irredeemable paper money. These were the infamous "greenbacks"; their fluctuating value was to plague the economy for years.

The momentum built up by the Civil War inflation continued in the post-war years to carry the economy along at a feverish pace. The principal area of malinvestment was the railroad. And the principal promoter was the U.S. government. Sparked by government subsidies and land grants, there ensued a speculative boom such as the world had never seen. The Pacific Railroad Bill provided vast subsidies in land and money. Later, the Texas and Pacific received 18 million acres of land and the Northern Pacific received 47 million acres. Subsidies were granted by state and local governments as well. With incentives like these there was an understandable rush to get into railroading. The vast profits of the infamous Credit Mobilier further encouraged an orgy of railroad speculation.

The distinguished banker Jay Cooke gained control of the Northern Pacific charter in 1869 and quickly sold in its behalf an initial bond issue of $4 million. By 1870 his Jay Cooke & Co., the largest bank in the country, was selling each month an additional $1 million in Northern Pacific bonds. Customers were eager to buy. And why not? Was not money plentiful? Did not this great new industry enjoy the whole hearted participation of the U.S. government? But construction costs were mounting and there was virtually no income to a railroad stretched through the then-desolate Northwest. (As the perceptive Commodore Vanderbilt observed a while later, "Building railroads from nowhere to nowhere is not a legitimate business.") Cooke soon found himself with $5½ million in overdrafts, and his house of cards was beginning to tremble. In January of 1875 the Credit Mobilier scandal broke, and investors began to take a hard second look at all railroads—including the precarious Northern Pacific. The house of cards shook, and on September 18, 1873, it collapsed. Jay Cooke & Co. was the foremost banking house in the country, and when it fell, thirty-seven other New York City banks fell with it on the same afternoon. Within days the entire economy, from one end of the nation to the other, ground to a halt. It did not recover for six years.

What had happened? The economy had been distorted by the needs of the Civil War and by the inflation attending it. Millions had been malinvested in capital equipment for which no true market existed at that time. But the problem was not "laissez-faire capitalism"; the problem was government manipulation of money and credit, aggravated in particular by government stimulation of what one historian accurately described as the "railway madness."

Panic of 1893. Another boom-and-bust cycle climaxed with the Panic of 1893. Once again the major factor was government distortion of credit, this time through the currency inflation resulting from the coinage of large volumes of silver. "Cheap money" has always been a favorite economic panacea, especially for those hard pressed by debt. The particular mechanism urged on the country in the 1870s and '80s was described by the political battle cry, "Free and unlimited coinage of silver at the ratio of sixteen to one." In 1878 Congress passed the Bland-Allison Act by which the Secretary of the Treasury was ordered to purchase and coin each month two to four million dollars worth of silver. Then, by the terms of the Silver Purchase Act of 1890, the amount was nearly doubled, approaching nearly the entire output of the nation. This second act also provided for the issuance of silver certificates. The flood of over-valued silver dollars generated the illusion of wealth and of demand. The result was another surge of malinvestment during the eighties and early nineties. But the illusion of demand could be sustained only as long as the process of inflation could be sustained. The silver treasury notes were redeemable also in gold, and by April of 1893 a final ominous drop in the Treasury's gold supply triggered the Panic of 1893. The Silver Purchase Act was quickly repealed by President Cleveland but the damage had already been done. The subsequent depression lasted about two years.

To summarize, the von Mises theory shows that the boom-and-bust cycle is not the product of "capitalism" but of government-inspired inflation. As we have seen, the von Mises theory is in full accord with historical fact. This is not to say that business fluctuations would not take place in the absence of government intervention, for businessmen will often guess wrong;

they will make mistakes, they will invest too deeply in the wrong place at the wrong time. Even in a free economy dislocations will occur and adjustments will be necessary. But the effects will be local and short-lived. Only with the steady and inexorable push of deliberate government policy will the entire economy find itself pushed along on a nation-wide wave of speculation which builds higher and higher—and then collapses in a national catastrophe.

A few of the boom-and-bust cycles have been described. The greatest economic disaster of all time, however, was yet to come: the Great Depression precipitated by the crash of 1929.

The Great Depression. The Great Depression was not just "in the cards"; it did not "just happen"—it was caused. Nor did it start in 1929. The groundwork was laid years before. The great boom of the '20s and the tragic depression that followed were again caused by government manipulation of credit, this time primarily through the policies of the Federal Reserve System.

The Federal Reserve System was created by law in 1913. It was to be the banker's bank, a central pool from which member banks could draw. In times of particular credit demand in one portion of the country the Fed would ease the shifting of funds to that area. In times of general stress, the Fed would support member banks that were under pressure. But private bankers had always been ready to pool their resources to support those who merited support; better had the nation's monetary system continued to evolve in private hands, for the Federal Reserve System proved to be a Frankenstein monster, an engine of inflation which all but destroyed the nation's economy. Between June of 1921 and June of 1929, the nation's money supply (currency plus currency substitutes, such as bank deposits) increased by a whopping 62%. The nature of the government-controlled fractional reserve banking system is such that this increase was generated by a much smaller increase in bank reserves, which, in turn, was generated by the Fed. A Federal Reserve System pamphlet describes the function of the Fed thus:

> The all-important fact brought out by this discussion is that the Federal Reserve, by adding to or extinguishing the member bank's reserves, can influence the bank to increase or decrease its demand deposits (the major component of the money supply) by several times the amount added or extinguished. This is why the dollars cre-

ated by Federal Reserve action that become bank reserves are often called "high-powered dollars" to distinguish them from ordinary deposit dollars....The commercial banks as a whole can create money only if additional reserves are made available to them....Thus, the ultimate capability for expanding or reducing the economy's supply of money rests with the Federal Reserve System.[4]

In short, the Fed controls the money supply by controlling bank reserves. Professor Murray N. Rothbard, in his book *America's Great Depression*,[5] identifies the three principal mechanisms by which bank reserves were manipulated by the Fed in the years preceding the Great Depression as 1) bills discounted, 2) open market purchases by the Fed of government securities, and 3) bills bought (called "acceptances").

1) Bills discounted. Let us suppose that a bank is loaned up to its limit of, say, one million dollars. It will find itself with I.O.U.s totalling that amount. One would assume that its lending would of necessity cease at this point. In order to "ease credit," however, the Fed will "rediscount" these I.O.U.s, which means that the bank can, in effect, borrow money from the Fed using the I.O.U.s as collateral. The interest that the Fed charges on this loan is called the rediscount rate. With its funds thus replenished, the member bank can continue lending. When the Fed was first set up in 1913 it was intended that the rediscount rate would be high enough to discourage rediscounting except in an emergency, but during most of the '20s the rate was kept very low. As a result, bankers were encouraged to lend to the hilt and then run to refill their bucket at the Fed well in order to lend some more.

2) Open market purchases. The major element in the forced increase of bank reserves (and the principal mechanism today) was open market purchases by the Fed of assets, such as government securities. It works like this: when the Fed Open Market Committee buys some asset in the open market, it pays by check which the seller then deposits in his own bank. When this member bank sends this check along to the Reserve Bank of its district, the sum is credited directly to the member bank's reserve account. With its reserves now expanded, the member bank can now greatly increase its lending role. (For more on this, see the following chapter.)

3) Acceptances. An acceptance is a sort of letter of credit, usually associated with international trade. Neither before nor after the 1920s has the acceptance market in the U.S. been of appreciable size, but during the 1920s it

was one of the major causes of the disastrous credit inflation. Rothbard describes it thus:

> The Federal Reserve policy on acceptances was undoubtedly the most curious, and the most indefensible, of the whole catalog of Federal Reserve policies. As in the case of securities, acceptances were purchased on the open market, and thus provided reserves to banks outright with no obligation to repay (as in discounting). Yet while the FRS preserved its freedom of action in buying or selling U.S. securities, it tied its own hands on acceptances. It insisted on setting a very low rate on acceptances, thus subsidizing and indeed literally creating the whole acceptance market in this country, and then pledging itself to buy all the bills offered at that cheap rate. This was an inexcusable policy on two counts—its highly inflationary consequences, and its grant of special privilege to a small group at the expense of the general public.[6]

According to Rothbard, the principal promoter of the acceptance policy was Paul M. Warburg, a former German investment banker who was one of the founders of the Federal Reserve System. As Chairman of the Board of the International Acceptance Bank of New York, the largest acceptance bank in the world, and as director of several other acceptance houses, Warburg was a major beneficiary of the Fed's acceptance policy.

The three principal means (there were others) by which the Fed generated cheap credit during the '20s, then, were low discount rates, open market purchases of various assets, and extensive purchases of acceptances.

But why? The reasons presented at the time for the cheap money policies were three. 1) To "help business." By easing credit it was expected that business prosperity would be encouraged and maintained. Secretary of the Treasury McAdoo had explained the Fed's easy-money policy thus:

> The primary purpose of the Federal Reserve Act was to alter and strengthen our banking system that the enlarged credit resources demanded by the needs of business and agricultural enterprises will come almost automatically into existence and at rates of interest low enough to stimulate, protect and prosper all kinds of legitimate business.[7]

2) To encourage foreign loans. Foreign loans would supposedly supply the money by which those countries could purchase American products, particularly agricultural. American agriculture was in a deep slump in the early '20s due in large part to the backlash of the highly protectionist

Fordney-McCumber Tariff of 1922. Unable to sell to us, Europeans had found it equally difficult to buy from us. The foreign loans would supposedly provide the Europeans with the purchasing power that the tariff had eliminated. Secretary of Commerce Hoover commented that even "bad loans" helped U.S. exports. (Wiser, of course, to reduce tariffs than to extend shaky loans, but this is not the way of enlightened statecraft even today.)

3) To protect England from its own inflation. Perhaps the least commendable motive behind the policy of deliberate inflation was an altruistic desire to protect England from the consequences of its own cheap money policies. Great Britain was losing gold to the U.S. at an alarming rate, and the officials of the Fed sought to save the British from embarrassment by deliberately debasing our own currency. By so doing, interest rates would be forced down (for a time) and capital balances would be diverted from this country to England. We were volunteered to be the goats. Benjamin Strong, influential governor of the Federal Reserve Bank of New York, wrote in 1924 to Secretary of the Treasury Mellon explaining,

> the burden of this readjustment must fall more largely upon us than upon them [Great Britain]. It will be difficult politically and socially for the British government and the Bank of England to face a price liquidation in England...in face of the fact that their trade is poor and they have over a million unemployed people receiving government aid.[8]

The American public was not informed that one of the reasons its currency was being debased was to make things easier for the British. Dr. Benjamin Anderson, at that time economist for the Chase Manhattan Bank, wrote in his definitive *Economics and the Public Welfare,*

> The governors of the other eleven Federal Reserve banks were called to Washington [in 1927]. They were not dealt with honestly. They were told that the proposed cheap money move was to "help the farmer." They were not told that the primary purpose of it was to make it unnecessary for England to honor her gold obligations to France, and to make it possible for England to continue an unwarranted degree of cheap money....The Chicago Federal Reserve Bank was suspicious and disapproved. The Chicago Federal Reserve Bank was in a better position to know what was really involved in the policy than the Federal Reserve banks of the more remote places. The Governor of the Chicago Federal Reserve Bank had less confi-

dence in Governor Strong than many of the other governors had. The Chicago bank refused to reduce its rate but the Federal Reserve Board at Washington overrode the Chicago Federal Reserve Bank, and by action of the board, not of the bank, the Chicago rate was reduced.[9]

And so, first by one means and then another, for a period of about eight years, the Federal Reserve System force-fed the fires of a raging inflation, increasing the money supply by about 62%.[10] (Interestingly, commodity prices did not increase greatly during this highly inflationary period. This was due primarily to the fact that productivity was also increasing at a rapid rate. This points up the importance of the correct definition for inflation: inflation is not merely "an increase in prices and wages"; these are sometimes the *consequences* of inflation, not its *cause*. Inflation itself is best defined as "an increase in the money supply over and above the supply of the precious metal standard.")

Worried about this out-of-control credit expansion, the *Chicago Tribune* called upon Fed Chairman Benjamin Strong to resign. The Fed reversed course for a brief period in the first half of 1928, but then resumed its expansionary policy later in the year. In 1929 the money supply was fairly stable, but it was way too late. The principal barometer of all this credit sloshing around was the soaring stock market. And whenever it threatened to sag, a timely reassurance from the Secretary of the Treasury or from President Coolidge himself was sufficient to send in churning upward again. In November of 1922 the *Times* Industrials had stood at 108; six years later, in November of 1928, the index had gone through the roof at 308.

But the end was in sight. It was October, 1929.

On an average day perhaps four million shares would exchange hands. On October 23, 2.6 million shares were traded in the last hour alone. The *Times* averages dropped from 415 to 384. The next day was Thursday, October 24. This was Black Thursday. On this day 12.9 million shares changed hands in a frenzy as wave after wave of selling drove the market downward. But then, "organized support" appeared as leading bankers pooled their resources and stemmed the tide. Fear disappeared and confidence returned. By the end of the day the market had recovered amazingly well, losing only 12 points, a third of the loss of the previous day. Through Friday and half-day of Saturday the market was relatively firm.

But Monday was bad: 9.25 million shares were traded and the *Times* Industrials plummeted 49 points. This time there was no "organized support." Tuesday was worse, with an unbelievable 16.4 million shares and a drop of another 43 points. But on Wednesday, perhaps due to the words of reassurance from President Hoover's Secretary of Commerce, the market rallied, moving up 31 points. The next day it recovered another 21 points. The market was closed Friday, Saturday and Sunday, but things were looking up—or so it seemed. On Monday the market lurched downward again, 22 points. Tuesday was a New York City election day and the market was closed. On Wednesday it dropped another 37 points. On Thursday and Friday the market was steady. But the first three days of the next week it lost another 50 points. And there was no end in sight. Rothbard writes,

> And so ended the great inflationary boom of the 1920s. It should be clear that the responsibility for the inflation rests upon the federal government—upon the Federal Reserve authorities primarily and upon the Treasury and Administration secondarily. The United States Government had sowed the wind and the American people reaped the whirlwind: the Great Depression.[11]

The Great Depression was not caused by "greedy businessmen" or "underconsumption" or "overproduction." Nor was it "just one of those things." John Kenneth Galbraith notwithstanding,[12] economic theory and historical fact demonstrate that the boom-and-bust cycle is generated by government-inspired credit inflation. And, as we shall now see, it was a continuation of such interventionist policies which prolonged the depression for nearly ten years.

4: The Great Depression

Both the Hoover and Roosevelt administrations directed all of the resources of government toward ending the depression. They managed only to prolong it.

T he Hoover Years. Herbert Hoover had been president only a year when the crash occurred. While Hoover is generally regarded as a champion of laissez-faire capitalism, he was anything but. Rothbard's sketch is illuminating.

> When Hoover returned to the United States after the war and a long stay abroad, he came armed with a suggested "Reconstruction Program." Such programs are familiar to the present generation but they were new to the United States in that more innocent age. Like all such programs, it was heavy on government planning, which was envisaged as "voluntary" cooperative action under "central direction." The government was supposed to correct "our marginal faults"—including undeveloped health and education, industrial "waste," the failure to conserve resources, the nasty habit of resisting unionization, and seasonal unemployment. Featured in Hoover's plan were increased inheritance taxes, public dams, and significantly, government regulation of the stock market to eliminate "vicious speculation." Here was an early display of Hoover's hostility toward the stock market, a hostility that was to form one of the leitmotifs of his administration. Hoover, who to his credit never pretended to be the stalwart of laissez-faire that most people now consider him, noted that some denounced his program as "radical"—as well they might have.[1]

As Secretary of Commerce under Harding, Hoover had initiated a President's Conference on Unemployment which was attended by 300 prominent leaders of business, banking and labor. Hoover had taken the lead in promoting a more active role for government in curing depressions. In the mild recession of 1921 he had urged government action to stimulate home construction and had supported a bill calling for a public works program. A Hoover-endorsed public works plan had been presented to the governors' conference in 1928 and was warmly praised by William Green of the American Federation of Labor. The *Literary Digest* of December, 1928 reported that "labor is jubilant, because leaders believe that the next president has found...a remedy for unemployment which, at least in its philosophy and its groundwork, is identical with that of labor."

It is clear that the new president was quite ready to use the full power at his disposal to bring the business cycle under government control. It was Hoover's pernicious notion that high wages cause prosperity; it followed, then, that the way to cure a depression would be to keep wages high, even in the face of dropping prices and extinguished profits. Accordingly, at a series of White House Conferences in November he extracted assurances from every major business leader that wages would not be lowered. But this was the worst possible leadership, for in a depression it is essential that excessively high wages drop just as do the excessively high prices. If wages were kept high in the face of extinguished profits the result would be wide-spread business failures and soaring unemployment. This, of course, is precisely what happened.

Unfortunately, the business community tried doggedly to cooperate with the president. Wages were not cut. Even John Maynard Keynes commented on American success in maintaining wage rates, while in October of 1930 William Green presented Hoover to the A.F. of L. convention declaring,

> The great influence which [Hoover] exercised upon that occasion [the White House Conference] served to maintain wage standards—to prevent a general reduction of wages. As we emerge from this distressing period of unemployment we...understand and appreciate the value of the service which the President rendered the wage earners of the country.[2]

By 1931 hourly wages had declined by only about 4% while due to falling prices real wages had actually risen by around 11%. The problem, however, was that there were now eight million unemployed. But Hoover had other weapons in his arsenal. Back in June of 1929 Congress, at Hoover's request, had passed the Agricultural Marketing Act, by which was established the Federal Farm Board (FFB). The purpose of this board was two-fold: to make low-interest loans to farm cooperatives, and to support prices. To support wheat prices the FFB established the Farmers National Grain Corporation, with $10 million in government money. With an assured market at subsidized prices, the farmers, of course, grew still more wheat. Under the weight of the new surpluses prices sagged still further and the FFB was given another $100 million with which to continue the process.

Hoover then established the Grain Stabilization Corporation, while the Secretary of Agriculture hopefully urged farmers to reduce acreage. Needless to say, wheat surpluses continued to pile up throughout all of Hoover's term. The FFB had similar success with cotton. In 1931 chairman Stone urged frantically that every third row be plowed under. By the end of Hoover's term the wheat and cotton programs had cost the taxpayers $300 million.

Triumph followed triumph. The FFB had equal success with wool, butter, beans, pecans, figs, grapes, raisins, potatoes, apples, sugarbeets, honey, nuts, maple syrup, tobacco, poultry, eggs and rice. Benjamin Anderson comments dryly that "Those who condemn the New Deal for its agricultural follies in 1933 and succeeding years...should not credit Roosevelt's New Deal with originality on this point."[3]

Few economic acts are more insidiously harmful than the protective tariff, yet in mid-1930 Congress passed the infamous Smoot-Hawley Tariff which imposed the highest rates in U.S. history. On the day the bill was passed, the hard-pressed stock market shuddered in agony and dropped 20 points. Hoover, ignoring the advice contained in a petition signed by 1028 economists, signed the act into law, triggering a wave of destructive protectionism around the world. International trade was impeded, and the American farmer was not helped by the subsequent loss in sales to Europe. Anderson described the Smoot-Hawley Tariff as "the crowning financial folly of the whole period from 1920 to 1933."

In the latter half of 1930 Hoover called for an "ample supply of credit at low rates" (more inflation) and urged a further increase in public works. In February of 1931 he signed into law a $1 billion public works bill, the Wagner Wage Stabilization Act. In 1932 he chose to burden the weary economy still further by sharply increasing taxes. His major achievement of the year, however, was creation of the Reconstruction Finance Corporation (RFC), the purpose of which was to make loans to shaky businesses—businesses too unsound to merit private support. But do such measures stimulate recovery or postpone it? The depression is caused by malinvestment—by investment in things for which no real demand exists. Only when capital is withdrawn from these areas and reinvested in useful things can recovery ensue. Accordingly, programs such as the RFC, in propping up unsound positions, served only to delay the liquidations and readjustments without which recovery was impossible. Nonetheless, in 1932 the scope of the RFC was broadened still further to embrace loans to agriculture and to cities and states for relief and public works.

There were now 12 million unemployed. The nation's first federal relief program was passed in 1932. During this period the Fed continued heavy purchases of government securities in order to increase bank reserves and thereby inflate the money supply once again. By now, however, worried banks were reluctant to lend to their full legal limit and the Administration's attempts were frustrated. Angrily, RFC chairman Atlee Pomerene declared, "Now...and I measure my words, the bank that is 75% liquid or more and refuses to make loans when proper security is offered, under present circumstances, is a parasite on the community!"[4]

In accepting his party's nomination in 1932 Hoover declared,

> We might have done nothing. That would have been utter ruin. Instead we met the situation with proposals to private business and to Congress of the most gigantic program of economic defense and counterattack ever evolved in the history of the Republic. We put it into action....No government in Washington has hitherto considered that it held so broad a responsibility for leadership in such times....For the first time in the history of depression, dividends, profits, and the cost of living have been reduced before wages have suffered.

And nearly 14 million, representing 25% of the working force, were now unemployed. Hoover's term was over. He had indeed resorted to "the most gigantic program" of economic interventionism the nation had ever seen or even conceived of. It was a tragic failure. Dr. Rothbard concludes,

> America had awakened, and was now ready to use the State to the hilt, unhampered by the supposed shibboleths of laissez-faire. President Hoover was a bold and audacious leader in this awakening. By every "progressive" tenet of our day he should have ended his term a conquering hero; instead he left America in utter and complete ruin: a ruin unprecedented in length and intensity.

What was the trouble? Economic theory demonstrates that only government inflation can generate a boom-and-bust cycle, and that the depression will be prolonged and aggravated by inflationist and other interventionary measures....The guilt for the Great Depression must, at long last, be lifted from the shoulders of the free-market economy, and placed where it properly belongs: at the doors of politicians, bureaucrats, and the mass of "enlightened" economists. And in any other depression, past or present, the story will be the same.[5]

The Roosevelt Years. The depression could hardly become more severe than it already was. There was no place to go but up regardless of who was elected in 1932. Nonetheless, many procapitalists had good reason to be disenchanted with the Hoover administration, and in Roosevelt they thought they saw prospects for a quicker return to economic sanity. During the campaign Roosevelt had promised a balanced budget, a 25% cut in government spending, adherence to the gold standard, and an end to the proliferation of government bureaus. This was heartening stuff, and many businessmen worked actively in his behalf. They were to regret it. Anderson comments ruefully,

> Colonel House and I had cooperated in the effort to elect Governor Roosevelt president and had cooperated in the effort to keep his campaign utterances sound, and to offset the influence of the new group of "brain trusters" whom neither of us at the time regarded as particularly important. We subsequently learned better.[6]

The New Deal set about immediately to introduce the nation to the delights of the managed economy. Much has been said about going off the gold standard, but of more lasting significance was the confiscation of privately-held gold. When there exist no restrictions on the ownership and use of gold, people are ultimately free to accept or reject paper money depending on their assessment of the integrity of those who have issued it. Private ownership of gold, therefore, represented a potential roadblock to New Deal plans. Accordingly, the administration quickly set about to acquire both physical possession and legal title to all gold in the nation. The steps in this procedure were as follows.

1) Immediately upon taking office, Roosevelt achieved passage of an act of Congress (March 9, 1933) granting to the administration wide discretionary powers over money. On April 5th, a portion of this power was invoked: by presidential order (#6102) private parties were directed, under threat of heavy penalty, to exchange all gold bullion, gold coins, and gold certificates for other forms of currency. Banks were directed to deliver their gold supply to the Federal Reserve Banks in exchange for credit or payment. The Federal Reserve Banks in turn were to deliver the gold to the Treasury. It was not yet clear that this was other than a temporary measure, for the Secretary of the Treasury declared, "Those surrendering the gold of

course receive an equivalent amount of other forms of currency and those other forms of currency may be used for obtaining gold in an equivalent amount when authorized for proper purposes."[7]

2) During the previous campaign Roosevelt had endorsed "100%" a speech by Democratic Senator Glass pledging Democratic support to the gold standard. Now, however, with gold out of private hands, the gold standard was abandoned. In addition to a series of highly inflationary provisions, the Thomas Amendment[8] gave to the chief executive discretionary power to devalue the dollar by up to 50%. "It's dishonor, sir!" cried Senator Glass in dismay. "This great government, strong in gold, is breaking its promise to [those] to whom it has sold Government bonds with a pledge to pay gold coin of the present standard of value. It is breaking its promise to redeem its paper money in gold coin of the present standard of value. It's dishonor, Sir!"[9]

3) On June 5, 1933 Congress declared invalid the gold redemption clause in private contracts. In addition, it repudiated the gold redemption clause in all government obligations. Senator Thomas Gore, the blind senator from Oklahoma, said to Roosevelt, "Why, that's just plain stealing, isn't it Mr. President?"[10]

4) Next, in accordance with the Gold Reserve Act of January 30, 1934, the state finally took legal title to all of the gold now accumulated in the Treasury, paying for it in so-called "gold certificates." However, these certificates failed to state just what value in gold they represented. Anderson was one of those who testified before the Senate Committee on Banking and Currency; he wrote that he protested the vague nature of these certificates whereupon he "was taken aside by one of the administration Senators who grinned and said, 'Doctor, you don't understand about these certificates. These are not certificates that you can get gold. These are certificates that gold has been taken away from you.' "[11]

5) With all gold (except for jewelry, antique coins, etc.) now legally and physically in the hands of the government the rest was anticlimax. In accordance with the Gold Reserve Act (above) the president finally devalued the dollar to a fixed level of about 60% of its original worth. The government made a quick profit of about $2.8 billion since the paper dollars with which it had purchased the gold were now sharply depreciated in value.

Government confiscation of gold was not only an immoral act, it was economically self-defeating. Seizure of the private property of American citizens on a nation-wide scale was hardly designed to restore business confidence. The real significance of these measures lay elsewhere, however: previously, the Federal Government had exercised considerable control over the nation's money, but now, with all gold in the hands of the state, that control was total.

Prior to the final devaluation (step #5 above) Roosevelt's "brain trusters" engaged in some heady experimentation in "money management." One of the fashionable theories of the day held that the level of commodity prices could be adjusted simply by varying the gold content in the dollar. Roosevelt, who was quite unconfused by any understanding of economics, eagerly adopted the scheme. He announced,

> I am authorizing the Reconstruction Finance Corporation to buy newly-mined gold in the United States at prices to be determined from time to time after consultation with the Secretary of the Treasury and the President. Whenever necessary to the end in view we shall also buy or sell gold in the world market. My aim in taking this step is to establish and maintain continuous control. This is a policy and not an expedient.[12]

Day by day the administration juggled the gold content of the dollar by varying the price at which the government stood ready to buy gold. It started at $31.26 per ounce. Then a little more the next day, and a little more the day after in a manner quite unrelated to the economic facts of life. Secretary of the Treasury Morganthau described years later how the day-to-day price of gold was actually arrived at:

> Every morning Jesse Jones and I would meet with George Warren in the President's bedroom, to set the price of gold. Franklin Roosevelt would lie comfortably on his old-fashioned three-quarter mahogany bed....The actual price...made little difference....One day when I must have come in more than usually worried about the state of the world, we were planning an increase of from 19 to 22 cents. Roosevelt took one look at me, and suggested a rise of 21 cents.
>
> "It's a lucky number," the President said with a laugh, "because it's three times seven." I noted in my diary at this time, "If anybody ever knew how we really set the price of gold....I think they would really be frightened."[13]

Needless to say, the scheme did not work. As usual, the New Deal was dealing only with symptoms, not with underlying realities. The result was not to raise commodity prices but to depress business activity. How much was a dollar worth? Would it be worth anything the next year or the year after? How could an interest rate be established? Senator Glass declared, "No man outside of a lunatic asylum will loan his money on a farm mortgage!"[14] But the "brain trusters" were already prepared to fill the vacuum in private credit which their own policies had helped create. With lending organizations such as the RFC, the Farm Credit Administration and Home Owners Loan Corporation, the financial capital of the nation was no longer in New York City; it was in Washington, D.C. "Washington," said Roosevelt grandly, "has the money and is waiting for the proper projects to which to allot it."[15]

Rarely did a piece of New Deal legislation achieve its advertised goal. All of these measures had one thing in common, however: all involved a still greater concentration of power in the hands of an aggressive and skillful political elite.

One of the more drastic New Deal programs was the ill-famed National Recovery Act. Its purpose was to set industry-by-industry codes of minimum prices, rates, wages, etc. The business community, attracted by the prospect of legally-enforced immunity from the rigors of competition, initially supported the act. It was with considerable justice that NRA critics dubbed it "Chamber of Commerce Fascism." Business enthusiasm waned, however, when it appeared that the NRA would enforce not only rigid prices but rigid wages, shorter hours, and increased hiring. The alleged goal of the NRA was to increase prices and increase purchasing power—both at the same time.

The wage policies of the NRA represented the same philosophy that had prevailed during the Hoover years—that if wages could arbitrarily be kept high, prosperity would somehow be assured. But the higher labor costs imposed an intolerable burden on business, aggravating (if not actually causing) a slump in industrial production of about 25% in the six months after the NRA became effective. Moreover, as will always be the case, minimum wage laws served only to price the marginal worker out of a job. Charles F. Roos, at one time the Director of Research for the NRA, estimated that its minimum wage codes forced about one-half million blacks on relief in 1934. Among its other goals the NRA sought to raise the prices of manufactured goods. At the same time, however, the AAA was trying to raise the prices of agricultural goods relative to manufactured goods. Anderson felt that the whole thing was incomprehensible. But was it? From the standpoint of economic recovery the New Deal was all but incoherent, but as a program for extending political control it had a consistency all too apparent. NRA regimentation became so intense that a New Jersey tailor, Jack Magid, was arrested, convicted, fined, and sent to jail for charging thirty-five cents for pressing a suit; the NRA code stipulated forty cents. In the famous Schecter case a wholesale poultry dealer was convicted for, among other things, permitting "selection of individual chickens taken from coops and half coops." This practice was a violation of the NRA "Live Poultry Code." The case finally went to the Supreme Court which declared that Congress could not delegate power virtually without limit, and the entire NRA was finally declared unconstitutional.[16]

Because the Supreme Court was now striking down quite a number of New Deal measures, Roosevelt sought to increase the size of the court in order to pack it with his own appointees. Congress finally rebelled, however, and his plan was defeated. But it made little difference, for the justices were slowly coming around to the New Deal point of view anyway. As the saying went, the Court may not follow the Constitution, but it does follow the election returns.

During the New Deal years the economic theories of British economist John Maynard Keynes came to dominate virtually all government and academic circles. Keynes was no champion of the free economy. He had written in 1932 in the *Yale Review,*

> The decadent international but individualistic capitalism, in the hands of which we found ourselves after the war, is not a success. It is not intelligent, it is not beautiful, it is not just, it is not virtuous—and it doesn't deliver the goods. In short, we dislike it and are beginning to despise it. But when we wonder what to put in its place, we are extremely perplexed.[17]

But Keynes was not perplexed for long. In 1935 he summed up his views in his book *General Theory of Employment, Interest, and Money* which became (unfortunately) one of the most influential books on economics ever written. In short, Keynes urged all-out intervention. The principal instruments of government policy would be variations in the interest rate, budgetary deficits and surpluses, public works, redistribution of the wealth, etc.

But to control the economy is to control the entire nation and everyone in it. Accordingly, to those with a yen for regulating other people's lives, Keynesian doctrine had an irresistible fascination. In 1929 a book (with a laudatory preface written by Mussolini himself) appeared entitled *Universal Aspects of Fascism*, which declared,

In fact, Mr. Keynes' excellent little book, *The End of Laissez Faire* might, so far as it goes, serve as a useful introduction to fascist economics. There is scarcely anything to object to in it and there is much to applaud.[18]

Keynesian doctrine was embraced with equal enthusiasm by the men of the New Deal, for it lent the illusion of academic respectability to those already dedicated to the concepts of statism. Did the political leaders wish to control banking? Quote John Maynard Keynes on the virtues of the managed currency. Did they wish to consolidate their political power by means of vast federal expenditures? Quote John Maynard Keynes on the wisdom of deficit spending. Did they wish to place within their own grasp the levers and controls by which the nation's economy is operated? Quote John Maynard Keynes.

A favorite Keynesian weapon was "pump priming." Billions were spent, but the net effect was not to spur recovery but to retard it, for the state can inject into the economy only what it has first taken out, either openly through taxes or surreptitiously through inflation. When government spends, therefore, the economy drinks its own blood and, in the end, is weakened accordingly.[19]

Under the stimulus of a whole catalogue of New Deal nostrums the economy lurched ahead in 1936 and into 1937, but a sick economy is not cured by more intervention any more than a drug addict is cured by more drugs. Late in 1937 the weary economy collapsed once again, with industrial production dropping over 34% in the next nine months. This was the sharpest break in the nation's history. The decline between 1929 and 1932 was deeper, but at no time was it so abrupt. The New Deal had achieved a "first," a depression within a depression. There were once again ten million unemployed.

Every kind of interventionist gimmick had been tried—and the economy was no better off than before. The New Dealers were discouraged and out of ideas. Adviser Abe Fortas recalls a session in Benjamin Cohen's office in 1939 trying to think up some new program which might get the New Deal on track. But Cohen "walked over to a globe at the end of his long office, and he twirled it around slowly and said in his quavering voice, 'I don't think we're going to have much to worry about in this respect because I think that in a few years we'll be at war.' "[20]

On September 1, World War II began. Partly due to the flood of war orders from abroad, and partly because the long-overdue liquidations had finally been achieved, the depression at last came to an end.

The depression ended. But not because of the New Deal. It ended in spite of the New Deal. The nation had experienced a period of government manipulation, regulation and interference unprecedented in U.S. history, and in 1938 unemployment stood at ten million, higher than it had been in 1931! Yet even today the demagogue and the ignoramus mouth the slogan that "Roosevelt got us out of the depression." Hardly. He prolonged it for six long and bitter years. Politically, the New Deal was a rousing success, but as a prescription for economic recovery it was a blundering failure.

Conclusion. Coercive government control of the economy has not brought stability; by disrupting the feedback mechanisms of the marketplace it has brought repeated dislocations.

Will there be another Great Depression in the near future? Probably not. To be sure, some of the parallels are striking—such as a roaring stock market which now seems to have run out of steam. The disarray of Asian economies is a further worry. But the basic pre-condition of a serious bust—an out-of-control increase in the money supply—has not been there. As noted before, during the eight years preceding the '29 crash the money supply had increased by a whopping 62%. In contrast, over the eight year period of 1988–1996 the money supply (M2) increased by a comparatively modest 28%. We may have a severe recession in our future, but a '29-style collapse seems unlikely.

In the event of an economic downturn, the challenge will be to restrain political leaders from engaging in the kind of counter-productive intervention which aggravated and prolonged the Great Depression. The best prescription would be an agenda of less government, lower taxes, and less regulation. Unfortunately, this is a prescription which generally runs counter to the perceived interests of the professional politician.

5: Capitalism and the Intellectuals; Radical Pique

For centuries, capitalism has been the object of intellectual distaste. The interesting question is "Why?"

The intellectual's disdain for capitalism began in earnest with the industrial revolution. As Bertrand Russell declared;

> The industrial revolution caused unspeakable misery both in England and in America. I do not think any student of economic history can doubt that the average happiness in England in the early nineteenth century was lower than it had been a hundred years earlier; and this was due almost entirely to scientific technique.[1]

Russell was merely restating the opinions of several generations of eighteenth and nineteenth century writers, clergymen and assorted social critics who tended to lay at the factory doorstep the blame for every social woe, real or imagined. The intellectuals of the day looked about and suddenly noticed that there was poverty. But the poverty had been there all along. Why, then, the passionate distaste for the very system which was gradually improving man's material lot? Possibly capitalism was its own worst enemy in this respect, for in raising the general standard of living it made more conspicuous the poverty that remained. But whatever the explanation, industrialization was roundly denounced from the rostrums, pulpits and newspapers of the time. Thomas Malthus wrote in 1798 that "The increasing wealth of the nation has had little or no tendency to better the conditions of the laboring poor." J. R. McCulloch declared that "there seems, on the whole, little room for doubting that the factory system operates unfavorably on the bulk of those engaged in it." Engels declared, "The proletariat was called into existence by the introduction of machinery....The consequences of improvement in machinery under our present social conditions are, for the working man, solely injurious, and often in the highest degree oppressive. Every new advance brings with it loss of employment, want and suffering." W. H. Hutt lists a further series of complaints registered by nineteenth century English reformers:

Thackrah lamented the fact that children were no longer contented with "plain food" but must have "dainties." The Reverend G. S. Bull deplored the tendency of girls to buy pretty clothes "ready-made" from shops instead of making them themselves, as this practice unfitted them to become the mothers of children. Gaskell saw decadence in tobacco....He also saw moral decline in the growth of workmen's combinations. The men were no longer "respectful and attentive" to their "superiors"....[Thackrah declared that] "Higher wages, moreover, very often, if not generally, lead men to intemperance."[2]

Child labor, of course, was a particular target of the early reformers. William Cooke Taylor wrote in 1844 about those reformers who witnessed children at work in the factories and thought to themselves, "How much more delightful would have been the gambol of the free limbs on the hillside; the sight of the green mead with its spangles of buttercups and daisies; the song of the bird and the humming of the bee."

But, as Taylor observed, "We have seen children perishing from sheer hunger in the mud hovel, or in the ditch by the wayside."[3] For many of these children the factory system meant quite literally the only chance for survival. Today, we overlook the fact that death from starvation and exposure was a common fate prior to the industrial revolution, for the precapitalist economy was barely able to support the population. Entire families worked in order to earn enough to buy the scarce and expensive necessities of life. As Professor Ludwig von Mises put it,

> The factory owners did not have the power to compel anybody to take a factory job. They could only hire people who were ready to work for the wages offered to them. Low as these wage rates were, they were nonetheless much more than these paupers could earn in any other field open to them. It is a distortion of facts to say that the factories carried off the housewives from the nurseries and the kitchen and the children from their play. These women had nothing to cook with and to feed their children. These children were destitute and starving. Their only refuge was the factory. It saved them, in the strict sense of the term, from death by starvation.[4]

Only as goods were produced in greater abundance at lower cost could men support their families without sending their children to work. It was not the reformer[5] or the politician who ended the grim necessity for child labor; it was capitalism.

Anticapitalist writers in nineteenth century England were particularly scandalized by the drab and dilapidated conditions in housing. Engels declared: "Everything which here arouses horror and indignation is of recent origin [and] belongs to the industrial epoch." But the state was not helping matters. Ashton points out that one of the principal reasons for the shortage of workingmen's housing was the great difficulty encountered by builders in borrowing the needed money. The usury law forbade an interest rate of more than 5%, and with the government paying 4½% for loans with which to prosecute the war against Napoleon, the builder was starved for capital. Moreover, brick was subject to heavy tax, while the duty on the higher grade Baltic timber was all but prohibitive. Then, as now, the heavy hand of government did little to stimulate progress. Ashton comments:

> if the towns were ridden with disease, some at least of the responsibility lay with legislators who, by taxing windows, put a price on light and air and, by taxing bricks and tiles, discouraged the construction of drains and sewers. Those who dwell on the horrors that arose from the fact that the products of the sewers often got mixed up with the drinking water, and attribute this, as all other horrors, to the industrial revolution, should be reminded of the obvious fact that without the iron pipe, which was one of the products of that revolution, the problem of enabling people to live a healthy life together in towns could never have been solved.[6]

In England a great deal of the antagonism toward the rising capitalist middle class had political origins. The Tories, who represented the country gentlemen whose position was threatened by the growing influence of capitalist businessmen, were not averse to discrediting the factory system at every opportunity. W. H. Hutt relates the episode of the "Sadler Committee Report" of 1832.[7]

Parliament had established a committee headed by Sadler to investigate the widespread reports of the gross cruelties of the factory system. It had been agreed that Sadler would call his own witnesses first, to be followed by the rebuttal witnesses. But the rebuttal was never heard, for Sadler published his findings immediately upon the close of that session of Parliament. None of Sadler's witnesses had testified under oath, and the one-sided report was as inaccurate as it was sensational. Some of the testimony was found by a second committee to be "absolutely false," and even Karl Marx's lieutenant, Friedrich Engels, described the report as "emphatically partisan, composed by strong enemies of the factory system for party ends....Sadler permitted himself to be betrayed by his noble enthusiasm into the most distorted and erroneous statements."

Even so, the Sadler report was immensely influential, becoming the bible for indignant reformers well into the twentieth century. The Hammonds described it as "one of the main sources of our knowledge of the conditions of factory life at the time. Its pages bring before the reader in vivid form of dialogue the kind of life that was led by the victims of the new system." Hutchins and Harrison described it as "one of the most valuable collections of evidence on industrial conditions that we possess."

One suspects that much of the anticapitalist bias of today could be traced back to fire-breathing reformers like Sadler. Were Bertrand Russell and Matthew Josephson influenced by the Sadler Report or by the works of the Hammonds or of Hutchins and Harrison? No doubt they were. And no doubt that influence has extended as well to the anticapitalist intellectuals of today who remain convinced that it is only continued and expanded government control which protects us from the horrors of capitalism.

For two hundred years and more intellectuals have been generally hostile toward capitalism. For every Adam Smith there were a dozen Sadlers; for every Milton Friedman today there are a dozen John Kenneth Galbraiths. The intriguing question is "why?" Why have intellectuals been so unfriendly toward the economic system which has improved the material lot of hundreds of millions? One reason is that capitalism is based on self-interest, a motivation which many intellectuals regard as ignoble. As Bertrand de Jouvenal has observed,

> The world of business is to the intellectual one in which the values are wrong, the motivation low, the rewards misaddressed. A convenient gateway into the intellectual's inner courtyard where his judgments are rendered is afforded by his deficit preference. It has been observed that his sympathy goes to institutions which run at a loss, nationalized industries supported by the treasury, colleges dependent on grants and subsidies, newspapers which never get out of the red.[8]

A second reason for the anticapitalist bias might be seen in the process of natural selection by which people end up as professional intellectuals. Consider a graduating class at a university: those with an entrepreneurial spirit go into business, or start a medical practice, or open a store, or go into private industry. The rest become the social workers and the politicians, or become the academics and historians and opinion makers[9]—the professional intellectuals.

This intellectual elite, then, from which the entrepreneurial spirit has been largely filtered out, will now naturally tend to be indifferent or downright hostile to the alien values of the marketplace.

But there is a third reason, probably the most important, why intellectuals as a class have been overwhelmingly unfriendly toward capitalism. The reason is Radical Pique.

Radical Pique

Capitalism has never enjoyed a great press. Arthur Schlesinger, one of the nation's more prominent anticapitalist intellectuals, used to talk about the "confused and frightened business community" and "the frightened, ignorant and despairing rich, driven by dark impulses beyond their own control to conspire in their own destruction."[10] And today one need only peruse any op-ed page to find similar expressions of liberal contempt for what has been the most successful economic system in the world. The intriguing question is "why?" Why do so many intellectuals, including their journalist cousins, and so many middle-class radicals, repudiate the economic system on which their own comfortable lifestyle depends?

Far from being the struggling masses of Marxist folklore, the anticapitalists comprise a comfortable and prominent elite. Generally affluent and well-educated, they are bright, articulate and idealistic people. But they are also impatient and resentful. They have (or think they have) all the answers to the problems of poverty, the environment, the economy, etc.—*but the marketplace does not pay attention to what they are saying!*

Here is the essence of Radical Pique: resentment toward an economic system which responds to what people actually want rather than to what these bright people *think* they should want. Worse, capitalism rewards those who cater to those wants. But a system so vulgar that it gives more encouragement to a rock star than to a tenured faculty professor, or so materialistic that it pays more attention to the consumer than to Ralph Nader, or so unjust that it rewards the "selfish" businessman more generously than his "unselfish" critic, is obviously rotten to the core!

Many intellectuals despise capitalism, then, not because it is undemocratic, but precisely because it *is* democratic: Capitalism responds to the inelegant tastes of the marketplace rather than to the more "progressive" judgements of its resentful critics. In the process it places economic power in the hands of crass business people who, in the activist's opinion, are less enlightened, less intelligent, less well-educated and less worthy than he is. Hence Radical Pique.

The phenomenon of Radical Pique touches upon a mystery which has bedeviled observers literally for generations: Why do so many well-fed intellectuals spend so much time trashing the economic system on which their own affluent life style depends? Sixty years ago economist Joseph Schumpeter addressed this question as the "Sociology of the Intellectual."[11] Radical Pique may be what Schumpeter was getting at.

> "The time has come," the chairman said,
> "To speak of many things:
> Of duty, bread and selfishness,
> And the evil that it brings.
> For, speaking thus we can amend
> That irony of fate
> That gives to unenlightened minds
> The power to create!"
> —from *Tom Smith and His Incredible Bread Machine*

The dangerous intellectual. Intellectuals, especially liberal intellectuals, invariably have a "plan," and the plan generally requires imposition by government. Listen again to Arthur Schlesinger:

> In any case, taxation and inflation are technical problems far more manageable once the national will has decided in favor of definite goals.[12]

But the concept of a "national will" or a "national goal," is the very essence of tyranny. In a free society governments do not have "goals"; only people have goals, and it is the proper function of government to maintain that climate of liberty in which those individual goals can be sought. But Schlesinger continues,

> As we develop a sense of national purpose, we will surely decide that extra available income could be better spent for public ends than for an increased flow of ever shinier consumer's goods. And we have in taxation the instrument by which we decide where our national resources should be allocated.[13]

And who is "we"? At best "we" in Schlesinger's equation is "the majority"; at worst it is an elite of intellectuals, politicians, bureaucrats and assorted opportunists. In either event, the individual is forcibly subordinated to a monolithic "national purpose." It is a concept as old as tyranny: "The function of government is to direct the physical and moral powers of the nation toward the end for which the commonwealth has come into being." Schlesinger again? No. Robespierre.[14]

The most dangerous animal on the planet is not the cape buffalo, but the intellectual with "a plan." Especially the intellectual willing to impose his creation upon others by force. As British historian Paul Johnson observes,

> It is not the formulation of ideas, however misguided, but the desire to impose them on others that is the deadly sin of the intellectual. That is why they so incline by temperament to the left. For capitalism merely occurs, if no one does anything to stop it. It is socialism that has to be constructed, and as a rule, forcibly imposed, thus providing a far bigger role for intellectuals in its genesis.
>
> So, one of the lessons of our century is: Beware the intellectual. Not merely should they be kept well away from the levers of power, they also should be objects of particular suspicion when they seek to offer collective advice. Beware committees, conferences, leagues of intellectuals![15]

Amen to that, for the resort to force will corrupt even the noblest aims. From the French Revolution to Auschwitz, and from the Gulags to the killing fields of Cambodia, well-meaning intellectuals with "a plan" have always been in the vanguard. Some of the greatest evils in history have been committed not by people who set out to do evil, but by people who set out to do good—by force.

As noted thus far in Part I, the dominant theme of government activity over the past 200 years has been regulation of the economy in behalf of this-or-that favored group. The process continues to the present day, as we shall see in the following chapter.

6:Regulation Today

Much of business regulation today is based less on fundamental concepts of justice than on murky and ever-shifting notions of "ideological law."

Robespierre, one of the architects of the French Revolution's reign of terror, was not a wilful murderer. On the contrary, he was an intellectual, an idealist and a humanitarian. Unfortunately, he was also a practitioner of what might be described as "ideological law."

"But I have done nothing," wept the young seamstress on her way to the guillotine in Dickens' story of the Revolution, *A Tale of Two Cities.* And there, in a nutshell, is the problem with ideological law. Her crime, if any, was not against some individual, for she hadn't robbed or killed anybody. Her offense was against an abstraction: "The Revolution."

Unlike English common law, the central concern of ideological law is not the individual who has been wronged, but the furtherance of some abstract Greater Good: the Revolution, the Party, the Workers, the Fatherland, or whatever.

Much of business regulation today, especially antitrust and SEC, is based on ideological law: concerned less with real people who have suffered actual harm, than with abstract and ill-defined notions of "fairness," "integrity of the marketplace," or "greed," or "sleaze," or whatever. This is not to say that these concerns are not legitimate, but in a free society the law—especially criminal law—must be referenced to some identifiable offense to some identifiable victim. Without this anchor to reality, the law is adrift. *Liberté, égalité, fraternité,* fairness, the level playing field; these are all noble concepts in the abstract, but as legal criteria they are worthless. Where the rule of law requires objective standards, touchy-feely notions about "fairness" or "sleaze" or whatever can mean anything to anybody. A prime example of ideological law is the murky issue of "insider trading."

The myth of insider trading. The popular wisdom on insider trading was neatly summarized by the lady law student mentioned by Henry Manne in his influential book, *Insider Trading and the Stock Market:* her contribution to a classroom discussion on this issue was to stamp her foot and declare, "I don't care. It just isn't right."[1]

But when enforcement depends only on a gut feeling that "it just isn't right," lady law students aren't the only ones who become a bit rattled trying to explain their position. In a subsequent law journal article Manne described the unfriendly responses to his book from his fellow law professors:

> one of the leading academics in the field of securities regulation stated to me personally, "We didn't need any book on insider trading. I know it's wrong and that's all there is to it."[2]

This degree of certitude may be comforting to the true believer—but not to the bewildered defendant. Consider, for example, the 1984 SEC suit brought against Barry Switzer, the former football coach at the University of Oklahoma. At a track meet, Switzer had overheard an oil company executive discussing a pending corporate takeover. Switzer and some associates bought stock in the target company and ended up making a profit of around $600,000. To the SEC this was insider trading.

No one disputes that wrongful acts such as breach of contract or theft should be punished. But Switzer had betrayed no fiduciary obligation, nor had he stolen this information. He was charged exclusively because he had an informational edge which was construed to be "unfair." The SEC finally lost this case, but the fact that it got into court at all tells us something about the confused nature of insider trading doctrine.

The rationale behind insider trading enforcement is that trading with the advantage of "material non-public information" perpetrates a fraud on the other, less well-informed party. However, this notion is simply a myth, *for the other party to the trade is going to sell (or buy) anyway.* The SECs own chief economist acknowledged this crucial point in a 1987 study:

> When traders with better information (whether gained legally or not) profit from their investment positions, they presumably do so at the expense of less informed investors. The anonymous nature of most stock trading makes it difficult to determine who loses what the information specialist gains. Those selling into the market when the better-informed are buying probably would not have sold had they possessed the same valuable information. *However, they still would have sold if the information specialist had refrained from buying,* especially if the trading of the specialist did not affect significantly the stock price. This holds true whether the trading is based on insider information or on careful analysis and successful anticipation of the event.[3] [Emphasis added.]

In itself, then, a trade in the anonymous marketplace is ethically neutral because it has no effect on the other party's decision. If there is a wrongful act it will not be in the trade, but in some prior offense, such as betrayal of a fiduciary duty, theft of information, etc.

Nonetheless, regulators are repeatedly bringing charges not because of some objectively wrongful act, but simply because this or that trading activity is construed to be "unfair."

For example, consider the recent indictment of Alvin DeShano, an accountant for the Carl's Jr. hamburger chain: On the first trading day after learning of a discouraging quarterly report he sold all of his available company stock and saved himself around $7000. As a result, he faced criminal penalties of up to 5 years in jail and a $250,000 fine.

Proponents of insider trading laws would argue that DeShano committed fraud by withholding important information—similar to the person selling a used car knowing the wheels were about to fall off. However, the analogy will not hold up, for the buyer was going to buy this stock anyway, if not from DeShano then from someone else.

In reality, DeShano defrauded no one. Of course, if he had *caused* the poor quarterly showing, or in some other way had violated his fiduciary obligation to the company, that would have been different. But in that event Carl's Jr. could have taken appropriate action through existing common law remedies. Perhaps this thought occurred to the jury, because it rejected the government's case, and DeShano was acquitted.

Not so fortunate was William Banowsky, the respected former president of Pepperdine University. An outside director of Thrifty, Inc., Banowsky mentioned to members of his family that there might be a merger with Pacific Lighting. Word got around, and as the stock climbed rapidly Banowsky's relatives made around $442,000. This was construed as insider trading, and as the law is now interpreted Banowsky was personally responsible, even though he didn't trade in the stock himself. The civil penalty was a fine of $754,000 plus a badly tarnished reputation.

But again, where were the victims? Who was cheated? The sellers were selling anyway, and if they hadn't sold to Banowsky's relatives they would have sold to someone else—and probably at a lower price! Nor is it "unfair" that the profit ended up in the hands of those with the more complete information; on the contrary, it would have been unfair were it otherwise. Moreover, insider trading permits the stock market to do precisely what it is supposed to do: reflect quickly and accurately a new set of economic realities. If Banowsky committed an indiscretion (which he obviously did) that was between him and Thrifty Corporation.

Manne has suggested that a corporation should be free to state publicly its policy of permitting or forbidding insider trading by its officers. Then, investors could decide for themselves whether to buy that stock or avoid it. In fact, the sophisticated investor might well prefer the corporation which permitted insider trading, because he would then be assured that the stock price reflected the true state of affairs. Says Manne, "I personally would prefer to invest in the shares of corporations which did allow insider trading."

Manne's views are not shared by the courts which remain faithful to the myths of insider trading. In 1997 the Supreme Court confirmed that the SEC could indeed go after those who merely traded on inside information, even though they had no fiduciary duty whatever. Accordingly, even the person who overhears information in the men's room and trades on it is subject to prosecution. Justice Ginsberg explained that the purpose of the Securities Exchange Act of 1934 was to ensure "honest securities markets and thereby promote investor confidence."

This is nonsense. There is not a shred of evidence that public concern about things like insider trading has in any way kept people out of the stock market. On the contrary, the desire of most investors is to get some of that special information for themselves. Hence the wide demand for newsletters and assorted tip sheets, the avowed purpose of which is to provide precisely the informational edge which the SEC so selectively deplores.

But the real problem with "fairness," of course, is trying to define it. Conceptually, any action which leads to a profit could be construed as "unfair," because somebody obviously had an edge over somebody else. When ideological law is on the prowl, who can tell what's legal and what isn't?

Not defined by any actual harm to any actual victim, the "law" is whatever the regulators say it is. And in the case of insider trading they aren't saying until it's time to pounce. For example, former SEC enforcement chief Gary Lynch, in Congressional testimony, explicitly opposed clearer definition of the rules because it would make prosecution "more difficult." For the same reason, Congressman Dingell, former Chairman of the House Energy and Commerce Committee, has declared flatly that "there will be no definition of insider trading."[4]

It is outrageous for regulators to refuse to define what it is they are going to punish. The name of the game for the SEC these days is to watch and wait and then pounce, declaring after-the-fact, "We just now decided that what you did was illegal." This is not law, but ideology.

It's worth noting that in no other country in the world is insider trading such a bugaboo as in the U.S. Hong Kong adopted an insider trading prohibition in 1974 but then repealed it a few years later. Japan has no such legislation, although the stock exchange has certain of its own prohibitions. France has very limited laws on the subject, while in the United Kingdom insider trading was not addressed until 1980, and since that time there have been only a handful of convictions and no prison terms. Only in the United States has insider trading been hyped into White Collar Crime #1.

This doesn't mean, of course, that there is no such thing as fraud. On any day of the week there are scores of truly fraudulent operations under way, from telephone bucket shops which will "invest your money in precious metals" and then disappear, to penny-stock scams whose promises are little better than bald-faced lies.

In the 1970s Bernard Cornfield of Equity Funding pulled off the biggest insurance scam of all time by writing up thousands of phony policies and selling them to unwary reinsurers. The scheme was uncovered by private analyst Ray Dirks. Whereupon the SEC expressed its thanks by charging Dirks with insider trading because he had warned his clients that something was fishy at Equity Funding! (The SEC pursued Dirks for ten years before finally losing before the Supreme Court in 1983.)

Surely, there are plenty of fraudulent schemes out there to occupy the talents of the SEC. Federal regulators, however, confused by abstract notions of what's "fair," seem unable to tell the difference between the businessman and the con man. Three contemporary cases illustrate the point: Michael Milken, Microsoft, and Intel.

Michael Milken. When the colorful oil man T. Boone Pickens launched a hostile takeover of Unocal, its irascible CEO Fred Hartley was outraged. He raced to Washington where his ire was directed not only at Pickens, but at Michael Milken who had backed several such moves with his innovative high-yield bonds (known by their detractors as "junk bonds").

Hartley represented everything that Pickens had been criticizing for years about some corporate managers. He had once had the side of his corporate jet opened up, at a cost to the company of $50,000, to install a piano. He had been pouring millions into the extraction of oil from oil shale, but when questioned about an investment which could never make economic sense, his response was to curse the questioner and pour in more money—close to a billion dollars and counting. Pickens, who knew a dry hole when he saw one, said that he would have closed down the shale oil operation "by sundown."

Hartley regarded Unocal as "his" company, and his attitude to shareholders was dismissive at best. At a shareholders meeting in 1984 a stockholder had the temerity to ask why the dividends were so low, and Hartley responded, "You look like an elderly fellow. Why don't you sell your stock and go have a good time?" A Unocal director confided to Pickens that he had once asked Hartley the same question, and the response was, "You're crazy. Why would you want to give a bunch of money to people we don't even know?"

The hostile takeover was a mechanism by which a dissident group of stockholders could replace complacent or inept management. The formula for the corporate raider was elegantly simple: if the assets of a corporation were being under-utilized, the stock price would be low relative to the value of the underlying assets. The corporate raider, bankrolled perhaps by Milken's high-yield bonds, could buy up the under-valued stock, even at a premium, and still come out ahead by imposing needed efficiencies and by selling off those under-utilized assets. The process generally served a legitimate economic purpose, but it is not surprising that the targeted executives, who might lose their cushy jobs, were infuriated.

In Washington, Hartley complained bitterly to a senate committee,

> If the Russians had somehow quietly managed to murder five of the nation's leading oil companies—and were stalking the rest—surely I'm certain that Congress would be in an uproar, demanding action....You may be looking at a target right now—you may be looking at the next guy to be murdered.[5]

Hartley had influential friends in and about the Bush White House, and important people were soon writing important op-ed pieces. One article in the *Wall Street Journal* was entitled "Junk Bonds and Other Securities Swill."[6] The government, through the machinery of the SEC, was soon mobilized to do what governments always do: protect established and influential economic interests. The story presented to the public, however, was quite different: to defend against the "greed" and "sleaze" of the malevolent Michael Milken.

The flimsiness of the SEC case was evident in the original 98-count indictment which referred to "the victims of these unlawful activities," but then never named any. This is not surprising, of course, considering Milken's remarkable track record in making other people rich. (See "Eight Curious Myths," at the end of this chapter.)

Much of the indictment was repetition, with allegations repeated again and again under different headings. The core of the indictment was a series of innocuous acts dug up by the prosecution and preceded by the magic words "unlawfully, wilfully, and knowingly." Some of this stuff might have risen to the level of minor technical violations, but to describe any of it as "criminal" was nonsense.

However, Milken was very rich and very secretive, and woefully inept in explaining to people that business activity might have something to do with the profit motive. Accordingly, it was pile-on time in the media. Connie Bruck wrote a best seller the title of which told it all: *The Predators Ball.* Benjamin Stein's article in *Barrons,* "Betrayer of Capitalism," was the first in a series of broadsides. A typical anti-Milken piece was a sneering article in *Playboy* entitled "Money-Mad Mike," which described him as "the Jimmy Swaggart of Junk" who "spread his greedy gospel around the globe."[7] The media described the corporate restructurings of the period only in terms of "greed" and "displaced workers," ignoring the long-term benefits to the economy—benefits which we enjoy to the present day.

> A prize cartoon depicted Smith
> With fat and drooping jowels,
> Snatching bread from hungry babes,
> Indifferent to their howls!
> —from *Tom Smith and His Incredible Bread Machine*

After four years of this Milken was probably the most despised person in the nation, and he wanted it to end. He thereupon made the biggest mistake in his life: he accepted a plea bargain.

The plea bargain of April 1990, contained just six counts: three securities law violations derived from Milken's association with Ivan Boesky, who really was a crook, one count of mail fraud, one tax count, and one conspiracy count linking the other five. The original charges of insider trading and stock manipulation did not appear, while none of the counts had any connection with junk bonds as such.

The weakness of the case can be inferred from Count Three, which pertained to what had previously been a minor civil offense called "parking."[8] Boesky, a compulsive plunger, parked stock with Milken so that Boesky would then be able to overstate his net capital to the SEC. Milken probably did not initiate these transactions, but he did accommodate them. It should be noted, however, that no one is defrauded here; there is no "victim." In fact, parking had previously been treated simply as a minor civil transgression to be satisfied by an injunction or a fine. Parking was elevated to criminal status only with Boesky's plea bargain in 1986. Accordingly, parking was criminalized not by Congress or the courts, but by zealous government prosecutors who hyped a minor technical violation into a major criminal charge.

Prior to the sentencing, Judge Kimba Wood called for a special hearing (called "Fatico," after a case of that name) at which the prosecution could present evidence of wrongdoing beyond these six counts. Here, at last, was the prosecution's big chance to lay out the full sordid story behind that well-publicized 98-count indictment.

The Fatico hearing was a bust. There was nothing there. The *Los Angeles Times* headline declared, "Smoking Gun Was a No-Show."

The sentencing was scheduled for November, 1990. Milken and his lawyers expected perhaps a four-year sentence, one more than Ivan Boesky. What they got left them stunned and unbelieving. Judge Wood, a woman quite unconfused by any knowledge of business or finance, declared,

> When a man of your power in the financial world, at the head of the most important department of one of the most important investment banking houses in this country, repeatedly conspires to violate, and violates, securities and tax laws in order to achieve more power and wealth for himself and his wealthy clients, and commits financial crimes that are particularly hard to detect [read: we couldn't find any victims], a significant prison term is required in order to deter others. This kind of misuse of your leadership position and enlisting employees whom you supervised to assist you in violating the laws are serious crimes warranting serious punishment and the discomfort and opprobrium of being removed from society.

But when Kimba Wood referred to crimes "that were particularly hard to detect," she gave the game away. What she meant was that no actual victims had been discovered. But no matter. She then sentenced Milken to 10 years in prison,[9] essentially for being "greedy." This was not law, but ideology.

Robespierre would have understood.

Whether Milken was the dark prince of sleaze as described by the prosecution and the media is really beside the point. Milken was not indicted for sleaze or greed or for being "unfair"; he was indicted for securities fraud. But when it came to explaining what was misrepresented, or who was actually defrauded, the original indictment as well as the final plea were mute. Where were the victims? What were their names?

Moreover, how could insider trading be charged in the initial indictment when the SEC's own chief economist acknowledges, as noted above, that it has no effect whatever on the other party? And how could stock parking be prosecuted as a criminal offense when the acts occurred *before* parking was magically elevated from a civil to a criminal matter in 1986? What can one say in defense of "laws" such as these which are created not by Congress, or even by the courts, but merely by the boundless ingenuity of bureaucrats?

The question, then, is not simply whether Milken "broke the law," for the law is so fuzzy that anyone can be found guilty of anything. The question is whether these picky and ever-shifting rules and regulations are defensible to begin with. Securities regulation has become (along with antitrust) the most capricious, disruptive and irrational body of law on the books today.

> The rule of law in complex times
> Has proved itself deficient!
> We much prefer the rule of men—
> It's vastly more efficient!
> —from *Tom Smith and His Incredible Bread Machine.*

Microsoft and Intel. Microsoft and Intel, two of the latest targets of Antitrust, are repeating the profound strategic error committed by Milken's high-priced lawyers: trying to fight the battle exclusively on terms defined by the government. But when the law is whatever the bureaucrat says it is, even innocence will be no defense, for the regulation will simply be shifted and reinterpreted to describe whatever the accused *did* do. The better defense would be to challenge the validity and constitutionality of rules which are designed not to protect rights, but merely to further the amorphous goals of ideology: "fairness," "the level playing field," etc. Perhaps the challenge would not succeed—but it would beat losing by default. (Ask Michael Milken!)

The Microsoft dispute had its origin in the Bush administration with an inquiry into Microsoft's licensing agreement with computer manufacturers. Antitrust intervened, and by terms of a consent decree signed in 1994, the licensing arrangement was terminated. In addition (and this was the fateful part), Microsoft agreed not to tie any of its other software programs to the sale of its popular Windows program. However, "integrated" features were explicitly allowed. The current dispute is over Microsoft's browser program, Internet Explorer, and whether it is a separate program or an integrated feature.

A rival company, Netscape, has a competing browser called Netscape Navigator. Prompted by Netscape, Antitrust says that Microsoft is violating the consent decree by "bundling" its browser with Windows. Microsoft says it isn't in violation because its browser is an integrated feature, just like many other features now taken for granted. For example, software supporting fax modems and e-mail, once available only as separate add-ons, are now commonplace ingredients of any operating system—and a great deal cheaper. IBM and Sun Microsystems have packaged browsers with their own systems, while some manufacturers, including IBM, Hewlett-Packard, Compaq and others, have bundled *both* browsers along with Windows.

An analogy to the "integrated feature" might be the air conditioner in an automobile. It's true that the purchaser could buy a separate air conditioning unit and install it himself—but is this really what customers want? And who decides? Consumers in the marketplace? Or Antitrust?

In the case of Microsoft, Justice Department chief Janet Reno evidently opts for the latter. In the touchy-feel language of ideological law, she has described the Microsoft practice as "plain wrong."[10]

But why is it "plain wrong"? If Netscape has a superior product, it's free to promote it and find its own niche. In fact, Netscape once held 90% of the browser market—now down to around 50%. Why is it "plain wrong" that competition, much of it from Microsoft, now offers consumers a wider choice? Moreover, Netscape has always been easily loadable into Windows, if the customer so desires. If Gates' business practices really are unreasonable, as antitrust alleges, he will ultimately pay the price as customers and competitors find ways to escape his evil clutches. Alternate technologies, such as the Java platform, are already out there. These are issues to be resolved by the marketplace, not by antitrust.

The irony here is that companies such as Netscape might not even exist were it not for the pioneering efforts of Bill Gates. Gates is the Henry Ford of computer software, and his efforts have helped create an entire industry, opening the door for hundreds of new companies and hundreds of thousands of new jobs. Gates is the Tom Smith of the era. He should not be harassed by Antitrust; he should get a medal.

However, the government continues to treat Gates like a bullying predator. One wonders what the response would be in Washington if he were to declare one day, "I'm out of here. I've had it with you people. We're moving to Vancouver and taking our multi-billion dollar corporation with us."

One suspects that there would finally be a serious attitude adjustment at Antitrust.

The latest target of antitrust (the FTC) is Intel, the hugely successful manufacturer of the Pentium chip. The complaint is that Intel has withheld technical information from other companies, including Digital, Intergraph and Compaq. Explains an Intel spokesman, "We withdrew that information in cases where we were either a defendant or about to be made a defendant in an intellectual property dispute. We believe that our actions are well within our rights under existing intellectual property and antitrust laws."

Again, whether Intel's actions are "reasonable" or "fair" is not the point. What *is* the point is that this information is the creation of, and the property of, Intel, to be used wisely or unwisely. Says William Baxter, former head of Antitrust, "The most time-honored way of protecting intellectual property is simply to keep it a secret, and that's all Intel has done here. The claim is that they have done it in a discriminatory and exclusionary way, but that's a very elusive concept."[11]

Elusive indeed. In second-guessing Intel's decisions the FTC assaults the very concept of property rights, on which the market economy is based. Companies such as Microsoft and Intel have helped to make the U.S. the world leader in computer technology, and that position will not be advanced by subjecting their business decisions to the whims of ideological law.

Today, consumers can purchase for under $2000 a computer and software which can perform 600 million instructions per second. This is six times faster than a system which would have cost $1 million just a decade ago. It has been noted that this advance would be equivalent to an automobile selling today for $2 and going 600 miles on a thimbleful of gas!

Microsoft and Intel have played major roles in this astonishing success story. Yet to the ideologues of antitrust the people responsible are exploiters and predators! When Janet Reno says it is "plain unfair," it is enough to make one gag. Alan Greenspan was right when he noted years ago that "The entire structure of antitrust statutes in this country is a jumble of economic irrationality and ignorance."[12]

Amen to that.

Across the spectrum of economic activity regulators continue to chip away at the structure of a free economy. What is missing throughout is an understanding of the principles on which a free society is based. This search will be the subject of the following section (which is really the core of this book), "The Three Principles of Capitalism and the Free Society."

Appendix to Chapter 6: Eight Curious Myths About Michael Milken and Junk Bonds

1) *Junk bonds caused the collapse of the S&L industry.* In fact, only about 5.3% of S&Ls held any junk bonds at all, comprising only about 1% of all S&L assets. The S&Ls failed primarily because of a collapse in real estate prices.

2) *Junk bonds were a Ponzi scheme which led to huge losses.* Junk bonds took a hit in 1989–90, but soon rebounded, with more new issues appearing in 1992 than in any previous year. Junk bonds continue to be solid investments, and an important source of investment capital for new and expanding businesses.

3) *Milken engaged in widespread fraud.* In fact, no "victim" of Milken has ever been discovered. Those individuals and institutions which dealt with him came away richer rather than poorer.

4) *Milken-backed junk bonds generally ended in default.* According to Salomon Brothers figures, the default rate on high yield securities issued by Drexel between 1977 and 1990 was a modest 9.6%, compared to 19.3% for Merrill Lynch, 43.1% for Paine Weber, etc.

5) *Hostile Takeovers, leverged buy outs, mergers, etc., were a creation primarily of junk bond financing.* In fact, only about 10% of these restructurings were financed by junk bonds, with around 73% coming from banks. In any event, Dr. Michael Jensen of Harvard Business School estimates that between 1976 and 1990 these restructured companies increased in stock value by around $650 billion.

6) *Junk bonds led the economy into an ocean of debt.* In fact, according to GAO figures, high yield bonds accounted for only about 9% of total corporate debt in the late '80s, up from 1% a decade earlier.

7) *Junk bonds led to widespread business failures.* In fact, economist Glen Yago notes that companies which went into bankruptcy or default consti-

tuted "only about 10% of the junk bond market at its peak in 1990 and less than 4% for the decade."[13]

8) *Junk bond activity contributed little to the economy.* In fact, junk bond financing raised over $200 billion in new capital during the '80s, much of which went to new and expanding companies. Yago reports that between 1980 and 1986 these issues accounted for around 82% of job growth among those public companies which report employment. George Gilder writes, "More important still was the critical role of junk bonds in financing such crucial American businesses as fiber optics, telecommunications and television. Drexel managed multibillion dollar issues for Turner Broadcasting, MCI, TeleCommunications, Inc., McCaw Cellular, and many other companies without firm collateral—companies that could not possibly have raised comparable sums anywhere else. These firms, backed by Milken, have been critical to U.S. competitiveness."[14]

But if Milken's activities were essentially productive and legitimate, why did he end up in prison? As indicated before, there were three underlying factors—and they had nothing to do with criminal conduct: hostility from within the corporate community, an unfriendly media, and a body of business law based upon ideology rather than objective standards and actual victims.

Part Two:
The Three Principles
of Capitalism
and the Free Society

7: Why Principles Matter

Today, as in the past, those who try to operate without principles are sailing without a rudder.

The phenomenon of Radical Pique discussed previously may describe why many intellectuals, journalists, et. al., dislike capitalism. But how is it, in spite of an unbroken string of socialist failures around the world, that these people continue to exercise so much influence? How is it, for example, that a utopian socialist like Ira Magaziner could become the principal architect of the Clinton health plan? Why have the babblings of these people been taken so seriously for so many years and decades?

The answer is that there is no explicit "philosophy of capitalism" against which to measure their proposals. Paul Johnson touched upon this problem: "For capitalism merely occurs, if no one does anything to stop it. It is socialism that has to be constructed."

Unlike socialism, capitalism is simply what happens in the absence of central planning. When Americans moved west they didn't have a blueprint from the Agency for Economic Planning; they did what came naturally: they farmed and bought and sold and traded. That was capitalism, and people simply took it for granted.

Americans (unlike the French) are notoriously non-ideological; they do what works, and don't worry much about some underlying philosophy. In a way, this has been a blessing. But it has also been a weakness, for without a philosophical rationale of its own, capitalism is intellectually vulnerable to the insults of every socialist-communist-fascist-Marxist crackpot with "a plan" who comes down the road. Compulsive meddlers like Magaziner are influential not because they are right, but because there is no widely-recognized "philosophy of capitalism" with which to combat them.

Without *principles*, the game is lost, for a bad idea can only be defeated by a better idea. What is missing is *principles*.

The importance of principles. Without principles, how do we tell what is right and what is wrong?

Can we assume that a thing is right if it is *legal?* But slavery was once legal; Nazism was legal.

Well, can we assume a thing is right if it is endorsed by *majority rule?* But a lynch mob is majority rule. Is a thing sure to be right, then, if it comes about *through the democratic process?* But fascist dictator Juan Perón of Argentina was democratically elected by majority rule on two occasions. It appears that these various criteria all have their shortcomings.

Well, how about the *Constitution?* But again we run into difficulties, for the Constitution can be amended to say anything the society wishes it to say. Suppose, for example, the Constitution were amended to permit the lynching of blacks—would this practice become ethically correct merely because the Constitution permitted it?

And so the answer still eludes us. Where are the standards by which we can reliably determine what is right and what is wrong?

How about "the greatest good for the greatest number"? But does this popular slogan really constitute a sound principle? For example, what about the human sacrifices of the Mayans? The entire society achieved a sense of spiritual security at the expense of only one person. The "greatest good" of the French army was served by its refusal to admit its error in sentencing Captain Dreyfus to Devil's Island. In fact, the "greatest good for the greatest number" is served if a man is robbed and his property split among ten thieves!

So, what is right and what is wrong, and how do we decide? Do we flip a coin? Indeed, in a society ruled by "practical" politics, anything goes if enough people are for it. But the result is utter confusion: If a farmer were to seize the property of his neighbor we would call it stealing; but when the state does it for him, we call it a "farm subsidy." When one is compelled by force of law to serve the "Fatherland" we are repelled. Call it the "public interest," however, and we are enraptured. The politician dispenses wealth which other men have produced, and we say he is "compassionate," while the businessman who produces the wealth is dismissed as "greedy" and "materialistic." If an individual were to impose a contract upon another by threat of punishment, we would call it extortion; but if city hall does the deed, we call it "rent control." If the majority violates the rights of the individual we call it injustice; if it has voted on the matter, we call it "democracy."

When people have no clear idea of what is right and what is wrong, when they believe that everything is "relative," the result is ideological chaos resulting in the gradual disintegration of the very fabric of a free society. What is it, then, that is lacking? An historian once observed that "facts are like beads, it takes a theory to string them together…no theory, no history." The same idea applies to politics (or political philosophy or whatever we wish to call it). Why is this program right and that one wrong? It is principles that we seek, for it is principles that "string things together."

Principles are not legislated or invented, however. They are discovered. A principle was discovered, for example, when rational people first realized that it was not to their ultimate advantage to rob one another. Since mutual plunder led to mutual impoverishment, it was "wrong" (i.e., destructive of life) to steal. This was not an "arbitrary social convention," but a fact of life. It was a matter of survival. It was the discovery of a principle of correct human behavior. The Ten Commandments were not legislated; they were discovered.

For centuries people were ignorant of the laws of physics—but they were subject to them nonetheless, and it was only when those principles were discovered that the great advances in the physical sciences could take place. So it is with human action. To the extent that the principles of freedom have been ignored or rejected, people have suffered poverty, stagnation and political tyranny. To the extent that those principles have been recognized and practiced, people have enjoyed abundance, progress and liberty. The three principles which follow are true, then, not merely because this or that writer says they are true; they are true because they are consistent with man's nature. And because they are consistent with nature, they work.

The three principles of the free society—individualism, the institution of private property and the market economy—will be discussed at length in the following three chapters. But first, is it possible that principles have been rendered obsolete by the "modern" society? There are many over the years who have said so. In 1955 that great icon of liberalism, Hubert Humphrey, wrote in *The American Scholar*:

> The liberal approach must be experimental, the solution tentative, the test pragmatic. Believing that no particular manifestation of our basic social institutions is sacrosanct or immutable, there should be a willingness to re-examine and reconstruct institutions in the light of new needs.

No particular manifestation of our basic social institutions is sacrosanct or immutable? What of freedom? What of human life? What Humphrey and the "pragmatists" of today argue is not a political philosophy but the denial that political principles are necessary or even possible. Yet it is precisely such nonabsolutists who have been most wrong most often. It was the well-meaning nonabsolutists who flocked to the Soviet Union in the 1920s to write in glowing terms about that "great experiment in social engineering." George Bernard Shaw was an apologist for the Soviets even during the darkest days of Stalinism, while in the early thirties columnist Walter Lippmann assured us that Hitler would provide Germany with responsible government. Rejecting the idea of fixed principles, many intellectuals lacked the means by which they could have assessed accurately the communist and fascist systems—systems which were explicitly violating all three of these principles.

When people ignore principles, they are headed for trouble. As Richard S. Wheeler once put it, "Today we abhor lampshades made of human skin; but tomorrow...who knows? It is precisely those persons who are not anchored to a set of eternal values who hanker the most for novelties."[1]

It is no surprise, of course, when an anticapitalist rejects these principles. Yet, even among sincere procapitalists there is considerable uncertainty as to the basic assumptions on which their beliefs are founded. The conservative who says he favors individualism, but then declares in the next breath that "the public interest takes precedence over individual rights" is simply contradicting himself. A procapitalist position not based explicitly on the primacy of individual rights is doomed to failure. For example, consider the rise and fall of "classical liberalism."

Among the first champions of modern capitalism were the "classical liberals" of nineteenth century England. These original liberals (quite unlike the "liberals" of today!) sought to liberate the marketplace by discarding the restrictions, the regulations, the petty interferences of the state. It was the triumph of classical liberalism which freed men's minds, and it freed their hands as well. For virtually the first time in British history government was largely confined to its proper task of protecting rather than regulating the individual. Politically, the ascendency of liberalism meant not the passage of new laws, but the repeal of old ones. Between 1833 and 1854 the crime of usury was abolished. In 1844 the crimes of "forestalling" and "regrating"[2] were abolished. The corn laws were repealed in 1846. The restrictive Navigation Laws were repealed in 1846 and 1849, and by 1867 the last protective tariffs had been eliminated. During this period a vast undergrowth of coercive restrictions was swept away. Never before had the individual been so free from interference in the conduct of his own life and in the disposition of his own property. As a result commerce flourished, and

England experienced the greatest surge of material progress in its history. Of all the countries of Europe, England was the freest and it prospered the most. The men who brought about this unprecedented state of economic liberty were the "classical liberals," men like John Locke, Adam Smith, Jeremy Bentham, Herbert Spencer and John Stuart Mill. What they had wrought was limited government—a government confined to its proper task of protecting liberty rather than violating it; a government which used legalized force—legalized physical compulsion—to protect private property rather than to control it.

Classical liberalism had a fatal flaw, however. The classical liberals championed the marketplace—but for the wrong reason. Generally, they supported it not as a matter of inalienable individual rights, but as a matter of "social utility," and when, toward the end of the nineteenth century, leaders became convinced that still greater "utility" could be achieved by regulating commercial activity once again, the structure of classical liberalism began to crumble. Under the guise of "humanitarianism" and "reform," new controls were imposed, and the British government once again became the master rather than the policeman. The trend continued unabated as England declined for decades into a coercive and stagnant welfare state.

Classical liberalism was a good structure, but it was built on sand: its defense of capitalism was premised on social utility rather than on individual rights. Any attempt to justify capitalism by its "value to society" will fail, for who decides what *is* of value to society? "Society," of course! But when the goals of the economy are charted by "society" the result is not capitalism, but socialism. Thus perished classical liberalism, and it died for lack of the correct premise.

Conservatives in this country frequently commit a similar mistake when they seek to oppose some obnoxious program only because it is "too expensive" or "too complicated," or whatever. An example of this tactical error is seen in the unending fight over the National Endowment for the Arts (NEA). Conservatives rail against the "bad" art of Maplethorpe or Finley, and the debate quickly degenerates into a food fight over artistic taste. But the issue here is not bad art versus good art; the real issue is whether the individual should be compelled to support *any* art.

The elitist supporters of the NEA have no business expropriating the earnings of Joe Sixpack to subsidize *their* artistic interests. If Joe had any choice in the matter, he might prefer that his money be spent on a new pair of bowling shoes, and that's his decision to make. The real issue here is one of individual rights in a free society, and when conservatives permit themselves to be goaded into irrelevant quarrels over taste, they have been out-maneuvered. They have abandoned the high ground of principle and the argument is already lost.

Those who try to operate without principles are sailing without a rudder. Another case in point is the failed presidency of George Bush. Bush was bewildered by the very concept of a political philosophy. This was "the vision thing," and he had no interest in it. But without a set of unifying principles he waffled unpredictably from issue to issue, infuriating friend and foe alike. Ultimately, it was Bush's philosophical incoherence which destroyed his presidency. A similar fate awaits Bill Clinton: a person devoid of any perceptible conviction, value or principle, he will likely go down in history as one of the least consequential presidents of this century.

Principles matter. Their absence can be crucial—to the classical liberals, to George Bush or to Bill Clinton or to any of us.

What, then, are the all-important principles of a free economy and a free society?

The three principles. The three principles of the free and progressive society are individualism, the institution of private property, and the market economy. These are the three "basic ingredients" of the American experience, and of what we loosely describe as "capitalism." In fact, these are the three unique elements of Western civilization itself, especially as it evolved in England, of whose political culture we are the fortunate heirs. No other civilization—not Chinese, not Indian, not Islamic, not African—has been based on the combination of these three elements.

Today, capitalism is being embraced around the world. Still, the continuing failure to identify and explicitly champion the principles on which it is based has left it vulnerable to assault at any time from the left—and often from the right as well. Today, with some of the world's major economies faltering, calls for expanded government control will increase. Without an explicit understanding of the principles of freedom the capitalism of today will suffer the fate of the classical liberalism of nineteenth century England, to be inundated by a new dark age of socialism.

Principles matter.

Of these three principles the most important is the first, for individualism (or self-interest or "ethical egoism") is the basic *moral* premise on which the rest depends. Individualism, the most difficult and controversial of these three principles, will be the subject of the following chapter.

> "So," people cried out, "Give us light!
> We can't tell what's wrong from right!"
> —from *Tom Smith and His Incredible Bread Machine*

8: Principle #1: Individualism (versus Altruism)

The moral basis of capitalism is not "service to others," but the right of each individual to live his own life, for his own sake.

As noted before, one of the more profound mistakes that Michael Milken made in the 1980s was his failure to recognize that the basic premise of a free society is self-interest, not altruism. His public pronouncements and PR ploys were full of glop about "helping others," but if this was his goal what was he doing with all that money? Why didn't he give it all away as Ralph Nader urged? And why didn't he renounce the profit-motivated capitalist system?

Beguiled by altruist fluff about "helping others," Milken was philosophically emasculated. Unable to justify his role in a system based on private profit, he was excoriated for his "greed," and his image as the nation's wealthiest hypocrite was assured.

The premise of capitalism is not altruism but individualism (or self-interest or "ethical egoism"). The businessman does not go into business to "help others" but to make a profit. True, he can only do this by providing the goods and services which other people want, but "helping others" is the *consequence* of capitalism, not its *moral justification*. Adam Smith touched upon this distinction 200 years ago, noting in *The Wealth of Nations* that the self-interested businessman,

> is in this, as in many other cases, led by an invisible hand to promote an end which was no part of his intention. Nor is it always the worse for the society that it was no part of it. By pursuing his own interest he frequently promotes that of the society more effectually than when he really intends to promote it. I have never known much good done by those who affected to trade for the public good.[1]

The businessman's moral legitimacy does not depend on what he does for "others" but on his right as an individual to live his own life, for his own sake, in accordance with his own values. So it is with all of us.

Still, confusion on the issue of self-interest has bedeviled the business community for 200 years. Many critics concede that capitalism is highly productive—*but still reject it on moral grounds!* The reason is that the profit motive is based on "selfishness" which, as everybody knows, is a crude and ignoble impulse.

The underlying conflict is between two opposing and irreconcilable premises: individualism and altruism. There can be no coherent middle ground, for any attempt at holding two opposing premises at the same time will lead only to confusion and contradiction. The premise one adopts will establish one's attitude on every social, economic and political issue ever raised.

The perfect metaphor for this conflict is the sports team.

The Metaphor. One of the most perplexing issues in political philosophy concerns the relationship between self-interest and a decent concern for "the group." The Marxist, of course, would insist on the complete subordination of the individual to the collective. In contrast, the individualist would regard the group not as an end in itself but rather as a means to the realization of *individual* goals. This relationship is shown in the chart on page 112.

This distinction is quite clear in the priorities of a sports team. It's not likely, for example, that the college football coach would urge his players to spill their guts for the glory of the state of Michigan or Mississippi or whatever; he is much more likely to emphasize personal gratification and to note that the players will remember the Big Game to their dying day. Teamwork and team spirit are vitally important, of course, but the ultimate motivation is self-interest.

At least in American society. But not so in Japan.

The contrast between individual and collective values is strikingly apparent in the Japanese national pastime of *besuboru*—baseball. In his entertaining book, *You Gotta Have Wa*, Robert Whiting notes that baseball has been a national passion in Japan since the late nineteenth century. Professional teams, in two leagues, have been in existence since 1935, and their fortunes are the subject of intense popular interest. Indeed, the fanatical Japanese fan makes the American fan look like a couch potato.

Where Americans emphasize the individual, the Japanese emphasize The Team. In fact, the Japanese term for individualism, *kojinshugi*, is "almost a dirty word." Explains Whiting,

> The concept and practice of group harmony or "wa" is what most dramatically differentiates Japanese baseball from the American game. It is the connecting thread running through all Japanese life

and sports. While "Let It All Hang Out" and "Do Your Own Thing" are mottoes of contemporary American society, the Japanese have their own credo in the well-worn proverb, "The Nail That Sticks Up Shall Be Hammered Down." It is practically a national slogan.[2]

As one prominent Japanese manager put it, "Lone wolves are the cancer of the team." When a top-notch pitcher once ignored a coach's instructions, the coach punched him between the eyes. The *pitcher* was fined and obliged to apologize for his lack of "wa."

The presence of inner-directed Americans on Japanese teams (limit of two per team) is a source of constant conflict. The culture clash was exemplified by one American player named Chuck Manuel who was once ordered by his drill-sergeant manager to run ten extra sprints. "Fuck no, I ain't!" declared Manuel, and walked off the field, leaving it to the interpreter to explain this bit of "wa," American style, to the glowering manager.

But what really cut it was when Manuel, as provided for in his contract, left the team in the middle of a pennant race to attend his son's high school graduation back in the states. To Manuel it was simple: "I can play baseball any time. My son's graduation only comes once."

His contract said he could leave, so he left. But to the Japanese management, and to the fans and sports writers as well, this was a betrayal of the team; a betrayal of "wa." Manuel returned as promised, and helped the team to a pennant, but the ill-feeling remained and Manuel was gone after that season.

The American ballplayer on a Japanese team is the perfect metaphor for the clash between two opposing philosophies. To the Japanese it's the primary obligation of the individual to serve the interests of the group; to the American the group is important—but only as a vehicle for the achievement of individual goals.

Which system is better? Well, the proof is in the pudding. Japan turns out mechanically excellent players, but they rarely achieve the spontaneous flair of good American players. Size is no longer a major factor; lots of Japanese players these days are six feet tall and over. Still, visiting American teams have yet to lose a series. In 1986 a group of American All-Stars, led by Met manager Davey Johnson (who had played in Japan and "had something to prove"), thumped the Japanese All-Stars six games to one. Lamented one of the Japanese players, "We're like a team of Little Leaguers playing adults."

But, of course, baseball is only a metaphor. The real issue is the relationship between individualism and group-ism in the broader society.

Individualism. Cleveland industrialist James Finney Lincoln represented the best in American capitalism. When he died in 1965 he had been for nearly forty years president of the Lincoln Electric Company, the world's largest manufacturer of electric welding equipment. Back in 1934 Lincoln adopted what was at that time a highly unusual program: an employee incentive plan. The plan was so successful that in the years that followed the Lincoln Company was consistently able to undersell the competition while at the same time paying Lincoln employees nearly double the prevailing wages in the industry. The most intriguing part of the story, however, concerns the straightforward reason that James Lincoln gave for introducing the incentive program. "Selfishness," he explained, "is the motivating force of all human endeavor."

Lincoln obviously did not mean selfishness in the sense of concern for one's self "at the expense of others," but rather the natural desire of most persons to act in their own rational self-interest by means of their own productive efforts. People are indeed selfish in this sense. They seek their own food, shelter, clothing, etc. If they did not, they would die. It is as simple as that. People will and should pursue their own welfare. Lincoln recognized this basic fact of nature and acted accordingly, with results that were highly beneficial to all concerned.

The philosophical doctrine which recognizes the moral correctness of selfishness—as defined above—is called "egoism." Individualism, a somewhat broader term, introduces the consequent relationship of the individual to the group. Individualism maintains that the individual is justified in pursuing his own self-interest, and that, accordingly, he is not morally obligated to place the welfare of the "group" above his own. *Webster*[3] defines individualism as, "The doctrine that the individual himself should be paramount in the determination of conduct; ethical egoism. The conception that all values, rights, and duties originate in individuals, and that the community or social whole has no ethical significance not derived from its constituent individuals." In short, individual rights are not subordinate to the demands of the group; the individual is sovereign over his own life.

Does this mean that the individual rejects any sense of obligation to others? Not necessarily; but it does mean that he recognizes as obligations only those which he has voluntarily assumed. For example, he recognizes his obligation to his children, to his friends, to his employer or employees, or to any individual or group with which he has, in his own self-interest, voluntarily associated himself. But he does not regard it as a "moral obligation" to (for example) pay farmers not to grow wheat, or to give assistance to every bum who demands a dollar for a cup of coffee. Because he values human life he may assist those who are in genuine need—but the obligation is to his own values, not to someone else's. The individualist does not regard it as an obligation to subordinate his own self-interest to the desires of others, and he would certainly resist any attempt to impose that alleged obligation upon him by force.

"But how far can such a principle be carried," it is asked. "Can it seriously be argued that the individual has no obligation to society? Does he not eat the food grown by other hands? Does he not wear the clothing that others have produced? Is it not particularly true in our complex society that the individual (unless he chooses to be a hermit) benefits incalculably from the society of his fellow men? Should he not be obliged—by law, if necessary—to do his part?"

But this argument misses the point. It is quite true, of course, that we all benefit from association with others, but the real issue concerns the terms on which this association takes place: is it voluntary or is it compulsory? Is it based on trade or is it based on force? Individualism does indeed recognize the need for cooperative association—but it insists that the association be of a voluntary, marketplace nature. Moreover, it is only upon the premise of individualism that genuine cooperation can be based, for it is only when people are free to act in their own self-interest that genuine cooperation can exist. If people are compelled by law to serve the interests of others, it is not cooperation, but servitude.

Only upon the premise of individualism can a free society be built. In fact, individualism was the implicit philosophical principle underlying the American concept of government as servant rather than master. The real significance of the American Revolution lay not in a military triumph (for other nations have won independence only to lapse back into tyranny), but in the partial triumph of the philosophy of individualism. The Bill of Rights did not establish the sovereignty of "society" but of the individual; the individual was not obliged to serve the State or the king or the nobility or society or the rich or the poor or the public interest or the fatherland or humanity. As long as he respected the same right for others, he was free to live his own life for his own sake in accordance with his own convictions.

Upon the premise of individualism the rest depends. If it is accepted, the two remaining principles of a free society—the institution of private property and the market economy—inescapably follow. But if the opposing premise is adopted, the institution of private property will be rejected, and the market economy abandoned. The result will eventually be tyranny rather than freedom.

The opposing premise is called "altruism."

Altruism. According to the dictionary the philosophical opposite of individualism is altruism. *Webster* defines altruism as "regard for and devotion to the interests of others as an ethical principle," and goes on to quote the *Dictionary of Political Economy* as stating: "Altruism is an ethical term...opposed to individualism or egoism...and embraces those moral motives which induce a man to regard the interests of others." Altruism, then, holds that true virtue lies not in pursuing one's own rational self-interest, but in "devotion to the interests of others." Collectivism, a somewhat broader term, introduces the subsequent relationship of the individual to society as a whole.

But what is wrong with having a decent regard for the interests of others? Nothing, in itself; in fact, the individualist might have an equal regard. But the individualist will be motivated ultimately by his own values, while the altruist will be motivated by an assumed moral obligation to place the values of others above his own. This is no mere quibble in semantics. It is the difference between black and white. As noted before, there can be no coherent middle ground, for any attempt at holding two opposing premises at the same time will lead only to confusion.

Now let us look at altruism a little more closely.

The word that best describes the morality of altruism is "sacrifice."[4] Self-sacrifice for the sake of "others" is, in a nutshell, the altruist ideal. And it is a concept of vast emotional appeal. But there are sacrifices and there are sacrifices, and the crucial distinction should be made: sacrifice for whose ultimate benefit?

Does the individual gain or lose by his sacrifice? For example, contrast the following situations: Jones is approached by a friend in serious financial trouble. Jones can help only at considerable personal sacrifice. But he makes that sacrifice because of the genuine satisfaction it gives him to be able to help a person whose happiness he values. Jones actually gains in the transaction because his friend's welfare is of greater value to him (evidently) than are the material goods he gives up.

Now consider Smith who finds himself in the identical situation except that he is approached by a person whom he despises. But Smith, also at great personal sacrifice, helps him anyway. He derives no net benefit from this act; he performs it only because of an assumed "moral obligation" to serve the interests of "others." Smith loses in the transaction; only the recipient gains.

Jones was the individualist; Smith was the altruist. In short, a sacrifice in response to *one's own values* is to be commended, but a sacrifice for the primary or exclusive benefit of "others" must be looked upon with suspicion.

Other examples of "sacrifice" within the context of individualism: A parent might give up a new suit in order to buy his child a bicycle. But the parent has not lost in the bargain, for to him his child's joy is of greater value than the suit. Similarly, the priest may dedicate his life to the church, but he probably does this not out of a blind sense of "duty to others," but because this is the avocation which brings a sense of meaning to his own life. Yet, the altruist philosopher Immanuel Kant would deny that there was moral worth in either of these actions since the parent and the priest were both acting for selfish reasons. According to Kant, an act has moral worth only if done out of a sense of duty. In his *Metaphysics of Morals* he gives the example of the tradesman who deals honestly with his customers, "but this is not enough to make us believe that the tradesman has so acted from duty and from principles of honesty: his own advantage required it....Accordingly the action was done merely with a selfish view."

Altruism, with its subtle emphasis on indiscriminate self-sacrifice, is not a healthy moral code. Still, many people, beguiled by what they feel is a doctrine of humanitarian benevolence, think of themselves—or would like to think of themselves—as altruists. If you really think you are an altruist, consider the following situation: suppose you come upon two children drowning. Suppose one of them is your own child and the other a stranger. Suppose the situation is such that you can save one of them, but not both. Which one would you save? Surely you would—or should—save your own child. Altruism, however, urges selfless devotion to the interests of others; specifically it would mandate that you place the happiness of the other family above that of your own. Altruism requires, then, that you "unselfishly" save the other child and let your own drown. Do you still think you are an altruist?

Altruism is not a livable philosophy. Nonetheless, it seems that most of the philosophers in history have been altruist oriented. John Stuart Mill, for example, wrote in his essay *Utilitarianism* that, "[Only in an imperfect world can man] best serve the happiness of others by the absolute sacrifice of his own [happiness]. Yet as long as the world is in that imperfect state, I fully acknowledge that the readiness to make such a sacrifice is the highest virtue...self renunciation...devotion to the happiness...of others."

Yet, from Mill's altruistic statement one must conclude that the most virtuous person of all must be the slave! Is it not those in slavery who are sacrificing to the greatest degree their own happiness for the good of others? But Mill no doubt meant that the sacrifice must be *voluntary*. All right then, it is the *willing* slave whose actions would be, according to Mill, the most virtuous; it is the slave who says, "Master, you can remove the chains, and I will not run away, for I have just read John Stuart Mill and I now realize that true virtue lies in sacrificing my happiness to yours."

The individual who consistently practiced altruism would regard it as a moral obligation, at every opportunity, to sacrifice his happiness for others, his welfare for others, and ultimately his own life for others. People can preach altruism but they cannot live it. Nor should they, for the genuine altruist voluntarily enslaves himself (or herself[5]) to the needs and desires of every other person. The genuine altruist—if there could really be such a thing—is not a person but a doormat.

Moreover, altruism can be dangerous to one's health. "Isn't it much better for people to work for the good of everybody?" asked 1960s terrorist Diana Oughton a few days before she blew herself up while making a bomb wrapped in nail-studded tape. (See Chapter Twelve.)

An intriguing question: was Jesus an altruist? The most revered image of Christianity is of Jesus on the cross sacrificing his life "for others." But did Jesus really die for others or, like Socrates or Joan of Arc or Sir Thomas More, did he die for the beliefs which brought meaning and purpose *to his own life?* Was Jesus an altruist—or a remarkably dedicated individualist?

Take your choice. But one element of the Judeo-Christian code is unambiguous: free will. Individualism and free will are essentially one-in-the-same. Accordingly, a political philosophy of individualism, and the Judeo-Christian religion, emerge from the same moral premise.

Altruism and politics. Even as a guide for purely personal conduct it should be apparent that altruism is not a coherent moral code. But when altruism serves as the underlying premise of a political dogma, the real trouble begins. True virtue still lies in service to "others," but "others" now means some empty political abstraction such as Society, the State, the Fatherland, or whatever.

Most of the political philosophers in history have based their arguments on one form or another of the altruist premise, and at best the result has been total confusion. The Roman emperor-philosopher Marcus Aurelius, for example, wrote in his *Meditations* that "that which does no harm to the State does no harm to the citizen." But would it have been true, let us say, in Nazi Germany that "that which does no harm to the State does no harm to the citizen"? Aurelius goes on, "For whatsoever either by myself or with another I can do, ought to be directed to this only, to that which is useful and well suited to society." Most people today would quickly agree with this noble-sounding sentiment. But suppose the society in question were a society of cannibals? Should the individual leap into the cooking pot, joyful in the knowledge that he was achieving true virtue by doing that which was "useful and well suited to society"? Once one adopts the self-sacrificial morality of altruism the concept of individual rights goes out the window, and it should be apparent that the result is ideological chaos.

At best, a political philosophy based on the premise of altruism leads to confusion. At worst, it leads to tyranny. When the German philosopher Hegel declared that "the highest duty of an individual is to be a member of the state," others were happy to carry this view to its logical conclusion. "To be a socialist," declared Nazi socialist Joseph Goebbels, "is to submit the I to the thou; socialism is sacrificing the individual to the whole."[6]

A favorite slogan in Nazi Germany was *Gemeinutz vor Eigennutz* (common interest before self). Stalin was equally explicit in asserting that true virtue lay in self-sacrifice to the collective:

> True Bolshevik courage does not consist in placing one's individual will above the will of the Comintern. True courage consists in being strong enough to master and overcome one's self and subordinate one's will to the will of the collective, the will of the higher party body.[7]

In any of the above statements the underlying premise is the same. But the doctrine of self-sacrifice is no longer in the ivory tower—it has entered the political arena, and the philosophical "thou ought" has finally become the legislated "thou must." What was previously only a "moral obligation" has now become a "duty." Every tyranny in history has been based on some variation of the altruist theme. Under Stalin and Lenin it was the duty of the individual to serve the Proletariat. Under Hitler it was the Fatherland. Under Mussolini it was the State. The altruist ideal of service to some other "greater good" is the cornerstone of tyranny.

It is true, of course, that Hitler and the rest directed their appeal as well to self-interest, promising jobs, welfare, a rising standard of living, etc. But we are not concerned with the ritualistic promises made by every political leader, good and bad—we are interested in the particular mechanism by which the despot then proceeds to beguile most of his countrymen into willing obedience to tyranny. That mechanism is invariably the exhortation to sacrifice for "the common good."

In American politics today the most powerful weapon in the arsenal of the political left is *moral intimidation* derived from the unchallenged assumptions of altruism. For example, those hapless Republicans who seek to reduce taxes or restrain spending will be reviled as "selfish," and "mean-spirited." The left seizes the moral high ground while bewildered Republicans are shamed into silence. As long as people accept the idea that self-interest is "greed," and that virtue rests only in service to "others," demagogues of the left (or the right) will be more than happy to see that "virtue" prevails.

In summary. The basic conflict in political philosophy is between the opposing premises of individualism (self-interest) and altruism. Which has priority, the individual or the group? We can't have it both ways; it's one or the other. Attempts at holding two opposing premises at the same time will lead only to confusion and contradiction.

It is asserted here that the basic premise of a free society is individualism, from which is derived the institution of private property, from which is derived in turn the market economy. The opposing principles are collectivism, restriction of property rights, and the economy controlled by and for a favored political class. These relationships are compared in the chart on page 112.

The second principle of the free society is the institution of private property, which will be the subject of the following chapter.

"Smith placed himself above the group
To profit from his brothers!
He failed to see the Greater Good,
Is Service, friends, to Others!"
   —from *Tom Smith and His Incredible Bread Machine*

9: Principle #2: Private Property

Private property is more than the key to material abundance; it is essential to the exercise of political liberty.

I f the premise of individualism is accepted, then the institution of private property[1] will naturally follow, for it can not be argued with any coherence that the individual has the right to his own life, but not to the products of that life. If the opposing premise of altruism is adopted, however, then the institution of private property will be rejected, for when it is the duty of the individual to serve others, then the products of his life are equally at their disposal. But the premise of altruism is unworkable and unlivable, and those societies which have attempted to abolish private property have invariably stagnated.

The Plymouth colony. The experience of the Plymouth colony provides eloquent testimony to the unworkability of collective ownership of property. In his history of the Plymouth colony, Governor Bradford described how the Pilgrims initially farmed the land in common, with the produce going into a common storehouse. For two years the Pilgrims faithfully practiced communal ownership of the means of production. And for two years they nearly starved to death, rationed at times to "but a quarter of a pound of bread a day to each person." Governor Bradford wrote that "famine must still ensue the next year also, if not some way prevented." He describes how the colonists finally decided to introduce the institution of private property:

> [The colonists] begane to thinke how they might raise as much corne as they could, and obtaine a beter crope than they had done, that they might not still thus languish in miserie. At length [in 1623] after much debate of things, the Gov. (with the advise of the cheefest amongst them) gave way that they should set downe every man for his owne perticuler, and in that regard trust to themselves....And so assigned to every family a parceel of land....
>
> This had very good success; for it made all hands very industrious, so as much more corne was planted than other waise would have bene by any means the Gov. or any other could use, and saved him a great deall of trouble, and gave farr better contente.

The women now wente willingly into the feild, and tooke their litle-ons with them to set corne, which before would aledge weakness, and inabilitie; whom to have compelled wold have bene thought great tiranie and opression.

Reflecting on the experience of the previous two years, Bradford goes on to describe the folly of communal ownership:

The experience that was had in this commone course and condition, tried sundrie years, and that amongst godly and sober men, may well evince the vanitie of that conceite of Platos and other ancients, applauded by some of later times;—that the taking away of propertie, and bringing in communitie into a comone wealth, would make them happy and florishing; as if they were wiser than God. For this communitie (so farr as it was) was found to breed much confusion and discontent, and retard much imployment that would have been to their benefite and comforte.

For the yong-men that were most able and fitte for labour and service did repine that they should spend their time and streingth to worke for other mens wives and children, without any recompense. The strong, or man of parts, had no more in divission of victails and cloaths, than he that was weake and not able to doe a quarter the other could; this was thought injuestice.

The colonists learned about "the wave of the future" the hard way. However, once having discovered the principle of private property, the results were dramatic. Bradford continues:

By this time harvest was come, and instead of famine, now God gave them plentie, and the face of things was changed, to the rejoysing of the harts of many, for which they blessed God. And in the effect of their perticular [private] planting was well seene, for all had, one way and other, pretty well to bring the year aboute, and some of the abler sorte and more industrious had to spare, and sell to others, so as any generall wante or famine hath not been amongst them since to this day.

The Virginia colony had similar problems with communal ownership. Captain John Smith wrote:

When our people were fed out of the common store, and laboured jointly together, glad was he could slip from his labour, or slumber over his taske he cared not how, nay, the most honest among them would hardly take so much true paines in a weeke, as now for them-

selves they will doe in a day; neither cared they for the increase, pre-
suming that howsoever the harvest prospered, the generall store
must maintain them, so that wee reaped not so much Corne from
the labours of thirtie, as now three or foure doe provide for themselves.[2]

Communal ownership of property had been tried and it had failed.
Even among "godly and sober men" it was an unworkable and unlivable
system. Only when the institution of private property was introduced did
the colonists achieve abundance.

The "Tragedy of the Commons." In 1968 there appeared in *Science* an article whose title, "The Tragedy of the Commons,"[3] has become a metaphor
for the most persistent of social pathologies, the tendency to exploit and
misuse public resources, the "commons."

The author, Garrett Hardin, explained the problem in terms of herdsmen over-grazing a "public" meadow. If a herdsman gains another cow, he
puts it out to graze with the others. He will gain a bit, although the
meadow is further depleted. The other herdsmen will do the same, until
the meadow is exhausted and all are worse off. Each herdsman, acting in
his own self-interest, has contributed to disaster for all. Hence, the "tragedy of the commons."

Hardin concluded that the key to the riddle is privatization. With each
herdsman owning his own plot, the tendency is not to exploit but to husband and preserve.

An example of the problem, and its solution, can be seen in the management of the nation's timberlands. During the nineteenth century, when
timberlands were "public," they were devastated by whoever could get in
and out the quickest, while privately-owned tracts today are carefully
farmed and reseeded for the obvious reason that future profits depend on
future trees. Even environmentalists, who are instinctively anti-business,
have acknowledged with surprise that private timber companies do a better
job of conservation than does the non-profit U.S. Government.

But what do we do about common areas which cannot be defined by
property lines? Hardin explained,

The tragedy of the commons…is averted by private property, or
something formally like it. But the air and waters surrounding us
cannot readily be fenced, and so the tragedy of the commons as a

cesspool must be prevented by different means, by coercive laws or taxing devices that make it cheaper for the polluter to treat his pollutants than to discharge them untreated.

Air pollution? O.K. If a polluter dumps his soot in our lungs, it's an invasion of *our* property, and government should act, as Hardin suggests. Waterways, however, are possibly more susceptible to private ownership than Hardin supposed. Consider the California town of Lake Arrowhead, an attractive and popular resort community centered about a privately-owned lake. The immediate consequence of this private ownership is elimination of that utter paralysis which everywhere plagues the administration of "unowned" public property. Lake Arrowhead is clean, and is kept that way by the private, profit-seeking corporation which owns it.

In principle, there is no reason why other bodies of water could not also be privately owned, even parts of the ocean. For example, lobstermen might "homestead" patches of seacoast. The immediate result of this private ownership would be careful reseeding of beds rather than quickie exploitation to scrape the bottom of the barrel lest someone else do it first. Hundreds of square miles of ocean might one day be fenced off for private farming.

Professor Oscar Cooley speculated twenty-five years ago on what would happen if Lake Erie were converted to private ownership:

> The company would want to maximize its income from the lake, as from a tract of owned farm land, residential property, forest, coal-bearing land, or other asset. It might do so by selling rights to fish, to sail, to bathe, to transport passengers or freight, and by selling water to cities. It would undoubtedly improve its property by stocking with desirable species of fish, deepening ship channels, improving beaches, and so forth.[4]

Initially, perhaps the stock in the new Lake Erie Corporation could be distributed among those municipalities and individuals and commercial interests along the shore who already had a proprietary interest in optimizing the quality of that waterway. Or, maybe the waterway could simply be sold to the highest bidder. How an equitable distribution of ownership might be achieved is not the point at the moment; the point is only to suggest a concept which should be pursued.

And the concept isn't all that far-fetched. In England, water rights along streams and rivers are often privately owned, and the owners have a vested interest in maintaining these assets for commercial and recreational use. And they do not hesitate to sue polluters. In 1951, years before the environment became much of a political issue, the Anglers Cooperative Association won its first big case against two chemical companies which were dumping sewage, hot water and tar into the Derwent River.[5]

People will look after what is theirs. William Tucker defines the issue in terms of the historical function of the "landlord":

> But a true understanding of the historic role of landlords should make us realize that it is the property owner's "land ethic" that ultimately keeps us from destroying our natural heritage. True stewardship and conservation are only nurtured by the experience of individual ownership—in a system where landlords are left free to preserve the value of their property and are protected from the universal political tendency to exploit someone else's resource without paying the costs. Until the impulse to protect the environment is harnessed to the private desires of landlords to care for their own property, environmental problems will never be solved. We are all going to have to learn to become landlords.[6]

The key to preserving the environment does not lie in the endless expansion of government control, but in the broadest possible application of the institution of private property.

Property rights and political liberty. Without property rights, no other rights can be secure. Genuine freedom of religion (for example) would be impossible if church property were owned or controlled by government. Freedom of assembly would be a fiction if all gathering places were regulated by the bureaucrat. When property is controlled by government, such civil rights as freedom of assembly, freedom of the press, etc., even if nominally observed, are not really regarded as rights at all, since their exercise is conditional, depending ultimately upon government approval.

When the government controls private property it is in a position to control all else. Accordingly, it is no mere coincidence that in each of the totalitarian dictatorships of this century private property was subject to total government control. In his book *Fruits of Fascism*, Herbert L. Matthews quotes Mussolini as declaring, "Property is not only a right but a duty. It is not an egoistic possession, but rather a possession which should be employed and developed in a human and social sense." But as Matthews observes,

That, in Fascist terminology, came to mean that private property, like everything else, had to be placed at the service of the State, and one may well ask to what extent the institution was infringed upon by taxation, forced investments, and the whole structure of governmental interference which told a man what he should produce, how much, with what labor and at what price. In short, can there be private property under a totalitarian system? Individuals are left with the title to their property, but since they can only use the property in certain ways specified by the regime, it becomes a form of state property as does everything else. You cannot have "a kingdom of your own" under Fascism.[7]

By controlling private property the totalitarian state can control every facet of society. Juan Perón insisted that there was no censorship in Argentina. In a way he was right. But the State controlled the paper mills, and those newspapers which displeased the regime soon found they had nothing to print on. In the former Soviet Union, since the printing presses and publishing houses were all controlled by the government, there was no means by which dissenting views could be heard.

It's worth pointing out that the Soviet Constitution made a great show of "guaranteeing" all civil rights—except the basic right of private property without which the others could not be exercised in any meaningful form. Without property rights, no other rights are secure.

Trashing property rights. The institution of private property is an essential ingredient of the free and prosperous society, yet our own government routinely trashes property rights in every way imaginable. A few examples follow.

Property forfeiture. Tina Bennis, a 38-year-old mother of five, was co-owner with her husband of a 1977 Pontiac. Unknown to her, her husband took the car for an assignation with a prostitute. He was arrested and the car was confiscated by the police and then sold, the proceeds going into police coffers. Bennis sued for recovery and the case went all the way to the Supreme Court which decided 5-4 against her. Chief Justice Rehnquist, citing cases back to 1827, declared in a 1996 decision that property may be forfeited if used for an illegal purpose, even if the owner was unaware of its use. Justice Stevens dissented strongly, condemning the "blatant unfairness" of the ruling. *USA Today* commented editorially on the abusive nature of the forfeiture laws:

> Believe it or not, Federal, state and local authorities have the power to take your business, home, bank account and personal property—all without indictment, hearing or trial. It only takes a flimsy assertion that the property might be linked in some way to a crime, no proof required. Even worse, the basic American presumption —innocent until proven guilty—is turned on its head: To get the property back, the owner must prove that it has not been used in a crime. Whether the owner was actually involved in the crime is irrelevant.[8]

The reach of the Drug Enforcement Administration is especially long. In New York State a 54 year old woman, Marcia Milbrand, had her 85-acre farm confiscated because narcotics agents discovered a handful of marijuana plants, evidently planted by her son, scattered among the vegetables. Given the Bennis ruling Marcia Milbrand was not hopeful about getting her farm back. "I have a feeling it's not going to go well. I hate to give up hope....I just don't know how much more they can take from people."[9]

Using forfeiture laws the FBI and the Drug Enforcement Administration seize around $1 billion in private property every year, retaining about half for their own purposes. Brenda Grantland, head of a group called FEAR (Forfeiture Endangers American Rights), notes that landlords have had their property confiscated because a tenant was selling drugs, and fishing boats have been seized for minor violations. She claims that federal and state governments are today "vying to see who can be the most abusive."[10]

Environmental laws. In Minnesota, John and Josephine Bronczyk suddenly found that 113 of their 160 acres, almost all of it dry land, would be declared a public waters wetland, and thereby essentially expropriated without compensation, the Fifth Amendment to the Constitution notwithstanding. Says Bronczyk in dismay, "There's nobody who's got more respect for wetlands than we do. But we also feel that a person's property rights are sacred."[11]

Not to EPA director William Reilly, who deplores "mainstream attitudes about private property and freedom of action." Reilly is concerned about the "tawdry gateways to some of our greatest national parks." By "tawdry gateways" Reilly is evidently referring to the motels and restaurants and service stations which make it possible for us commoners to make it to these national parks in relative safety and comfort. Reilly writes that "conscious public choice" (i.e., his) is needed or else "the market will decide which land gets developed and which remains as it is."[12]

But it is precisely the function of the marketplace, based on property rights, to allocate resources in a more-or-less balanced manner. The alternative has been tried in the Soviet Union, and the results were not pretty.

Zoning. The age-old rationale for zoning is expressed by the question, "You wouldn't want someone moving in next door with a pig farm, would you?"

Well, no. But if we are talking about a residential community the property value would be much too high for a pig farm. The more likely use would be for a new house.

Zoning is not an imperative. In fact, many communities do without it. Houston, Texas, for example, has never had zoning, and has been managing quite well for years. Back in 1965 Jo Hindman wrote the following syndicated article, as relevant today as it was then:

> Citizens are propagandized into believing that a city would lapse into chaos without zoning laws. Such is not the case. Zoned land use is not tolerated in some parts of the U.S.A. and in one thriving major city—Houston, Texas—zoning is firmly rejected each time it is brought before the voters [most recently in 1994]....
>
> In zoned cities, ordinances have stripped from owners and transferred to city hall the right to decide how land will be used. Worse, the zones can be changed at whim of city hall and owners made to conform or risk having their property condemned as nonconforming....
>
> Zoning is peddled to the public with promises to protect homeowners from noxious uses adjacent to their land. Anyone who sits through the kangaroo hearings of certain zoning appeal boards knows that in about 90 percent of the cases, zone-abiding citizens are overruled and the zone-breaking aspirant wins out. Whenever the losing citizens go to court to reverse the decision, invariably they lose again.
>
> In Houston, there is none of that; land still rests under control of its private owner—not city hall. How does this beautiful, large city do it, growing bigger and wealthier without zoned land use?
>
> M. W. Lee of Houston, businessman, university real estate instructor, finance and insurance company official, explained, "The fact that zoning justice cannot be obtained at the courthouse, but

that a zoning 'fix' may be obtained at city halls, is not lost on Houstonians....Deed restrictions, in most instances, have preserved residential subdivisions in Houson without the economic slowdown effects of zoning."

When time limits on deeds expire, owners in Houston may renew the restrictions, leave the land unencumbered, or sell for a more valued use. This spells timely financial returns to owners in aging sections of town, close to expanding business centers. While their homes, say, have deteriorated in value, their land has become more valuable. This free play of the market equalizes what otherwise would be lost under rigid zoning restrictions.

In the ensuing years the issue of zoning kept coming up and the people of Houston keep voting it down, most recently in 1994. A subsequent op-ed piece in the *Houston Chronicle* noted the difference between heavily-zoned California and un-zoned Houston:

For every blighted urban or suburban neighborhood in Houston I can show you 10 in the heavily zoned San Francisco Bay Area. For every "inappropriate" business in a residential neighborhood in Houston, I can show you thousands in heavily zoned California....

What does all this mean? Houston politicians are doing nothing more than trying to California-ize Houston. The Golden State may have a lot to offer, but Houstonians ought to think twice before they borrow what has already failed so miserably in California.[13]

Eminent Domain. Comments Isabel Paterson, "If you accept the principle of eminent domain, you are lost." Quite true, for if the "group" can expropriate the property of the individual any time it is deemed to be "in the public interest," what is the limit? There is none, for who decides what is "in the public interest"? At worst a political clique; at best the "majority." In either event the principle of individual rights has been abandoned, and it is for the state to seize private property when and where it may choose.[14]

Eminent domain was originally intended only for the achievement of certain "public" facilities such as roads. Gradually, however, that restriction has been eroded, and in 1954 the Supreme Court upheld Federal Urban Renewal, by which was permitted the seizure of private property for favored *private* use.

Overall, the program was a disaster. As Martin Anderson documented in his famous book *The Federal Bulldozer,*[15] entire neighborhoods were torn up, and the properties were sold to private developers for around 30% of cost. But then, most of the people who were evicted found that they could not afford to live in the more expensive new housing, and had to crowd into existing slums.

When government usurps control of private property, regardless of the good intentions, bad things seem to happen. Still, the reach of eminent domain steadily lengthens. The University of California Board of Regents acquired condemnation of a 315-unit apartment complex in order to take it over for the use of UCLA students. A few years ago a Hollywood man was forcibly taken from his home in order that it might be destroyed to make room for a privately operated museum. A tract called Chavez Ravine was seized by the city of Los Angeles to make room for Dodger Stadium. The principle of eminent domain has been so extended that there remains not a home or field or blade of grass that cannot legally be expropriated for virtually any purpose embraced by those with political influence.

The practice of eminent domain should be abandoned. If a demand exists for—let us say—a monorail system in Los Angeles, let whichever company wishes to make the effort, do so. Let it attain the right-of-way in the same fashion that many pipeline companies achieve rights-of-way, i.e., by acquiring "options to buy" along two or more alternative routes (to bypass the stubborn holdout) until one of the routes is complete.

Without the confiscatory power of eminent domain perhaps this-or-that project could not be achieved. So be it. The measure of human progress is not the grandiose public project, but adherence to the principles of a free society—the second of which is the institution of private property.

The third principle of the free and progressive society is the market economy, which will be the subject of the following chapter.

10: Principle #3: The Market Economy

The third principle of the free society is the market economy. But could the "unfettered" marketplace be trusted to function properly without the continuous scrutiny of the regulator?

Fifty years ago economist Joseph Schumpeter described capitalism as a process of "creative destruction" in which the old ideas, products and industries are constantly being displaced by the new. For example, of the 100 largest corporations of 1917, only 22 are in existence today.

The reallocation of resources from the less to the more productive use is a continuing and essential process—although not always a welcome one. In 1948, when Textron boss Royal Little closed a textile plant in Nashua, New Hampshire, 3500 jobs were eliminated and Little was hung in effigy. But he predicted that the town would one day thank him for taking this painful but necessary step. He was right. A few years later, the factory space which once housed 3500 low-tech, low-paying jobs housed 5500 high-tech, high-paying jobs. And in 1983 the town honored Royal Little at a banquet.

Even the corporate raider who closes down a plant, sells off the assets and walks off with a bundle is performing a vital if unpopular function, for these assets are soon directed to more productive use. To the general public, however, the hostile takeover may be just another example of the evils of the "unfettered marketplace." An excellent presentation of the opposing views on this contentious issue appeared in a highly unlikely place: in a wise and entertaining movie entitled *Other People's Money*.[1]

Other People's Money. A 1991 movie starring Danny DeVito and Gregory Peck did an outstanding job of illustrating the conflict inherent in the painful process of creative destruction.

Takeover artist Larry Garfield (DeVito) has made a tender offer for a fading company, New England Wire & Cable. As the story develops, Garfield has two goals: 1) to take over the company with the expectation of breaking it up and making a bundle, and 2) to get the company chairman's attractive daughter into bed.

Campaign #2 is put on hold, because the showdown for #1 is at the yearly stockholders' meeting where Garfield's offer will be put to a vote.

The Chairman of the Board, played by an avuncular Gregory Peck, addresses the shareholders first with a moving presentation of conservative values.

I'd like to talk to you about something else. I want to share with you some of my thoughts concerning the vote you are going to make, and the company you own. This proud company, which has survived the death of its founder, numerous recessions, one major depression, and two world wars, is in imminent danger of self-destruction. On this day, in the town of its birth.

There [pointing scornfully at Garfield] is the instrument of our destruction. I want you to look at him in all of his glory: Larry the Liquidator! The entrepreneur of post-industrial America, playing God with other people's money!

The robber barons of old at least left something tangible in their wake. A coal mine, a railroad, banks. This man leaves nothing. He creates nothing. He builds nothing. He runs nothing. And in his wake lies nothing but a blizzard of paper to cover the pain.

Oh, if he said "I know how to run your business better than you," that would be something worth talking about! But he's not saying that! He's saying, "I'm going to kill you, because at this particular moment in time, you're worth more dead than alive"!

Well, maybe that's true, but it is also true that one day this industry will turn! One day, when the yen is weaker; the dollar is stronger; or when we finally begin to rebuild our roads, our bridges, the infrastructure of our country, demand will skyrocket! And when those things happen, we will still be here! Stronger, because of our ordeal, stronger because we have survived. And the price of our stock will make his offer pale by comparison.

God save us if we vote to take his paltry few dollars and run! God save this country, if that is truly the wave of the future! We will then have become a nation that makes nothing but hamburgers, creates nothing but lawyers, and sells nothing but tax shelters! And if we are at that point in this country where we kill something because at the moment it is worth more dead than alive—well, take a look around. Look at your neighbor. Look at your neighbor. You won't kill him, will you. No. It's called murder, and it's illegal! Well, this too is murder! On a mass scale. But on Wall Street they call it "maximizing shareholder value"! And they call it legal! And they substitute dollar bills where a conscience should be. Dammit! A business is worth more than the price of its stock! It's the place where we earn our living; where we meet our friends; dream our dreams. It is in every sense the very fabric which binds our society together.

So, let us now, at this meeting, say to every Garfield in the land, "Here we build things; we don't destroy them! Here, we care about more than the price of our stock! Here, we care about people!"

At this point the Chairman takes his seat amid an enthusiastic and prolonged ovation. And then to scattered boos, Larry Garfield is introduced. He rises to his feet and takes the microphone. He waits for the catcalls to subside, and commences:

Amen.
And amen.
And amen.
You'll have to forgive me; I'm not familiar with the local custom. Where I come from, you always say "amen" after you hear a prayer. Because that's what you just heard. A prayer. Where I come from, that particular prayer is called a prayer for the dead.

You just heard a prayer for the dead, my fellow stockholders, and you didn't say "amen."

This company is dead. I didn't kill it. Don't blame me. It was dead when I got here. It's too late for prayers. For even if the prayers were answered, and a miracle occurred, and the yen did this and the dollar did that, and the infrastructure did the other thing, we would still be dead. You know why? Fiber optics. New technologies. Obsolescence.

We're dead all right. We're just not broke. And do you know the surest way to go broke? Keep getting an increasing share of a shrinking market. Down the tubes. Slow but sure. You know, at one time there must have been dozens of companies making buggy whips. And I'll bet, the last company around was the one that made the best goddamn buggy whip you ever saw!

Now, how would you like to have been a stockholder in that company? You invested in a business. And this business is dead. Let's have the intelligence—let's have the decency—to sign the death certificate, collect the insurance, and invest in something with a future!

Ah! But we can't, goes the prayer. We can't, because we have "responsibility." Our "responsibility to our employees; to our community; what will happen to them?"

I got two words to that: "Who cares?" [A gasp from the crowd.]

You care about them? Why? They didn't care about you. They sucked you dry. You have no responsibility to them! For the last ten years this company bled your money. Did this community ever say, "We know times are tough; we'll lower taxes; reduce water and sewer"?

Check it out. You're paying twice what you did ten years ago.

And our devoted employees who have taken no increases for the past three years, are still making twice what they made ten years ago. And our stock? One sixth of what it was ten years ago.

Who cares? I'll tell you. Me. I'm not your *best* friend; I'm your *only* friend!

I don't make anything? *I'm making you money!* And lest we forget, that's the only reason any of you became stockholders in the first place! You want to make money! You don't care if they manufacture wire and cable, fried chicken or grow tangerines! You want to make money!

I'm the only friend you've got! I'm making you money! Take the money. Invest it somewhere else. Maybe—maybe you'll get lucky, and it will be used productively. And if it is, you'll create new jobs and provide a service for the economy! And, God forbid, even make a few bucks for yourselves. [laughter]

If anybody asks, tell them you gave at the plant. [laughter]

By the way, it pleases me that I'm called "Larry the Liquidator." You know why, fellow stockholders? Because at my funeral, you'll leave with a smile on your face and a few bucks in your pocket! Now, that's a funeral worth having!

Larry takes his seat amid laughter and applause.

The vote is taken, and Larry the Liquidator wins.

Eventually, the Chairman's daughter, a savvy corporate lawyer, arranges for the restructured company to provide some special product to the Japanese, or something, and everyone is happy. Especially Larry, who can now get on with Campaign #2.

But more to the point, *Other People's Money* does an outstanding job of illuminating one of the more controversial events in the turbulent process of "creative destruction." There's a lesson here: The marketplace is not always neat and orderly and "fair." But it works a whole lot better than the alternatives.

The regulator versus the marketplace. One of the great myths of the twentieth century has been that a national economy is so big and complex and pervasive that it must be managed and controlled by a central authority. But consider the task of managing just one large company.

In a corporation such as General Motors there are tens of thousands of workers, managers, salesmen and engineers to be directed and paid. There are thousands of customers to be satisfied. There are hundred of thousands of parts to be designed, manufactured, catalogued, shipped and stored. There are millions of invoices, orders, receipts, checks and vouchers. And there are millions of purchases rippling out across the rest of the economy influencing prices from Maine to California. The complexity of such an organization is immense. But GM, in conjunction with a flexible market economy, does a pretty good job. And it does it without imposing a single fine, without jailing a single person, without confiscating a square foot of private property, and without seizing a single dollar from a single taxpayer. To suppose that government could do better is awfully naive.

And, in fact, with socialism discredited over most of the globe, the political class has generally given up on the notion of day-to-day hands-on control. The task is simply hopeless. So, the fall-back role of the regulator is "oversight"—the monitoring role of agencies such as the SEC and Antitrust, to assure the goals of "fairness," the "level playing field," or whatever. But in practice this requires reining in the process of "creative destruction" on which economic health and growth depend. We have already seen how these agencies operate, but one more example will further illustrate the impact of the regulator upon the marketplace.

U.S. v United Shoe Machinery Company.[2] The United Shoe Machinery Company was formed back in 1899. By 1917 it leased or sold 85% of the shoe machinery in the country. In its industry, United was the Microsoft of the day. The company's first run-in with Antitrust was in 1917, but the Supreme Court found that an efficient company offering a good product was not violating the law. In a 1922 antitrust suit the company was obliged to modify its leasing contracts somewhat, but its dominant position was still not in itself attacked.

A third antitrust suit was initiated in 1947, and the leasing conditions were again the major target. The final decision was handed down six years later. The judge attributed the company's dominant position to "superior products and services," and acknowledged that the machines performed well and were serviced by the company "promptly, efficiently and courteously." Further, the rates were found to be uniform and fair, and the customers had expressed no dissatisfaction.

Still, the judge supported the government lawyers in condemning the leasing arrangements even though leasing of shoe machinery had been the accepted practice in the industry since the Civil War. The arrangement was beneficial to both parties: it assured a steady and predictable cash flow to the lessor, and in addition permitted easy entry into the shoe manufacturing field. There were 1462 shoe firms in the U.S. at that time.

However, Antitrust claimed, and the court agreed, that the leasing agreements were "anticompetitive." For one thing, the ten year lease period was deemed to be too long. The judge explained that "a competitor may not get a chance to have his machine adequately tried out by a shoe manufacturer." It was ordered that the period be reduced to five years.

The second objection was United's policy that the lessee "shall use the leased machinery to full capacity upon all footwear." This evidently meant that if a customer leased a United machine it should use it and not a competitor's. Why the customer, having paid the lease fee, would do otherwise, is not clear. Anyway, Antitrust objected, the court again agreed, and this provision was ordered dropped.

The third objection was over the requirement of a return fee if the machine were returned prior to the lease expiration. However, the charge would be reduced if the machine were replaced by another United machine. Antitrust argued, and the court again agreed, that this was anticompetitive because the lessee would pay the full charge if the replacement were a competing machine. This was "discriminatory." Considering that the fee was only around $300, this hardly seems a significant issue, but the differential was ordered abolished.

The judge found that the company's free repair policy was "exclusionary" because it made it difficult for other companies to compete without offering a similar service. The company was ordered to sell its repair service as a separate item.

The court objected to the fact that leasing meant that there would be no used machine market; this was also deemed anticompetitive. The company was ordered to offer all of its machinery for sale as well as lease. (About half its line had been for sale all along.)

A final objection was to the company's dominance in "shoe factory supplies." The court acknowledged that "there's nothing whatsoever to the government's allegations that customers are coerced, or are subservient, or a captive, or are deliberately misled by United's representatives." No matter. The company was ordered to divest itself of its nail, tack, and eyelet subsidiaries.

No single order was all that onerous, but the sum was a wholesale meddling with common practices which had evolved over many decades. The judge explained that this was necessary to "root out monopolization." He further argued that the court's restrictions were not themselves "discriminatory" because they would simply reduce United to the position of its less efficient competitors. Great.

The government lawyers were still not finished with United. The Justice Department appealed the case to the Supreme Court in 1967 claiming that the lower court had not gone far enough, even though United's market share had dropped from 85% in 1953 to 60% in 1967. The Supreme Court complied, and ordered further divestitures. United was ordered to divest itself of a large chunk of its shoe machines, manufacturing assets and patents. A new, competing company was formed of these elements, to which United was obliged to provide service and parts. In addition, United was forbidden to compete for five years with the product line of which it had been divested. Finally, United was ordered to licence its own treasured patents to potential competitors.

For decades United had been bullied, battered and virtually dismantled by the True Believers at Antitrust. But a company culture of sound management, innovation and hard work built up over generations could not survive this kind of assault forever. Antitrust finally got its wish: In the years that followed United continued to decline, and today it has dropped out of the shoe machinery business entirely. Foreign companies now dominate this market.

U.S. v United Shoe is an old case, but the attitudes among antitrust lawyers have changed little. The successful company which wins a large market share through skillful management and a superior product is still regarded as some kind of public enemy. We see this attitude today in the Intel case, or in the Microsoft case, where commonplace licensing agreements are supposedly "exclusionary," "anticompetitive," "coercive," "monopolistic," or whatever. The idea that the marketplace should be the final arbiter is simply unthinkable to the True Believer. Antitrust all but destroyed United Shoe Machinery, and if it gets its way it will do the same to Microsoft and Intel.

"To be a merchant prince has never been my goal,
For I'm qualified to play a more important role:
Since I've never failed in business, this of course assures
That I'm qualified beyond dispute *to now run yours!*"
—from *Tom Smith and His Incredible Bread Machine*

The urge to second-guess the marketplace takes many forms. Back in the 1980s the big rage was for a "National Industrial Policy." Books were written on the subject, and soon every Democratic candidate for president had jumped on the bandwagon. A National Industrial Policy referred to an explicit federal program of loan guarantees, subsidies, tariffs and associated trade restrictions to bypass the marketplace in order to aid and direct this or that segment of the economy. Some of the proposals would target up-and-coming "sunrise" industries, the high-tech firms which would have the greatest potential for creating new markets, jobs and wealth. Because Japan subsidized and managed its economy, so the argument went, this country should do the same. But as Senator Proxmire warned at the time,

> Money will go where the political power is....It will go where union power is mobilized. It will go where the campaign contributors want it to go. It will go where the mayors and governors as well as congressmen and senators have the power to push it. Anyone who thinks government funds will be allocated to firms according to merit has not lived or served in Washington very long.[3]

Japan embraced the "managed" economy while the U.S., in spite of the regulatory impulses of Washington, stayed more-or-less with the "creative destruction" of the marketplace. How did things turn out fifteen years later? Writing in *The New Republic* in 1998, Charles Lane compares the results this way:

> the giddily unplanned United States, willing to endure corporate downsizing and other short-term costs of meeting foreign competition, has come out ahead. Our labor markets, once considered chaotic, are now celebrated for their flexibility. Our capital markets, once denounced as citadels of greed, are now hailed for their transparency. Our culture, once derided as compassionless, is now recognized as a vital crucible of individual creativity.[4]

The regulator, who has probably not spent a day of his life in the real world of the marketplace, simply does not comprehend the unruly process of "creative destruction." Accordingly, he is tireless in his efforts to restrict the takeovers, impede the leveraged buy outs, punish the efficient, bring down Microsoft, make things "fair," and in general make a nuisance of himself.

Yet, miraculously, the system continues to function. Lucky us, for the market economy is the third essential ingredient of the free and progressive society. Based on voluntary exchange, it is the only economic system consistent with human liberty.

And on top of that, it delivers the goods.

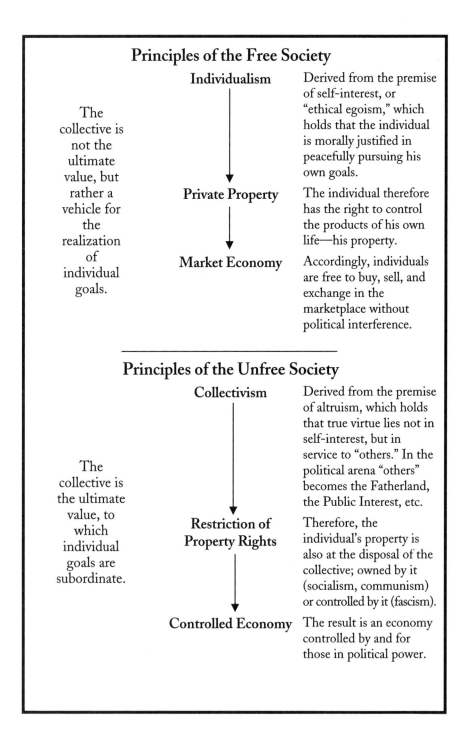

Principles of the Free Society

Individualism

The collective is not the ultimate value, but rather a vehicle for the realization of individual goals.

Derived from the premise of self-interest, or "ethical egoism," which holds that the individual is morally justified in peacefully pursuing his own goals.

Private Property

The individual therefore has the right to control the products of his own life—his property.

Market Economy

Accordingly, individuals are free to buy, sell, and exchange in the marketplace without political interference.

Principles of the Unfree Society

Collectivism

The collective is the ultimate value, to which individual goals are subordinate.

Derived from the premise of altruism, which holds that true virtue lies not in self-interest, but in service to "others." In the political arena "others" becomes the Fatherland, the Public Interest, etc.

Restriction of Property Rights

Therefore, the individual's property is also at the disposal of the collective; owned by it (socialism, communism) or controlled by it (fascism).

Controlled Economy

The result is an economy controlled by and for those in political power.

11: The Origin of Cooperation

What is the origin of cooperation? Is it government? Or is it rational self-interest?

There are standards of behavior which have nothing to do with politicians and regulators. Perhaps these standards arise from religious or cultural values. On the other hand, maybe they arise ultimately from a sense of enlightened self-interest. Maybe the Golden Rule is just good business.

But this raises an interesting question: if businessmen would tend to good behavior simply out of self-interest, this would mean that the concept of government as the essential arbiter of the marketplace might be a myth. Beyond the most basic policing of force and fraud, the regulator might be simply a meddlesome scold, needlessly interfering with a society which, if left alone, would work things out pretty well.

The ultimate question here concerns the *origin of social order*. Does it arise spontaneously out of individual self-interest, or is it the product of political authority? Most people believe that the source of social order is government. As Oliver Wendell Holmes, Jr. put it, "Taxes are what we pay for civilized society."

But if order evolves from political authority, what does political authority evolve from? A more likely sequence in the evolution of social behavior is that a cooperative structure of some sort emerges first and a political structure, for better or worse, is then superimposed upon it. For example, when the Hebrews left Egypt they were already well organized on a tribal and religious basis; only after many generations did a tax-supported political state emerge. But if a cooperative social order can evolve *in the absence* of political authority, then Holmes was wrong: the compulsory state is not a required element of civilization after all.

How, then, does cooperation evolve? This question was the basis of a fascinating computer tournament devised by Robert Axelrod of the Department of Political Science and the Institute of Public Policy Studies at the University of Michigan at Ann Arbor. The tournament was described in detail by Douglas R. Hofstadter in the May 1983 issue of *Scientific American*, and in Axelrod's subsequent book *The Evolution of Cooperation*.[1]

The computer tournament. Consider the following scenario: you want to buy a bushel of potatoes, and you encounter a potential seller. But the situation is such that cooperation is required: you must leave the money on a stump in the forest, and the seller will (he says) leave the potatoes on another stump in another part of the forest. If you both stick to the bargain, you get the potatoes and he gets the money. But suppose he reneges? He gets the money and you get nothing. Morality aside, would it not be wiser to renege yourself? You would have a chance of getting the potatoes free. And if you both defected, you would at least be no worse off. But then, what about the next time you need a bushel of potatoes?

Based on a classic problem in logic called the Prisoner's Dilemma, the question here is whether cooperation can evolve in a world of unfettered self-interest. As Hofstadter put it, "The first aspect is: How can cooperation get started at all? The second is: Can cooperative strategies survive better than their noncooperative rivals? The third is: Which cooperative strategies will do best, and how will they come to predominate?"

The game was simple: each entrant would encounter each of the others in a continuing round robin, learning from each encounter, and reacting accordingly at the next meeting. There was no external punishment for defecting and no "rules of conduct." The contestants were guided exclusively by self-interest, the goal being simply to amass the greatest number of points by whatever strategy could be devised.

At each encounter the player would respond with a "C" (cooperate) or a "D" (defect), taking into account any previous experience with that participant. Scoring was as follows:

		Player B	
		Cooperates	Defects
Player A	Cooperates	3, 3	0, 5
	Defects	5, 0	1, 1

That is, if both parties cooperate in an encounter each receives 3 points. If A cooperates but B defects, A gets zero points and B gets 5, etc. The maximum gain for a single encounter, then, would be to defect (i.e., cheat) when the other party does not. But, of course, the other party might not be so trusting next time.

The first tournament, held in 1979, had fourteen entrants. The longest program was 77 lines of instruction and the shortest was just four lines. Each program engaged each of the others a total of 200 times.

It was the shortest program which won, a program called Tit for Tat composed by Anatol Rapaport, a psychologist and philosopher at the University of Toronto. The program was extremely simple: cooperate on the first encounter, and thereafter do whatever the other party did on the previous encounter. If the other party cooperated, cooperate; if the other party defected, defect. That's all. But how could such a simple program defeat the complex stratagems devised by other experts? Said Axelrod,

> The analysis of the tournament results indicates that there is a lot to be learned about coping in an environment of mutual power. Even expert strategists from political science, sociology, economics, psychology and mathematics made the systematic errors of being too competitive for their own good, not forgiving enough and too pessimistic about the responsiveness of the other side.

Axelrod went on to perform a number of "subjunctive replays," introducing newly-devised strategies. Depending on the environment some of the new programs would occasionally win, but Tit for Tat continued to be a star performer. Axelrod studied the implications of this at length and identified two salient personality traits of Tit for Tat: be "nice" (don't be the first to defect), and be "forgiving" (be willing to cooperate again once you have "gotten even").

Axelrod then announced a second tournament, inviting all the original participants and also advertising in computer hobbyist magazines. To each candidate he sent a detailed discussion of the lessons learned in the first tournament. Accordingly, all of the entrants knew what the others knew—and could plan accordingly.

This time, sixty-two entries were received from eight countries, from eight academic disciplines and from all ages. One entrant was ten years old. The shortest program was again the four-line Tit for Tat and the longest was 152 lines. In general, the programs were more sophisticated, some employing subtle "character probes" in order to exploit any weaknesses among the more trusting programs.

To the amazement of Axelrod and the rest, the winner was again Tit for Tat. Subtlety and trickery did not pay off. The willingness of Tit for Tat to defect canceled out any transient advantage that might be gained over it. Thus, in this new and more challenging environment, Axelrod appreciated the importance of the third salient character trait of Tit for Tat: the willingness to retaliate in kind, which he called "provokability."

Again Axelrod replayed the tournament adding newly-fashioned programs. Tit for Tat continued to be a top performer. But the most significant replay was the "ecological tournament," consisting of a cascade of many generations, each one modified by the results of the preceding. That is, the more successful programs increased in number while the less successful waned in importance, finally becoming extinct.

A concrete example of ecological extinction was provided by Harrington, the only non-nice program among the top 15 finishers in the second tournament. In the first 200 or so generations of the ecological tournament, as Tit for Tat and other successful nice programs were gradually increasing their percentage of the population, Harrington too was increasing its percentage. This was a direct result of Harrington's exploitive strategy. By the 200th generation or so, however, things began to take a noticeable turn. Weaker programs were beginning to become extinct, which meant there were progressively fewer dupes for Harrington to profit from. Soon the trend became apparent: Harrington could not keep up with its nice rivals. By the thousandth generation Harrington was as extinct as the dodos it had exploited.

Tit for Tat, the simplest program of all, was the clear winner in the ecological tournament.

An interesting aspect of Tit for Tat's consistent success is that it never "defeated" anyone. Of course, this was the nature of the program: it might lose on occasion, but the most it could gain overall with any player was a tie. Says Axelrod, "Tit for Tat won the tournament not by beating the other player but by eliciting behavior from the other player that allowed both to do well. Tit for Tat was so consistent at eliciting mutually rewarding outcomes that it attained a higher overall score than any other strategy in the tournament."

By this time Axelrod had identified a fourth character trait which helped Tit for Tat compile its winning record: "clarity." The other entries, programmed to maximize their own gain, quickly recognized that they could prosper with Tit for Tat only by cooperating with it. Complexity would be self-defeating. Explained Axelrod, "Too much complexity can appear to be total chaos. If you are using a strategy that appears random, then you also appear unresponsive to the other player. If you are unresponsive, then the other player has no incentive to cooperate with you. So being so complex as to be incomprehensible is very dangerous."

It's interesting to note that the four personality traits which Axelrod identified in Tit for Tat are identical to those of a good parent: be "nice," but react to misbehavior ("provokability"); then be "forgiving," and throughout, be open and predictable ("clarity"). Would that all parents could develop these four simple traits.

But it's in the broader arena that the tournament is most instructive, for the contestants were real people engaged in the basic building block of social behavior, the one-on-one encounter. Each was seeking to maximize his profits by whatever "selfish" means he could devise, with no external authority to reward some and punish others. Yet, the result was not dog-eat-dog. Cooperative self-interest won the day!

Still, the computer tournament was not "real life." Could an actual society function without the guiding hand of the politician? Well, consider what things were like a few years ago in Peru where, thanks to the stifling inefficiency of an intrusive socialist government, two out of three urban workers were engaged in a vast underground economy which operated entirely outside the legal system. Yet the result was order, not chaos. In fact, Claudia Rosett's description, based on a two-year study by a Peruvian think tank called the Institute for Liberty and Democracy, sounds like a replay of the computer tournament:

> With this large volume of informal business, an underground legal code has developed that ignores the inefficient laws that drive people into the underground in the first place. This code is so powerful and pervasive that underground businessmen can dependably make deals with each other and the legal sector that could never be enforced in a government court. In Lima, for example, street vendors command prices of up to $759 for sale of their business locations, although they hold no legal titles to the spots.
>
> In an ironic twist, honesty and integrity are especially important factors in underground business success. Anyone who does business outside the law has nothing but his word to guarantee contracts, and will therefore tend to go to great lengths to preserve his good name. Also, an entire community can suffer a loss of credit if one member cheats on a deal. So profit incentives create community pressures that encourage fair dealings.

In fact, the underground makes honest men out of otherwise corrupt state judges. Informal contractors sometimes hire off-duty judges to arbitrate disputes. While some of these judges take bribes when working for the state, they cannot afford to do so when working for the underground. If word gets out that they are crooked, they will not be hired again.[2]

So perhaps the implications of the computer tournament are not so far-fetched after all. Perhaps Justice Holmes was wrong. Perhaps the real guardian of civilized behavior is not the political state at all, but the enlightened self-interest of the marketplace.

The three principles of the free society, then, are individualism, private property, and the market economy. When we violate these principles, bad things seem invariably to happen, as we shall now see in Part III, "The Principles Ignored."

Part Three:
The Principles Ignored—
How Political Force Disrupts Our Lives

12: The Death of Diana

Wrong principles can lead to bad results. "Isn't it much better for people to work for the good of everybody?" asked 1960s terrorist Diana Oughton, a few days before she blew herself up.

The history of 1960s radicalism—the New Left—is endlessly fascinating. How could so many bright people be so thoroughly wrong-headed? Looking back on it, Peter Collier puts it this way:

> It is true that history did not provide our generation with a great issue, as Stalin and Soviet Communism was for the Thirties....But there have been events over the past two decades—the fate of Vietnam, revelations about the Cuban gulag, the invasion of Afghanistan—that should have prompted a rethinking about who exactly we were in the Sixties, what we did, the way we viewed the world, and the heritage we left. The fact that there has been so little soul-searching reinforces the thought that many of us suppressed at the time—that the New Left, to put it charitably, was not a thinking movement. It was vaunt and braggadocio. Despite all the "struggle sessions," the intellectual nattering, and endless talk, the New Left always had an allergic reaction to ideas.[1]

Well, not quite. The problem with the New Left was not *no* ideas, but the *wrong* ideas. Diana Oughton, for example, a member of the violent Weatherman faction of the Students for a Democratic Society (SDS), was no nihilist thrillseeker. She was an idealist who believed fervently in the justice of her cause. And in a New York City townhouse in 1970 she was blown to bits while fashioning bombs wrapped in nail-studded tape.

The violence of the New Left has today been largely repudiated, but the vision which inspired it—the view of capitalism as world-wide exploiter of the poor—continues to be a dominant theme of intellectual and political debate. Accordingly, the perceptions which brought Diana to that townhouse are as relevant today as they were then.

The death of Diana. Diana Oughton, from a wealthy and close-knit family in Dwight, Illinois, would seem an unlikely convert to revolutionary terrorism. After attending public school through the ninth grade in Dwight, Diana attended the exclusive Madeira School[2] in Virginia, followed by the equally exclusive Bryn Mawr Women's College outside of Philadelphia. Recalls one young man who knew her, "It wasn't that she was particulary beautiful; she had a round face and a funny nose, but she was so sharp and kind of glowing that everyone fell half in love with her."[3] But Diana was starting to develop a different set of interests.

During her last year at Bryn Mawr, Diana joined a reading tutoring program for black children in Philadelphia. Volunteers were expected to tutor one child, but Diana, on finding these seventh-grade children could not read *at all*, soon had three under her wing and was taking the train two nights a week into Philadelphia. Later, she became involved in a voter registration drive for blacks in Cambridge, Maryland. Diana, who had already shed her midwestern Republican views, was becoming increasingly troubled by a view of America she had not dreamed of in Dwight, Illinois.

While her classmates went on to graduate school or a career or got married, Diana joined the Voluntary International Service Assignments (VISA) run by the American Friends Service Committee and was assigned to Guatemala. After three months of training in Guatemala City she arrived in the Indian village of Chichicastenango.

In the ensuing months Diana was numbed by the poverty she saw about her. The sight of drinking water alive with pin worms once moved her to tears, while the memory of an Indian woman with her sick and shivering baby wrapped in papers would stay with her all her life.

Diana worked hard these two years and brought modest improvements to the villagers in education and health. Against the background of millions on the edge of starvation, however, she was painfully aware of the insignificance of her own contribution. An acquaintance, an American Fulbright Scholar living in Guatemala City, expressed a view which Diana gradually began to share: that her efforts were merely "delaying the revolution." As she now saw it, a few wealthy families were keeping the poor in a state of virtual peonage, and her own country, through its repeated intervention in behalf of favored economic interests, was largely to blame.

Considering the long history of U.S. intervention in Latin American affairs, Diana's view of things was understandable. But there's a difference between the *political* capitalism of gunboats and puppet dictators, and the *private* capitalism of the marketplace. Neither Diana nor Karl Marx, however, chose to make such distinctions. It was all the same evil—the institution of private property—and Diana left Guatemala a confirmed radical socialist dedicated to the overthrow of "capitalism" whatever its form.

Back in the U.S. Diana became active in the radical SDS (founded by Tom Hayden) which, at the Chicago Convention in 1968, precipitated the first major confrontation between the New Left and the armed establishment in the form of Mayor Daley's police. As Diana moved farther toward the edge of the political spectrum the distance between her and her family increased. "I've made my decision, Daddy," she told her father. "There's no sense talking about it."

In the summer of 1969 Diana was one of a 36-member delegation which met with North Vietnamese in Cuba. The experience heightened the conviction of the young radicals that the U.S. was headed for a major military debacle, and that a revolution was a genuine possibility. After all, Castro had pulled it off with only 13 men. The Weathermen, as Diana's more radical faction of the SDS was now called, were determined to become the cutting edge of their own revolution.

Diana's individuality was rapidly being submerged into the revolutionary movement. Her sister, Pam, begged Diana to attend her wedding but Diana explained, "My life isn't my own. I don't make the decisions about how I use my time."

Diana was now living in Weathermen collectives in Flint and Detroit. A major "Days of Rage" demonstration was scheduled for Chicago in October, and as the crucial date approached, life in the communes became increasingly savage as Weathermen sought to transform themselves into disciplined revolutionaries. In his book *Diana: The Making of a Terrorist*, Thomas Powers described it thus:

> In practice "everything for the revolution" meant nothing for anything else. As a result, the collectives turned into foul sties where beds went unmade, food rotted on unwashed plates, toilets jammed, dirty clothes piled up in corners....
>
> Inside the collectives the Weathermen were cruel to themselves and each other. Hurt feelings and smoldering grudges poisoned the atmosphere; suffering themselves, people tended to attack each other with increasing violence. Individuals were sometimes attacked so brutally in group criticism sessions they were left whimpering and speechless. Individuals who seemed to hold back some part of themselves were subject to harsh psychological assault; if they persisted, they were sometimes purged. Everyone was overtired and underfed, nervous and fearful. People became stiff and unnatural, afraid they

would be attacked for the slightest error, a deliberate process which sometimes hid a desire literally to destroy.[4]

The Days of Rage demonstration was a flop. On the final day only about 200 took part. Although Weathermen publicly claimed a success it was apparent they were failing dismally in their attempt to precipitate a mass revolutionary movement. In just four months the contingent had shrunk from 2000 or so idealists to around 200 window-smashing vandals.

But if the violence thus far had not precipitated the inevitable revolution the solution was obvious: escalate the violence one more notch. It was time to go underground. The Weathermen broke up into groups of ten to thirty in order to conduct campaigns of urban guerrilla warfare.

Diana phoned her home for the last time. "You know, Diana," said her mother, "you're killing us both."

"I'm sorry, Mummy," Diana answered.

Diana was gaunt and ill when she visited a friend from the old days. She praised the Cuba she had visited. "Isn't it much better for people to work for the good of everybody?" she asked.

It was March 2. Diana had four more days to live. She phoned her sister, Carol, and talked at length about the family and about old friends. Diana abruptly asked, "Will the family stand by me no matter what? Will they help me if I need it?"

"Of course," Carol said. "Anything."

Diana left Detroit and soon joined a small group of Weathermen at 18 W. 11th St. in New York City. On the morning of March 6, using clocks, wire, batteries, blasting caps and two 50 pound cases of dynamite, she and Terry Robbins were fabricating bombs. Just before noon, one of them made a mistake. All they could identify of pretty Diana was the tip of one finger.

Diana Oughton is dead and the Weathermen long ago dispersed, but the questions are as intriguing today as they were then. For one, why were these youthful radicals so hostile to established wealth when they were themselves generally from comfortable middle-class or above backgrounds? Perhaps this seeming paradox merely affirms the general rule that people do not value what they have not earned; the wealth which was theirs to command had not been created by themselves but by others—by parents, grandparents, or great-grandparents. Feeling only contempt for their own unearned affluence they despised all wealth, unearned or not. The distinction between the producer and the dependent was not one which they were intellectually prepared to make.

The fact that these youthful bomb-throwers represented an unusually high level of formal schooling strikes another incongruous note. Diana had attended a "good" public school followed by exclusive private schools including the prestigious Bryn Mawr—yet she had evidently received from them no real understanding of the connection between economic freedom and material progress. If nothing else, the death of Diana stands as a grim monument to the condition of formal education in America today.

Above all, Diana embraced the unlivable morality of altruism. Accordingly, she regarded the profit motive as immoral and exploitive. American society in general seems equally befuddled on this issue. "Who wants to live in a society in which selfishness and self-seeking are celebrated as virtues?" asks neo-conservative Irving Kristol in the *Wall Street Journal*. "Isn't it much better for people to work for the good of everybody?" asked Diana a few days before she blew herself up.

Principles matter, and Diana embraced the wrong ones.

Diana was wrong about a lot of things. The real enemy of the poor over the years has not been capitalism, but a world-wide infatuation with political force, legal or illegal, as the way to solve problems. This subject will be pursued in the following chapter, "The War Against the Poor."

13: The War Against the Poor

Capitalism did not create poverty; it inherited it. The real obstacle to material progress is not the marketplace, but political interference with it.

Poverty has not been the consequence of private capitalism but of the world-wide infatuation with political force as the regulator of economic activity. For example, in 1968 a nationalist/socialist military regime ousted the elected president of Peru and immediately expropriated the assets of U.S. oil companies and other major segments of the economy. Capital fled the country and production plummeted. As price controls were imposed even farming became unprofitable. Food production declined so sharply that the socialist leaders were obliged to spend large amounts of foreign exchange to import food—this in a country which had been self-sufficient in food since the days of the Incas! During the twelve years of socialist rule real income dropped by 40%.

Nowhere has the perverse influence of political force been demonstrated more consistently than in the Third World countries of Asia and Africa, many of which have been ruled by doctrinaire socialists since independence, with uniformly wretched results. In India the per capita food supply has barely increased in fifty years, and private investment of any description—foreign or domestic—is treated with open contempt by a massive and entrenched bureaucracy. The state-run universities of these countries attach little importance to agriculture and the sciences, emphasizing instead the "soft" disciplines of interest to future bureaucrats. In India, three-quarters of college graduates go to work for the government. The market-oriented economies of Japan, Taiwan, South Korea, Singapore and Sri Lanka are reasonably prosperous, while the Indian masses continue to live out their lives in socialist squalor.

For decades, the U.S. Government has subsidized repressive regimes around the world with billions in so-called "foreign aid." The process continues today in part through the efforts of the International Monetary Fund (IMF). In Russia, for example, billions follow more billions in spite of well-documented reports that much of the money is going directly into the pockets of corrupt officials, to end up in Swiss bank accounts. Corruption is rewarded, the market economy is stifled, and the Russian people remain mired in poverty.

In the U.S. we have moved away from private capitalism, based on voluntary exchange, toward *political* capitalism, a system ordered and influenced by the state in behalf of this or that favored group. But for every beneficiary of government intervention there is a victim, and the most consistent victims are the unorganized poor, as the following examples will illustrate.

Professional groups insulate themselves from competition by a jungle of legislative restraints. Consider the case of legal secretary Rosemary Forman of Jacksonville, Florida, who for 20 years had been offering cut-rate legal assistance for standard procedures such as divorce, adoptions, wills, etc. Where lawyers were charging $300 or so for these services, she was charging around $60. She explained in a *60 Minutes* interview, "If you want to pay for a lawyer's three-piece suit, Gucci shoes and styled hair, live it up." But the Florida Bar Association was not amused and brought suit against her for practicing law without a state licence. When she ignored an order to "cease and desist," she was charged with contempt of court and sentenced to four months in jail and a $2500 fine. She was finally granted clemency—but only on condition that she close down her office. The Florida Bar can now breathe easy—but the poor have now lost a source of inexpensive legal help.

Another example: skilled and experienced midwives are willing and able to provide inexpensive care to those who desire it—but in California and in many other states medical interests have prevailed upon legislatures to outlaw such services. The explanation, of course, is that such restrictions "protect the public"; the outcome, however, is that the poor person who is unable to afford expensive hospital care may end up with no care at all. Retail druggists achieve restrictions against less expensive mail order suppliers; undertakers acquire legislative roadblocks to cremation; optometrists, teachers, dentists, barbers—every group imaginable—all enjoy the privileges of state-enforced monopoly. And the expense falls most heavily, of course, upon the poor.

One of the great myths of our time is that the poor are net beneficiaries of government activity because they escape the taxes which pay for it all. On the contrary, the poor are the hardest hit by *all* taxes. A corporation tax, for example, is simply a disguised sales tax passed on to the consumer, poor as well as rich, in the form of higher prices. Another passed-on cost is the heavy expense of government regulation: Dr. Murray Weidenbaum of Washington University once calculated the added burden at around $2200 per year for a family of four. So who is the real beneficiary of all this government activity? One clue: the two richest counties in the U.S., by family income, are Montgomery in Maryland and Fairfax in Virginia, the two "bedroom" counties for Washington, D.C. It's not the poor who benefit from the vast array of federal largess as much as the affluent bureaucrats who administer those programs.

One of the past glories of this country was its great "upward mobility"—the unobstructed ease with which even the poor person, if he so desired and had the ability and determination, could enter the economic mainstream through some kind of independent activity. Young Cornelius Vanderbilt, to take an extreme example, started out with neither connections nor capital nor education, yet was able to create a vast and profitable empire in shipping and in railroading. And for every Vanderbilt tens of thousands of others were opening restaurants or grocery stores or shoe shops or newsstands or barber shops or whatever. If a person had something of value to offer little would prevent him from offering it. Today, however, upward mobility has been vastly impeded by pervasive government. Rules, regulations, inspections, restrictions, orders, decrees, taxes, licenses, fees, uncertainties and red tape all heavily weigh the scales against the poor person trying to break into the world of independent economic activity.

Consider the fate of Leroy Barrett, a 60-year-old black man who started a driveway paving business in Los Angeles without benefit of a contractor's license. Having ignored an injunction brought against him by the State Registrar of Contractors, he was hauled into court, the Deputy District Attorney explaining that "the law is geared to protect the public." (The possibility that Barrett's customers were capable of judging for themselves was evidently not considered.) Nearly illiterate, Barrett claimed he had been unable to comprehend the injunction, but the judge was unmoved, declaring, "This time it is a fine. Next time it will be jail. I don't want to put a 60-year-old man in jail, but I don't want him to believe he can violate the court's orders with impunity, so next time it will be jail."[1]

Barrett paid a $500 fine and went out of business.

This episode took place twenty years ago, and the barriers are more complex today than they were then. For example, suppose a person in a poor area saw the need for a low-cost barber shop. One might suppose that with a few hours practice, a $15 set of clippers, a chair and a willing customer, he could go into business. Then, if he were industrious, and were truly able to provide a service of value to his neighbors, he would prosper. Perhaps one day he could open a bigger shop and hire two of his relatives. That is the way things are supposed to be in a "land of opportunity." But that is not the way things are. In California, this is what the law says he must do.

The first step for an aspiring barber is a barber's license granted by the state Board of Barber Examiners. But this requires either two years as an apprentice working for someone else or 1500 hours (!) at a state-licensed barber school at a cost upwards of $3500. (In either case this individual has already been prevented from opening his own shop, but let us continue anyway.) Then, it costs $50 to register for the state test. And then, if the test is passed, there's another $50 for the two-year state license. But there's still more, for the new shop must now be inspected and approved by the Board—for another $50. Then, a city business license ($106.43 in Los Angeles). Then the new shop (assuming it opened at all) would be subject to periodic snooping, not only by the Board but by the city Health Department. And, of course, state and federal business taxes must be computed and promptly paid—or else.

Now, assuming he were still in business, suppose the new proprietor hires an assistant. Deductions, contributions and fees must be accurately computed and paid. Just for starters there's Worker's Compensation and unemployment insurance (around 1.3% of the first $7000 in wages) paid for by the employer. Then, in California there's something called the Employee Training Tax, 0.1% of the first $7000. Then there is a Federal Unemployment Tax, $56 per year per employee.

Now come the payroll deductions. State Disability Insurance (SDI) is 15% of the first $31,767 in wages. Then there's State Withholding Tax (variable). Then come the federal calculations which include Withholding plus Social Security/Medicare (7.65% matched by the employer).

The paperwork for all this represents a severe burden even to people with a fair degree of schooling; to the person with only a meager education and perhaps only a scant familiarity with the mysteries of bookkeeping, these artificial barriers to business survival are simply overwhelming. But there is still more: most states enforce—or try to enforce—minimum price schedules. But a poverty area shop forced to charge these inflated rates would go out of business in a week!

Cosmetology is another intensively regulated trade. Ask SaBrina Reese, a young black woman who owns two hair braiding salons in California, employing nine people. The state cosmetology board has sought to shut her down because she has not attended a state-approved cosmetology school—for 1600 hours at a cost of $9000. The fact that the school offers nothing on the subject of hair braiding doesn't matter. She has already been fined $1000 (later reduced to $500) and final resolution of the case is pending. A competitor explained the real issue: people like Ms. Reese are "a threat to those of us who are licensed and went through the normal channels."[2]

Just about every kind of business activity is subjected to the type of obstructions, burdens and harassments mentioned above. In New York City a "medallion" permitting the operation of a taxicab costs around $160,000, thus permanently excluding all but the wealthiest operators. In contrast, the license fee in Washington, DC, is under $200 and (as Professor Walter Williams[3] observes) most of the operators are black. Our congested cities cry for transportation—but a person would be hamstrung in trying to run a one-man jitney service, since public transportation is invariably in the iron grip of city hall and the transportation unions. Every enterprise imaginable—dry cleaning, trucking, beauty parlor, grocery store, and on and on—is today under the thumb of the politician. And let us not suppose that the controls are merely "on paper," for an army of bureaucrats will assure that every regulation is adhered to and every assessment paid.

For those who already have capital, experience and education, the numberless "barriers to entry" erected by the state can be overcome, but to the undercapitalized poor, often with little experience and scant education, these barriers are virtually insurmountable. The illegal immigrant selling oranges at the off-ramp of a Los Angeles freeway is a truer capitalist than those businessmen who are constantly running to government for this-or-that favor or restriction. Insulated from competition from below, the rich tend to stay rich. And the poor tend to stay poor.

It is worth considering that young Cornelius Vanderbilt, who was poor and nearly illiterate, and had neither connections nor experience, would very likely find it impossible, simply because of the suffocating influence of government, to get a start in business today!

Controls designed to protect the poor invariably do more harm than good. For example, strict eviction procedures make it extremely difficult for the apartment owner to rid himself of the professional deadbeat, and this added operating cost will eventually be passed on to the other tenants in the form of higher rents, reduced maintenance, or both.

In Los Angeles the first step in an eviction is to serve the delinquent tenant with an Unlawful Detainer which costs around $100 plus an additional $75 or so if the matter goes to trial. But first, a friend of the renter can claim to be another occupant of the apartment who must also be served, thus setting the process back to square one. Then the tenant, possibly assisted by a tax-supported legal aid attorney, can file a legal response, thus buying another 3–4 rent-free weeks. The tenant need not even show up in court. But even if the owner eventually receives the judgment, the process can still be delayed several more weeks by a wide variety of legal ploys. Then, filing for bankruptcy can stretch things out for months longer. An eviction can often take four to six months, but with bankruptcy the determined deadbeat can frequently enjoy rent-free living for a year or more. Faced by such a prospect, the apartment owner will often pay the deadbeat a thousand dollars or more to leave. It is literally cheaper than the alternative, which could be six to twelve thousand dollars or more in legal fees and lost rents.

The biggest loser in all this will again be precisely the person these laws are designed to protect, the marginal renter. For example, consider a divorced mother with a spotty employment record: where an apartment owner might otherwise accept this high-risk tenant the laws today are such that he would be very foolish to take the chance. Thanks to all this "protection" the high-risk renter today will find it harder than ever to find a place to stay.

In Los Angeles it is next to impossible for an owner even to get drug dealers out of his apartment house. As long as the dealer pays his rent he is virtually untouchable. Charles Isham of the Apartment Association of Greater Los Angeles once reported that in the Crenshaw area some apartments had a 20% vacancy rate because drug-dealing tenants forced other occupants to leave, and the apartment owner was powerless to do anything about it short of calling the police, which, under the circumstances, would be highly imprudent.

When owners are denied the right to manage their own property, long-term paralysis and neighborhood decline are inevitable. The next step in the death spiral of rental housing is the slumlord. Ever-tightening regulation makes rental housing less and less attractive as a long term investment; as a result, the responsible owner finally calls it quits and the slumlord moves in to extract the last few dollars as quickly as possible. The final step is abandonment. The poor are now finally out in the street.

The ultimate measure in housing regulation is rent control, which will be the subject of the following chapter.

14: Rent Control Versus the Poor

When government messes with property rights, bad things happen. Especially to the poor.

Nobel laureate economists Milton Friedman and George Stigler once contrasted San Fransisco's housing shortage after the 1906 earthquake, and in 1946 after several years of rent control. The renter was better off with the earthquake.

The San Francisco quake destroyed more than half the housing stock, and the remaining structures had to accommodate about 40% more people. However, because there were no controls, higher rents quickly brought forth new accommodations and the crisis evaporated within a few weeks. In contrast, the shortfall in 1946 was only 10% but the housing shortage persisted as part of what the governor described as "the most critical problem facing California."

In a free market an increase in rents has the desirable effect of broadening the supply: people take in roommates, homeowners are encouraged to rent out a spare room, investors are encouraged to build rental units, etc. As a result, shortages tend to be self-correcting. When the feedback loop of the marketplace is severed by rent control, however, any incentive to increase the supply is destroyed. At best the supply remains static, and at worst it starts to contract as apartment owners find themselves caught between rising costs and fixed rents. Upkeep declines, and in the extremity owners simply abandon their buildings.

The paradox of rent control is thoroughly understood by economists, if rarely by politicians. An honorable exception was Senator Eagleton of Missouri, who once noted, "The sad truth is that rent controls—enacted for the best of motives to protect middle and low-income tenants—actually work against the very people they were designed to aid."[1]

Rent control creates a wide variety of side effects, but making housing more available to low income people is definitely not one of them. The phenomenon has been well documented for years in New York City. As one prominent developer put it, "We have plenty of low-income housing in New York. But there are high-income people living in it." A few years ago writer William Tucker listed a few:

- Mayor Edward Koch was paying $351.60 a month for a rent-controlled unit with a wrap-around terrace in Greenwich Village which would otherwise have rented for around $1700 per month. Koch has held the lease for 21 years, and obviously has no intention of moving.
- Actress Lauren Hutton was living in a chalet-style unit on the lower West Side that cost $468.81 a month; comparable uncontrolled apartments cost as much as $1600 a month.
- Alistair Cooke was paying $975.38 a month for a rent-controlled eight-room apartment overlooking Central Park which would otherwise have rented for around $4000 to $5000 per month.
- Abbie Hoffman, a noted noise-maker of the '60s, was paying a scant $95.15 a month for an apartment which would otherwise have cost $500 to $700 a month.

These are a few of the happy winners in the rent control lottery—but their good fortune is paid for by those latecomers to the game who must pay premium rents elsewhere—if they can find a place at all. The U.S. Senate Committee on Banking, Housing and Urban Affairs once commented on the influence of rent control on New York City housing:

> Interestingly enough, there is no evidence to show that rent control benefits the poor. Quite the contrary, it helps a small, privileged group of long-time residents, largely middle class, while driving up rents in uncontrolled units.[2]

Meanwhile, rent-controlled housing becomes less and less attractive to the investor. As the apartment owner is squeezed between rising costs and inflexible ceilings, the first thing to suffer is maintenance. As one prominent black newspaper in New York City put it,

> We would be vigorously supporting the continuance of rent control if that concept and that ideal had moved minority groups toward better and less expensive housing. But unfortunately, this has not been the case....The result is that the property, no matter who owns it, goes steadily downhill to eventually become another war-torn hollow shell—a victim of the war of rent control.[3]

During the forty years of rent control in New York City about 300,000 units have been abandoned, due in part to rent control, and perhaps there is some poetic justice in the fact that New York City today must shell out over $300 million a year in aid to the homeless.

Of course, cities without rent control have also suffered problems of urban blight. However, rent control has been a major factor in aggravating New York City's acute housing shortage, and it's unfortunate that this lesson is being ignored elsewhere—in places like Santa Monica, California, a.k.a. the "People's Republic of Santa Monica."

Rent control in the People's Republic. In 1979 Santa Monica, California, imposed one of the most stringent rent control programs in the nation, the proclaimed purpose of which was to "assure affordable housing to middle and low-income people." As would be predicted, however, the result was quite different: rent control forced apartment owners to subsidize their middle and upper income tenants—while the poor were gradually eased out of town.

The problem began with the inflationary years of the 1970s. Costs were spiraling upward, including rents, and those renters on a fixed income were caught in the middle. However, the renters blamed the landlords instead of the government-inspired inflation, and political activists, of which Santa Monica has more than its fair share, were quick to urge rent control. The popular view of the grasping landlord was reflected by a 1977 article in the *Los Angeles Times*:

> Rent control is an idea whose time has finally come to California. Tenants throughout the state are demanding relief from unconscionable increases in housing costs and, as a result, are turning to rent regulation as the only remedy.
>
> The tenants are opposed, of course, by an equally determined set of landlords. In 1976 a high-powered real estate lobby, fueled with nearly $100,000 in campaign contributions, nearly enacted legislation that would have barred local governments from stopping rent gouging.[4]

During the inflation-ridden '70s there were certainly instances of rapid property turnover, accompanied by sharp rent increases which were not always reasonable, even for those superheated conditions. Attorney Robert Myers, who drafted the rent control measure, described one four-unit apartment which changed hands four times in four years with the rent increasing by 85%. However, while anecdotal stories about "unconscionable rent gouging" were highly publicized, there was little concrete information about the overall rental picture. In fact, to this day the Santa Monica rent board itself has no statistical data on Santa Monica rents during the critical years preceding rent control.

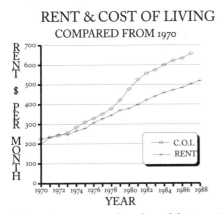

RENT & COST OF LIVING
COMPARED FROM 1970

Fig. 1. Average rent of ten Santa Monica units at 1143 Sixth St., compared to the cost of living from 1979 to 1988. Rent control was imposed in 1979. For comparison, the cost of living has been normalized to the rental figure for 1971. Cost of living data from Bureau of Labor Statistics.

Perhaps a more realistic picture of what was going on can be provided by the graph at left which shows the average rent of ten mid-town units from 1970 on. Rents were indeed rising steadily, but it can be seen that they were not out of line with the cost of living, and in fact were starting to lag behind. Overall, the problem was not an army of voracious apartment owners, but the inflationary spiral being created back in Washington, D.C.

But with rents moving inexorably higher, the dismay of renters, especially those on fixed incomes, is understandable.[5] A rent control measure had been defeated in 1978, but a powerful grass-roots movement was now being generated by a liberal-left-radical coalition called SMRR—Santa Monicans for Renters' Rights. A major component of the coalition was the local chapter of the Campaign for Economic Democracy (CED), the political movement founded by Santa Monica resident Tom Hayden, the husband of actress Jane Fonda. Rent control was once again on the ballot in April of 1979 in the form of a charter amendment.

The campaign was intensely emotional. Derek Shearer, a local activist and CED theoretician, later described it this way:

> You have to understand that political campaigns are not educational vehicles.…What you do is play on [voters'] feelings and sentiments about what's going on in society [which could mean producing campaign literature that shows an elderly tenant couple looking] a little bit like an Auschwitz picture [or perhaps a cancer victim saying] "Before I die, I'm voting for Ruth Yannatta and rent control."[6]

The charter amendment won by a comfortable margin, and rent control was at last established in Santa Monica. The result, however, has been unending turmoil and bitterness. Ironically, the owner who suffered the least was the "greedy speculator" whose rents were already at a high plateau, while the owner who had exercised restraint during the '70s was trapped between rising costs and an unreasonable ceiling. One of the anomalies of Santa Monica rental housing today is that the rent for virtually identical units on the same street, or even in the same apartment house, may differ by $150 a month or more.[7] Near the beach, where parking is especially hard to find, a garage rents for more than some rent-controlled apartments!

Another consequence of rent control is the widespread black market in renters sub-renting their apartment for more than the legal maximum. As one young woman testified at a rent board hearing, "Of course I'll make a profit at it if I can. Why shouldn't I? Lots of people are doing this!"[8]

Bargain rents soon created a permanent seller's market, the effect of which could be seen every day in the crush of applicants for the rare vacancy. A 1986 *Los Angeles Times* article noted that would-be renters cruise the streets looking for moving vans moving people out, or for painters renovating a vacant apartment. Apartment owners rarely advertised; one new owner made that mistake and lamented that "After the calls had reached probably 400 I took the phone off the hook."[9] But when the apartment owner is faced by such a flood of applicants he can obviously be highly selective, accepting only the family with the highest family income and an impeccable credit rating. The blue-collar worker, or the young family with children, or the old couple with a marginal income, need not even bother to apply. Moreover, even those marginal renters who already have a place may find themselves without one if the apartment owner, caught between rising costs and below-market rents, elects finally to go out of business, as many were soon doing.

In his 1986 book *Middle Class Radicalism in Santa Monica*, Mark Kann, who is generally sympathetic to radical aims, describes the rental market this way:

> The handful of available rentals were going to affluent professionals who could invest the time, energy, and resources necessary to campaign for vacancies; who sometimes shelled out up to $1,000 to former tenants, landlords, or agencies in black market efforts to crack the housing market; who were deemed more responsible and reliable than low income tenants in the view of landlords; and who were in the best position to purchase their units if the landlords were able to

push through a referendum allowing for conversions. I know one professional woman who tried to get a Santa Monica apartment for more than a year without success, but she broke into the city, finally, by marrying someone who already had an apartment there.[10]

With rent control, the apartment owner is caught in an intolerable bind, for it is the explicit purpose of the controls to keep rents *below* the market level. In Santa Monica, rent increases are limited to about two-thirds of the Consumer Price Index,[11] and as shown in Fig. 1 on page 136 there was in 1988 a gap of about 30% between what these rents were and what they realistically should have been.

With rising costs bumping into an unrealistic ceiling, the first casualty of rent control was maintenance. Rent control officials were fully aware of the trend: "Landlords are not making the repairs," complained one of them, and in retaliation the board proposed permitting tenants to deduct up to $80 per month for failure to replace worn carpets or drapes, or to repaint. As one exasperated apartment owner asked, "Are you going to specify what color of paint? Are you going to specify the quality of drapes?"[12]

Santa Monica rent control permitted the apartment owner to petition for a rent increase, but the process involved a detailed eleven-page questionnaire, plus extensive documentation. The assistance of an accountant was generally needed, and possibly of a lawyer as well. Then, the owner had to plead his case before an elected board of political activists whose avowed mission was to prevent increases. As a result, apartment owners not only deferred maintenance, they were increasingly reluctant to engage in capital improvements the cost of which might never be recovered.

The process was slow, but inexorable. A Rand Corporation study[13] concluded that each year around 8% of the relative price reduction achieved by rent control was converted into undermaintenance. The death spiral of rental housing under rent control was underway in Santa Monica.

As the squeeze intensified, a prolonged contest developed between apartment owners seeking escape and officials seeking to prevent it. Conversion of rental units to condominiums was quickly outlawed. Tearing down an apartment to replace it with any other kind of structure was also forbidden: rental units could only be replaced with an equal number of other rental units.

As the rent control officials saw it, they were only doing what they were elected to do. A spokesman explained, "Our eye is always on [maintaining] the number of rental units in this city…affordable to low and moderate income earners. That is what we were voted in for."[14]

One property owner, however, who was prevented for years from tearing down a vacant eyesore, saw it quite differently: "There used to be a time you could be proud to own land. Now a bordello owner would have more respect."[15]

The state legislature finally became concerned about what was happening in the People's Republic, and in 1986 passed the Ellis Act which reaffirmed what most Americans had always assumed: that a person had the right to go out of a particular business if he chose to. To the dismay of Santa Monica officials, another loophole was the exemption of three-unit or less apartments occupied by the owners—the famous "mom-and-pop" landlords. But rent control supporters lamented that these uncontrolled, and therefore especially valuable properties, were then being bought by "upwardly mobile attorney-types"[16] who then raised the rents, forcing out those who couldn't pay. The solution proposed by SMRR was to eliminate the exemption completely.

Even if all loopholes were finally closed, however, the fundamental paradox of rent control would remain: bargain rents attract a flood of applicants for each vacancy, which means that low-income families are automatically screened out. As one rent control commissioner delicately put it,

> One of the mandates of the rent control law is to provide housing for low-income people, and we've found that rent control does control rents, but not always guaranteeing that those units are occupied by low income people.[17]

The unmistakable trend was toward an ample supply of luxury apartments, condominiums and hotels,[18] while the small apartment owners, who provided most of the middle and lower-income housing, were slowly driven out of business. Sam Hall Kaplan, once vice chairman of the East Harlem planning board, says of Santa Monica's rent control crusade,

> People's Republic? If it really was the People's Republic rent control wouldn't be such a hot topic and the people would be taken care of. The yuppies have gotten the best of it. They've saved so much on their apartments they can eat out every night, which is why Santa Monica has so many trendy restaurants. Also why they can afford big cars. Look at the cars under the apartments that the landlords can't afford to fix up![19]

Because 70% of Santa Monica voters are renters, it was unlikely that rent control would ever be relaxed from within the city. Relief finally came from Sacramento, however. In 1995 a measure was passed permitting vacancy decontrol. That is, when a tenant moves out the rent on that apartment can be increased by 15%. After 1999 the rent can be raised to the full market level when a tenant leaves. (Controls on current occupants, however, remain in place.) Other units, those which went on the rental market after January 1, 1996, will be free of all controls after January, 1999. Maybe the real world is starting to intrude on the People's Republic.

Progressive hypocrisy. The gradual squeezing out of the poor was something of an embarrassment to those who gained office by promising to increase the availability of low-income housing. However, Santa Monica's middle class radicals have always been somewhat ambivalent on this issue. When they won control of the City Council in 1981 an advisory group recommended raising the density limits to achieve more low income housing, but the proposal was immediately brushed aside. When it came to choosing between low income housing and a low density "human scale environment," the radicals immediately confirmed the priority of their own middle class interests. One local activist observed,

> Middle income renters living in rent-controlled apartments will respond to low and moderate income housing in their neighborhood the same way as their homeowner counterparts, with opposition....The young, professional, middle income renter has more in common with the typical Santa Monica homeowner than with many of the residents of the [low income] Pico Corridor.[20]

The worthy goals of a "human-scale community," "decentralization," "greater control over one's own life," etc., quickly fell victim to the contradictions inherent in an ideology based exclusively on political force. As Carnoy and Shearer explained in their book *Economic Democracy*, "As has been stressed throughout this book, the government—at all levels—is the key arena in the struggle for economic democracy."[21] But what this meant in practice, of course, was top-down authoritarianism. Kann described how a City Council task force took six months to affirm the principle of neighborhood power—and then finally recommended the *practice* of centralized city hall power. The board of directors of one neighborhood group, the Pico Neighborhood Association, published a letter to the editor which concluded,

Sadly, our observation of the new progressive city council's appointments leads us to conclude that while they may support some PNA projects, they have no intentions of sharing political power with our community in a real way or opening up the process of government to our residents.[22]

But the newly empowered officials were unmoved, one staff member explaining that "We support maximum citizen neighborhood involvement in the process, but we would never recommend releasing the decision making part to the neighborhood or providing them with veto control."[23]

The problem is that the worthwhile goals of autonomy, neighborhood power and the rest were contradicted at the outset by the means. An ideology centered on political control will obviously lead to—political control. "Participatory democracy" will last only until it's time to make the decision. Then it's not participatory any more. The city council simply behaved as any political body must; the only difference is that the Santa Monica radicals supposed that it could have been otherwise. If people are looking for "autonomy" and "neighborhood control," they will not find it in the political arena. (For an alternative, see Chapter Twenty, "Farewell to City Hall.")

Much has been said here about the adverse effect of rent control upon the poor—but let us not lose sight of the underlying ethical issue: rent control is essentially an act of extortion, and it does not become morally purified simply because city hall is in charge. French philosopher Frederic Bastiat identified the issue of "legal plunder" 140 years ago in his classic study, *The Law*:

> See if the law benefits one citizen at the expense of another by doing what the citizen himself could not do without committing a crime. Then abolish this law without delay, for it is not only an evil in itself, but also it is a fertile source for further evils.[24]

15: Big Labor

Government is force, and when it intervenes in behalf of this-or-that favored interest—such as labor unions—bad things seem to happen. Especially to the poor.

Rod Carter, a former linebacker for the University of Miami 1987 championship football team, was a UPS driver who elected to keep working when the Teamsters Union went out on strike in 1997. Said Carter, "They have the right to strike and I have the right to work. My family is more important than a union or UPS."

His wife received threatening phone calls. Then, when Carter was stopped at a red light, he was attacked by six striking union men armed with ice picks. Seriously wounded, he ended up in the hospital. The six assailants were apprehended and charged with attempted murder. Carter eventually recovered.

This is only one incident in a long and sordid history of union thuggery. Around 9000 attacks have been documented over the years, 181 of them fatal. Smashed windshields, slashed tires, physical intimidation—these are such common union tactics that they pass virtually without notice.

For years, the nation's media and political elites have averted their eyes, dismissing union violence as "regrettable," but "a small price to pay" for the social advances supposedly achieved by unions. In particular, by forcing wages upward, unions are largely responsible (it is alleged) for this nation's high standard of living.

However, it's not unions but capitalism which has powered this nation's prosperity. As F. A. Harper pointed out in his classic study, *Why Wages Rise*,[1] the standard of living in this country has risen steadily over the past 200 years even before the emergence of unions, and even during subsequent periods in which union membership declined. The non-relationship between unionization and prosperity has been conclusively demonstrated during the last four decades: union membership has declined steadily from around 30% of non-government employment in the 1950s to around 10% today, but economic growth continues, and material welfare continues to rise.

It should be acknowledged however that unions served a legitimate historical purpose—at least in earlier days. In the tumultuous early years of union growth, 100 years ago, too many employers tended to treat workers like cattle, and unionization was the appropriate free-market response. But those days are long over, and employers are today well aware that the way to maximize profits is to share the responsibilities and incentives of ownership. Around 11 million workers participate in stock ownership programs, up from around 25,000 in the '70s. Millions of others are part owners of American business through pension plans. Profit sharing and team management plans proliferate. As the old divisions between labor and management become blurred, the labor union becomes increasingly irrelevant.

How unions hurt the poor. Capitalism creates new wealth. The labor union, however, is a zero-sum enterprise. A union can indeed force wages up for its members—but only at the expense of someone else. That someone is not the owners, who simply pass on the higher costs in the form of higher prices. The ultimate losers are generally those at the bottom of the economic ladder. Not only are they hit by the higher prices, they often find themselves squeezed out of the labor market by this-or-that union-backed measure. An example is the minimum wage law.

The minimum wage law was never designed to "help the poor." The measure was conceived by Massachusetts politicians in the 1930s as a means of destroying the competitive advantage of lower-wage Southern states. The Democratic governor of Massachusetts wanted to force Southern wages higher so that "Massachusetts [would] have equal competition with other sections of the country, thus affording labor and industry of Massachusetts some degree of assurance that our present industries will not move out of the state."[2]

Congress finally responded, and the first national minimum wage law was passed in 1938.[3] It has been impeding unskilled workers ever since. It is a major cause of high unemployment among black teenagers. Milton Friedman once called it "the most anti-Negro law on our statute books."[4] Paul Samuelson, at the other end of the political spectrum, has come to the same conclusion: "What good does it do a black youth to know that an employer must pay him [the minimum wage] if the fact that he must get that amount is what keeps him from getting a job?"[5] Thomas Sowell writes,

A growing number of studies by independent academic economists all over the country has shown repeatedly that minimum wage laws increase black teenage unemployment. By lobbying for such laws, labor unions price these youngsters out of the job market and thereby preserve their own wage scales, all in the name of "humanitarian" objectives. Somebody among the black leadership has to say, out loud, that their young people are idling away on street corners for the greater glory of the AFL-CIO—regardless of how much the NAACP or the Black Caucus in Congress are in hock to George Meany and Company.

It is of course much easier to blame black teenage unemployment on "racism" but then it would be hard to explain why their unemployment rate was only a fraction of its present level (and no different from white teenage unemployment rates) back in 1950, before the minimum wage law spread its coverage and began a series of escalations. Was there less racism then? We all know better.[6]

During the 1988 Congressional debate on the minimum wage, the non-partisan Congressional Budget Office reported to the House Labor Committee that the proposed increase from $3.35 to $5.05 per hour "could cause the loss of approximately 250,000 to 500,000 jobs." This was not what the liberal Democrats in charge of the committee wished to hear, and a new report was demanded without this damaging information. And now in 1999 a new round of minimum wage hikes is being proposed.

Larry Elders, a prominent black radio talk show host in Los Angeles, declares that the minimum wage law must be abolished. "I can't tell you how strongly I believe this," he says. Yet, even though the evidence is overwhelming that the minimum wage hurts the poor, we need have no doubt which way the politician will vote: labor unions have the political clout; the poor do not.

In South Africa a major bulwark of apartheid was the white-dominated labor union. The preferred jobs were reserved for whites, the menial tasks for blacks. The attitude of the labor union hasn't been all that different in this country. Thirty years ago Mayor Ibus W. Davis of Kansas City noted that "It's easier for a Negro to be invited to a garden party at George Wallace's home than to get into a plumber's union in Kansas City."[7]

Not much has changed. Consider the notorious Davis-Bacon Act, which is still on the books.

The Davis-Bacon Act was a depression-era measure designed to protect white union members from competition by migrant black workers. The measure directed that all government-contracted construction projects of greater than $5000 (later reduced to $2000) must pay workers "prevailing" wages. In practice, this meant union scale. The less-skilled black workers could not command these inflated wages, which, of course, was precisely the point. During the Congressional debates Rep. John J. Cochran (D.-Mo.) stated that he had "received numerous complaints in recent months about southern contractors employing low-paid colored mechanics getting work and bringing the employees from the South." Rep. Clayton Allgood (D.-Ala.) complained of "cheap colored labor" that "is in competition with white labor throughout the country." Others complained about "cheap labor," "cheap imported labor," "transient labor," etc.

Davis-Bacon was an overtly racist piece of legislation from the start, and it continues to the present day to make it more difficult for the less-skilled construction workers, who are often black, to be hired. But guess who are the most vocal defenders of Davis-Bacon? Unions, of course.

When unions interfere with the right of management to manage, it is the blue-collar jobs which are most at risk. Union practices such as mandated over-staffing, feather-bedding, niggling obstruction of management efforts to compete, are the hallmarks of labor union militancy. A constant bone of contention, for example, is "outsourcing": the subcontracting of work to outside firms, which may be non-union. For management, the incentive is simply to stay competitive; for the union, the goal is simply to protect union turf. The ultimate irony is that this kind of union pigheadedness does not "preserve jobs" at all—it jeopardizes jobs as companies replace union workers with machines, or perhaps move their blue-collar jobs out of the country entirely. But as these lower-skill jobs are shipped off to Mexico or China or Singapore, it is again those at the bottom of the economic ladder who end up paying the price.

The most effective anti-poverty program is a competitive and growing economy. A major burden upon the economy, however, is the short-sighted and obstructionist labor union. It wasn't always so. What went wrong?

Unions emerged during the last century as a marketplace response to reactionary employer practices. Unions grew vigorously without government assistance, and often in spite of persistent government hostility. In the 1930s, however, as unions demonstrated their political clout, government became not the antagonist of the union but its patron. As this symbiotic relationship flourished, labor leaders found it was easier to get their way through government intervention than through the give-and-take bargaining of the marketplace. Accordingly, labor leaders gradually became more attentive to their political alliances than to the long-term interests of their membership—interests which, it should be pointed out, are ultimately those of a capitalist, market-based economy. Maybe this growing disconnect with reality is one factor behind the steady decline in union membership. In any event, the labor union today is sustained less by a willing membership than by government, as we shall now see.

How government props up unions. The labor union today is largely the creature of government. Three measures in particular have provided unions with a power and influence they could not have earned otherwise.

The Norris-LaGuardia Act (1932) sharply limited the role of the federal courts in granting injunctive relief to employers suffering damage from illegal union activity, and the Wagner Act (1935) made "collective bargaining" compulsory and defined what were to be regarded as "unfair labor practices." In addition, the Wagner Act established the National Labor Relations Board (NLRB) as the administrative agency by which the provisions of the act were to be enforced.

Norris-LaGuardia Act. There are two kinds of what might be called "legal justice," (1) law, and (2) equity. Law metes out punishment for an illegal act after the act has occurred, while a court of equity can, by means of an injunction, prevent an illegal act from taking place. The distinction could be crucial to the employer faced by the prospect of irreparable damage arising from some sort of illegal union activity. For example, massed picketing is illegal since it physically prevents access to the struck plant. Those responsible can be punished under the law, but during the long legal process the massed picketing could continue and the employer could be put out of business permanently. The court of law would have been unable to protect him from the disastrous consequences of a coercive and illegal act. A court of equity, however, can halt such actions immediately by issuing an injunction. Prior to 1932 this procedure served as a slight counterbalance to union power, but with the passage of the Norris-LaGuardia Act the ability of the employer to gain injunctive relief in the federal courts was sharply limited.[8] In addition, this act made unenforceable in the courts any contract by which the employee agreed not to join a union (the so-called "yellow dog" contract).

The Wagner Act. The Wagner Act made "collective bargaining" compulsory. If, in an NLRB-conducted election, a majority of the workers in a company choose to be represented by a particular union, that union is certified by the NLRB as the exclusive bargaining agent for all of the employees of that company. The company is then legally compelled to bargain with that union.

In accordance with this feature of the law, then, a union could be dominated by mafia hoodlums, but if that union achieves the support of a bare majority of the employees voting, the owners of the company are compelled by law to negotiate with it. Thus the Wagner Act is at the outset an improper law, for if "bargaining" is made compulsory, it is no longer "bargaining" but extortion! Conflicts should be settled by the varied and voluntary negotiating tactics of the marketplace including, perhaps, a hard-line refusal to bargain at all. If a union genuinely has a service of value to offer, then sooner or later, by means of a strike or other peaceful measures, management will be brought to the bargaining table. In the absence of physical violence by either labor or management, a strike will succeed if union demands are justified, and it will fail if they are not. The proper arbiter of a labor dispute is not the bureaucrat, but the marketplace.

The NLRB. The Wagner Act established the NLRB to conduct certification elections, and to address charges of "unfair labor practices." As interpreted and enforced by the NLRB, however, virtually any management effort by which union power might be countered has been declared "unfair." Moreover, acts which are permissible when performed by unions frequently become "unfair" when performed by management.

For example, if a union solicits an employee to strike, that is quite all right. If the company solicits him *not* to strike, however, it is an "unfair labor practice."[9] If a union threatens to gain its end by closing down a company, there is no cry of indignation from the NLRB. But if a company threatens to close rather than deal with the union, it is an "unfair labor practice."[10] Or if a union presents a firm demand and sticks to it, there is no objection from the NLRB; but if a company presents a firm *offer* and sticks to it then it is "not bargaining in good faith" which is an "unfair labor practice."[11]

During an organizing drive, a union does not hesitate to promise that unionization will bring increased benefits. But if the employer attempts to discourage unionization by withdrawing, or by threatening to withdraw, benefits, it is an "unfair labor practice."[12] It is also "unfair" if he attempts to counter union efforts by offering wage increases or other benefits during the union organizing drive.[13]

If a union were to urge outside civic organizations to encourage unionization, it is unlikely that the NLRB would issue a cease-and-desist order. But if a company urges outside civic organizations to *discourage* unionization it is guilty of an "unfair labor practice."[14]

Professor Sylvester Petro listed the above items (and many others) back in 1957. Things are no different today. If a union delivers a pay raise to its members, that's OK. But when the Miramar Sheraton hotel of Santa Monica gave raises to two non-union employees, that was "unfair," and the NLRB ordered the hotel to grant identical raises to 228 union members as well.[15] If a union provides coffee and donuts to its striking picketers, that's OK, of course; but when Caterpillar provided free lunches for non-strikers, the NLRB decreed that it was an "unfair labor practice."[16] An employee can be disciplined by the union for perceived anti-union activity; but if an employee is disciplined by the *company* for perceived anti-*company* activity, it is an "unfair labor practice."[17]

If a union wins a certification election, the issue is closed. But if it *loses* the election, it can turn to the NLRB to overturn the results.[18]

One would suppose that direct and open communication between management and labor would be encouraged. Not by the NLRB, however. In 1992 the DuPont plant in Deepwater, N.J., was ordered to disband a quality circle program because it would tend to undermine union authority. Later, seven safety committees were also ordered abolished.[19] In 1998 Webcor Packaging Co. of Michigan was ordered to dismantle its management/labor committee for the same reason.[20]

And on and on and on.

Over the years the Democrat appointees to the NLRB have been unapologetic in pushing a pro-union agenda, while Republican appointees seem to lean over backwards to be "fair." The net result, as we have seen, is a federal agency constantly pushing the envelope in behalf of Big Labor. In the process there is not even a pretense of concern for the rights of the individual union member. Consider the NLRB's refusal to implement the terms of the Beck decision.

For years, dissenting union members have sought to prohibit the use of their dues for political purposes of which they disapprove. The right of employees to withhold such dues was affirmed by the Supreme Court in the landmark Beck decision of 1988, but the unions, backed by the ever-protective NLRB, have simply ignored this decision. The chairman of the NLRB, William B. Gould (once counsel to the United Auto Workers), went so far as to publicly campaign against Proposition 226, an unsuccessful effort in California to implement the Beck decision in that state. Gould's blatant impropriety was condemned by leaders of both political parties. However, the NLRB continues to refuse to implement Beck, and a backlog of 250 Beck-related cases continues to collect dust.

Forty years ago, Professor Sylvester Petro described the performance of the NLRB as "simply pitiable." It is still pitiable.

The Wagner Act has twice been amended: in 1947 by the Taft-Hartley Act, and in 1959 by the Landrum Griffin Act. In part, the Taft-Hartley Act outlawed the closed shop[21] and the secondary boycott. In addition, it sought to define certain "unfair" union practices. The Landrum-Griffin Act sought to prohibit a number of corrupt union procedures and in addition undertook the hopeless task of clarifying what is and what is not a secondary boycott.

These two amendments sought to repair the inequities in the existing situation by confounding it still further. The inequities were caused by the prior legislation; therein lies the basic trouble. For example, there would be no need for a Landrum-Griffin Act if dissatisfied union members were free to break away from a corrupt union to join an honest one. But the majority-rule, all-or-nothing provision of the Wagner Act greatly discourages such action. Only in the unlikely event of a decertification election will that union cease to be the exclusive bargaining agent for all employees. Nor would there be any need for "right-to-work" laws if employers were better able to withstand the union's demand for a union-shop contract. But employer resistance to such demands is severely weakened by measures such as the Wagner Act.

This, then, is the heart of the problem: the power of the labor unions grew to such disturbing dimensions only because the counter balances inherent in a free society were emasculated by pro-union legislation. The solution lies not in the passage of new laws, then, but in the repeal of such as these that are presently on the books. The Norris-LaGuardia Act and the Wagner Act should be repealed. The NLRB should be abolished. Conflicts between a union and a company should be settled in the regular courts or by negotiation or—if need be—through a strike. Workers must always be free to strike—but employers must be equally free to hire replacements should a strike occur. The proper role of government is not to put its heavy thumb on the scales, but simply to keep the peace and prevent violence. In short, justice for all concerned will be achieved not through picket line violence or government intervention, but only through the give-and-take bargaining of a free society.

Moving left. Propped up by government, union leadership becomes less responsive to the views and values of its declining membership. A symptom of the broadening gap between union headquarters and those it claims to represent can be seen in Big Labor's steady move to the fringes of liberal-left politics. Writing in *Commentary*, Arch Puddington comments on the cultural shift within the AFL-CIO leadership.

> Under Sweeney, even as a somewhat more conciliatory approach is being pursued on narrower issues involving cooperation between labor and management, the change in the composition of the machinery has intensified, to the point where a genuine radical-leaning culture has begun to take root within the AFL-CIO apparatus. This is most evident in the recruitment of personnel. One source is composed of operatives from left-wing splinter groups like the New party, the Labor party, and the Democratic Socialists of America (which Sweeney himself joined after his election as AFL-CIO president). Another and larger source is made up of individuals hailing from the environmental and feminist movements, the offices of liberal Congressmen, and even the Clinton administration. With this combined new crop of activists taking charge, AFL-CIO conferences and publications have regularly begun to showcase a view of America as a society built on the ongoing exploitation of the working class and the oppression of women and minorities.[22]

These people are the soul mates of Diana Oughton. However, the shift to the left may be the last gasp of Big Labor as we have known it. Union membership is declining steadily to begin with, and it is not likely that the remaining membership, 40% of which voted for Reagan and Bush, will be broadly supportive of the leftist ideologues who increasingly populate the corridors of Big Labor.

In spite of the best efforts of the NLRB, the labor union is becoming increasingly irrelevant. It served its legitimate historical purpose, but history is now passing it by. Just as well. The labor union is a zero-sum institution whose gains are generally at someone else's expense—and those someones are very often the poor.

16: The War on Drugs

As with Prohibition, the government's War on Drugs is another disaster, a domestic Vietnam which must eventually be abandoned in failure.

In her book *The March of Folly* historian Barbara Tuchman describes a number of episodes in history, from the Trojan War to Vietnam, in which destructive national policies were adhered to even in the face of overwhelming evidence that those policies were counterproductive. This nation's War on Drugs would be a fitting addition to Tuchman's list.

The death toll of drug abuse is trivial compared to that of alcohol or cigarettes.[1] The associated evils—pushers on the street corners, police corruption, warring gangs fighting over turf, the billions spent on enforcement activities—are not the consequence of drug use as such, *but of anti-drug legislation*. Decades of political intervention have escalated a manageable problem into a national catastrophe.

The idea that the nation's drug laws emerged as a response to a serious drug problem is largely a myth. During the nineteenth century drugs were inexpensive and readily available through physicians, druggists and patent medicines. The problems of addiction were becoming better understood, but at no time was drug abuse as extensive as alcohol abuse. Yet, the first federal prohibitions were directed not against alcohol but against opium. The reason was its association with a despised minority—the Chinese.

Starting around the 1850s tens of thousands of Chinese laborers were imported to work in the mines, factories, and on the transcontinental railways, and to the dismay of white Americans many elected to remain. Anti-Chinese prejudice was intense, and a particular object of scorn was the Asian practice of smoking opium. In 1875 San Francisco, which was a wide-open town in every other respect, passed an ordinance banning the opium den, and over the next few years many states enacted similar legislation. In 1887 Congress prohibited the import of smoking-type opium—except by Americans—and in 1890 its manufacture was also prohibited—except by Americans.

American labor was virulently hostile to the Chinese, and in 1902 Samuel Gompers, founder of the American Federation of Labor (AF of L), co-authored and published a pamphlet entitled *Some Reasons for Chinese Exclusion: Meat vs. Rice, American Manhood Against Chinese Coolieism—Which Will Survive?* Gompers declared that "the racial differences between American whites and Asiatics would never be overcome. The superior whites had to exclude the inferior Asiatics by law, or if necessary, by force of arms....The Yellow Man found it natural to lie, cheat, and murder and 99 out of every 100 Chinese are gamblers."[2]

Gompers described in lurid detail the fate of white children trapped in the sinister opium dens.

> What other crimes were committed in those dark fetid places, when these little innocent victims of the Chinamen's wiles were under the influence of the drug, are almost too horrible to imagine....There are hundreds, aye thousands, of our American girls and boys who have acquired this deathly habit and are doomed, hopelessly doomed, beyond the shadow of redemption.[3]

Just as opium was associated with Chinese, cocaine was widely associated with blacks. In 1910 a narcotics commission report, sent to Congress with a note from the President urging "appropriate action," concluded that "it has been authoritatively stated that cocaine is often the direct incentive to the crime of rape by the Negroes of the South and other sections of the country."[4] During debate on the Harrison Act of 1914, a Dr. Koch of the Pennsylvania Pharmacy Board reiterated that "Most of the attacks on white women in the South are the direct result of a cocaine-crazed Negro brain."[5] In a lengthy article in the *New York Times* entitled "Negro Cocaine Fiends Are a New Southern Menace," a Dr. Edward Huntington Williams assured his readers that the lurid tales of cocaine-induced mayhem were not exaggerated. With unconscious irony he noted that cocaine use was greatest in those areas of the South which, in an attempt to eliminate the "drunken negro," had outlawed saloons.

> These laws do not, and were not intended to, prevent the white man or the well-to-do negro getting his accustomed beverages through legitimate channels. They obliged him to forego the pleasure of leaning against a bar and "taking his drink perpendicularly," to be sure; but a large proportion of the intelligent whites were ready to make this sacrifice if by doing so they could eliminate the drunken negro....But unfortunately...a substitute was found almost immediately—a substitute that is inestimably worse even than the "moonshine whiskey," drug-store nostrums, or the deadly wood alcohol

poison. This substitute, as I have pointed out, is cocaine; and a trail of blood and disaster has marked the progress of its substitution.[6]

Marijuana was also associated with alien groups: during the 1930s with Mexican-Americans, and during the 1960s with the most disturbing element of all, long-haired and defiant youth.

Substance abuse has always been a matter of concern in this country (the first temperance organization was founded in Litchfield, Connecticut in 1789), but the so-called "illicit" drugs have been the object of special revulsion. The reason, it seems apparent, has been their association with alien cultures perceived as threatening or offensive to the established order. "Our" drugs (alcohol and tobacco) are acceptable, but "their" drugs (the opiates, cocaine and marijuana) are not. Until this profound cultural bias is recognized and resolved, the irrationality of the present struggle (for example, banning marijuana while subsidizing tobacco) will continue to bedevil us.

Whatever the genesis of our present drug laws, the reality is that they are astonishingly self-defeating. According to U.N. statistics the illegal drug trade generates around $400 billion per year in revenues—about 10% of all world trade. These immense profits generated by an illegal but coveted commodity assure an army of ready suppliers, and further crackdowns only increase the inducements. Moreover, the forbidden fruit has a special appeal, and if dealing drugs is "glamorous" in some quarters, it's the illegality that has made it so. Meanwhile all of the other well-documented consequences accumulate: needless deaths due to contaminated street drugs, jammed courts and prisons, street violence among competing dealers, and a general disrespect for all laws—even the good ones. Never has a crusade done so much mischief while accomplishing so little.

Perhaps the most troubling consequence of drug prohibition has been the corrupting influence upon law enforcement. Because drug use is a voluntary choice, there is simply not the condemnation that would be directed toward the robber or the murderer. Accordingly, the policeman's attitude is ambivalent. If the dealer is making all that money, why should he not get a piece of it?

Maybe that's what Rene De La Cova was thinking. He was the DEA supervisor whose photograph appeared in newspapers all over the country as he took custody of Manuel Noriega, former Panamanian strongman.

Five years later De La Cova pleaded guilty to stealing $760,000 in drug money.

The problem is rampant. Says former San Jose Police Chief Joseph McNamara,

> It's going on all over the country and corruption ranges from chiefs and sheriffs on down to officers. Every week we read of another police scandal related to the drug war—corruption, brutality and even armed robbery by cops in uniform.

McNamara describes the drug war as "an impossible job," and concludes that "The sheer hopelessness of the task has led many officers to rationalize their own corruption."[7]

Further casualties of the War on Drugs have been third-world countries. Secretary of State George P. Shultz declared in 1984, "attacking the world-wide network of narcotics production and trafficking" is "top priority in our foreign policy."[8]

And look at the results. Eradication programs in Southeast Asia and in South and Central America in the ensuing years have served only to enrich corrupt officials while embittering the people against the U.S. A peasant farmer can hardly be expected to understand why his livelihood must be destroyed to satisfy U.S. domestic policies. Over a 15-month period in 1983–84 U.S.-trained and financed strike teams destroyed some 4000 acres of coca fields in the Tingo Maria region of Peru, and the result was a disaster. As one U.S. development expert put it to the *New York Times*, "There are now a lot of resentful people around Tingo Maria. People are now anti-government and anti-American. You don't exactly feel welcome there."[9]

Until their final collapse, Maoist Sendaro Luminoso ("Shining Path") guerrillas were quick to exploit the bitterness, and an estimated 2000 or so of the local peasants soon joined their ranks. The strengthened guerrillas then launched a major offensive against U.S. and government facilities. Ten of 13 police stations in the area were destroyed, and 19 police were killed. Many local officials and schoolteachers resigned their jobs under threat, and families who had cooperated with the Americans moved away in fear for their lives. Most Americans were withdrawn from the area, and the $30 million eradication program was largely diverted to defending government installations. Not only did American policy fail to achieve any worthwhile goal, it managed to disrupt the social fabric of the area while making patriot heroes of Maoist guerrillas!

However, each new failure in American drug policy led to further escalation, and in July of 1986 armed helicopters manned by U.S. crews were ferrying Bolivian police on raids into cocaine-growing areas of that country. The U.S. presence steadily increased, and U.S. Special Forces were soon training Bolivian police who were then accompanied by U.S. "advisors" in raids on primitive jungle laboratories. Gradually, the War on Drugs was replacing the Cold War as the rationale for U.S. military involvement in many parts of the world.

About 60% of the cocaine on American streets comes through Mexico, which may soon overtake Columbia as a center of drug-associated violence. It is reported that the Arellano Cartel has been hiring foreign mercenaries to train its "soldiers" in advanced military tactics. In the meanwhile, President Clinton, over the strenuous objections of the DEA, has chosen to ignore the rampant corruption in the Mexican government by certifying it as a "partner" in the ongoing crusade.

U.S. drug laws have made billionaires out of drug racketeers who now undermine the institutions of Bolivia, Columbia, Peru, Mexico, Burma and other drug-producing countries. The United Nations International Narcotics Control Board noted back in 1984 that "Illegal drug production and trafficking financed by organized crime is so pervasive that the economies of entire countries are disrupted, legal institutions menaced and the very security of some states threatened."

This is certainly the case in Columbia. Columbia has now become a virtual battleground with raid and counter-raid, and with vast sections of the country beyond government control. There is a real possibility that the Columbian army may actually be defeated by well-armed and well-financed drug forces, in which case the government itself would no doubt cease to exist.

Drugs, like alcohol, can kill. Yet even conceding the potential dangers of the illicit drugs, the underlying question remains: how far can we go—or should we go—in attempting to protect people from the consequences of self-incurred risk? Should we outlaw cigarettes which kill far more people than do heroin and cocaine combined? Should we forbid eating fatty foods? What about skydiving? What about riding in the automobile, which kills about 50,000 people per year? Obviously, government can not be (nor should it attempt to be) the all-embracing nanny shielding each of us from the consequences of his own folly-of-choice. If someone wishes to use alcohol or marijuana, or crack, or elects to ride in an automobile, that is his choice and his responsibility.

But now a more difficult question emerges: What if the drug user then endangers the safety of others? For example, what about the Amtrak engineer in Maryland a few years ago who, under the influence of marijuana, drove his locomotive past warning signals and caused the deaths of 16 innocent people? It is understandable that such an episode would fan the flames of antidrug ardor—but was this tragedy really any worse than the one in Kentucky a few months later in which a drunk driver collided with a church bus and killed 27? Why should marijuana be banned if alcohol is not?

The point is this: If a drunk driver causes an auto accident, he goes to jail, as well he should. However, it's not the *drinking* that is illegal but the irresponsible act of *driving while drunk*. The identical distinction should apply to the illicit drugs. If someone wishes to ingest heroin or cocaine or marijuana that is *his* business. Only if he endangers someone else does it become *our* business, and *that's* when he goes to jail.

An objection to this liberalized policy, of course, is that the restraint comes too late; the victim of the drunk driver, or drugged driver, might already be killed or maimed. True, of course. But in a free society there is no realistic alternative. We cannot tailor all of society to the behavior patterns of the least responsible among us.

A further objection to legalization is that drug use would increase. Perhaps it would.[10] However, it's not obvious that drug *abuse*, as most people understand the term,[11] would increase markedly with legalization. For example, consider the current trend in smoking. Smoking is not (yet!) illegal, but as awareness of the health hazards has grown thousands have kicked the habit, and the smoker today is a virtual social outcast. If the illicit drugs were legalized, the user would no longer be the free-spirited outlaw defying authority, but merely, like the smoker, someone risking his health. In any event, if American society is truly bent upon self-destruction, as the anti-drug warriors seem to believe, no amount of enforcement could change things anyway.

Like Prohibition, the War on Drugs has generated a host of new problems, but the most destructive has been the erosion of individual responsibility. The key to restraint in drinking, smoking, eating, working or whatever, is self-control. But when people are controlled instead by authority the capacity for self-control atrophies. The over-protected child, for example, shielded from experience and temptation, will be less likely to mature into a responsible adult. By supplanting personal responsibility, the paternalistic War on Drugs assures an unending supply of irresponsible users.

In the continuing debate over drugs one aspect is invariably ignored: the possibility that occasional drug use might be a healthy and natural facet of human behavior. As psychiatrist Dr. Thomas Szasz notes in his provocative book *Ceremonial Chemistry*, the ritual use of drugs is as old as human history. Wine in Catholic Communion, or peyote use by some western Indian tribes are contemporary examples. Szasz suggests that the use of drugs, whether in a religious observance or among a group of friends sharing a joint (or sipping cocktails), is essentially ceremonial: an affirmation of shared cultural values.

Szasz objects to the fact that the drug issue is now monopolized by the medical profession, which is oblivious to the ceremonial aspect of drug use. As Szasz sees it, it's as though one were to try to understand holy water by studying only the chemical properties of H_2O. The failure to comprehend the ceremonial significance of drug use, Szasz suggests, is largely responsible for the singular myopia of current government policy.

Although one might not accept Szasz's striking analogies, the underlying reality can neither be changed nor ignored: people take drugs because they wish to. They believe it makes their lives better. Maybe they are right and maybe they are wrong. But if a free society means anything at all it must include the right of the individual to live and learn in accordance with his own values—even values which might be offensive to the rest of us. If someone chooses to take drugs, that is his decision, and it is not the business of nanny government to interfere.

But American officialdom is unwavering, and the War on Drugs is now endorsed by the leadership of both of the major political parties. As Ronald Hamowy notes in *Dealing with Drugs*, a solidly-entrenched constituency is now committed to a continued and ever-expanding struggle.

> There are large numbers of people, principally employees of law enforcement agencies, who have a vested interest in seeing to it that ever increasing amounts are expended to stamp out the distribution and sale of illicit drugs. These groups are economically dependent on the existence of restrictive drug legislation; and even though the evidence might point to relaxing or repealing our current laws, their

own economic benefit will best be served by supporting comprehensive legislation and a massive campaign of drug enforcement. Those whose primary concern is the enforcement of the nation's narcotics laws, together with all those who staff the institutions responsible for the treatment and rehabilitation of drug users—from administrators and physicians on down—all stand to lose if these laws were substantially liberalized.[12]

The real monkey on our backs today is not drug use as such, but the addiction to political force as the remedy for every social ill. We spend over $30 billion per year on the War on Drugs, and what we have to show for it is more drugs on the street, and around 400,000 people in prison for drug-related crimes, usually non-violent. And the hammer falls most heavily upon the poor. This time liberal columnist Robert Scheer was right when he declared,

> This is a war fought in a contradictory manner aimed primarily at the urban ghetto. Only 13% of drug users are black, but they make up far more than a majority of those imprisoned on drug charges. These people are in prison as sacrifices to the gods of the drug war who will not let go of their holy crusade no matter haw many lives are broken.[13]

The unwinnable War on Drugs is another March of Folly, a domestic Vietnam which must eventually be abandoned in failure. There is no "light at the end of the tunnel," and the costs of the escalating War on Drugs are far exceeding any conceivable benefit. It's time to cut our losses and get out. If someone chooses to take drugs, that's his business. Drug use must be legalized, and the sooner the better.

17: Environmentalism

Anti-growth activists employ regulation as a means of imposing their elitist values on the rest of society.

The old guard conservationists—John Muir, Teddy Roosevelt, the older generations of the Sierra Club and the Audubon Society—were essentially conservative in that they wished to preserve our natural resources for the use and enjoyment of future generations. It is these people we can thank for the setting aside of the national parks. One could argue that these congested assets would be better managed in private hands, but few would contest the worthiness of the goal.

Moreover, let us concede at the outset that government has a legitimate role to play in environmental regulation. If a polluter deposits his soot in our lungs, it is an invasion of our property and government should act. That's its job.

Over the years, however, a new kind of environmentalism has emerged which has little interest in the individual and still less in the concept of property rights. The new environmentalism is populated with savvy and aggressive political activists for whom the environment is primarily a vehicle for the promotion of their own agenda—which may have little to do with the environment.

The new environmentalists could be divided into three groups.

1) The first are the Leisure Class Environmentalists who employ "the environment" as a rationale for restraining economic development, thus defending their own privileged position from incursion by others.

2) The second group are the Doomcriers: the prophets of apocalypse who warn that civilization itself is in peril unless we repent our capitalist sins. The most prominent Doomcrier scenario today, of course, is global warming.

3) The third strain of contemporary environmentalism—and the most bizarre—is Neo-Paganism: an exaltation of "nature" over humans. This "deep ecology" rejects technology in all its forms, and condemns capitalism as a "cancer on the biosphere."

Throughout, the common denominator of these three strains, as we shall see, is a lofty indifference to the impact of their no-growth, anti-technology proposals upon the poor.

The Leisure Class Environmentalist. A major environmentalist victory of the '70s was the scuttling of a coal-fired plant on the Kaiparowits Plateau of Utah. With the plant sited on a vast reserve of low-sulphur coal and remote from urban areas, pollution problems would have been minimal. But after thirteen years of regulatory delay, spearheaded by environmentalist groups, the plan was abandoned. It is clear that the issue was not health and safety, nor could there have been much serious concern about scenery in this barren and isolated corner of the state.[1]

The project was overwhelmingly favored by the Mormon inhabitants of the region because the economic activity would have encouraged the young people to stay rather than move away. But as far as the Southwest Regional Vice-President for the Sierra Club was concerned, they could just move along. "I don't know how wise it is for people to try to make a living when it's not possible," she declared. And she added that the Sierra Club would see to it that the project was indeed "not possible."[2]

There was much handwringing for the Stephens kangaroo rat and the black-footed ferret, but the real goal of the environmentalists was painfully clear: to slow the economic growth of a society which, in their elitist opinion, was already too affluent for its own good. The *Wall Street Journal* did not overstate the issue when it declared editorially that "More callous disregard toward due process, property rights and ultimately the homes and settled existence of fellow humanity is being displayed these days by the defenders of nature than by any other American political movement with which we are familiar."

Reminiscent of Thorsten Veblen's *Theory of the Leisure Class*, William Tucker, contributing editor to *Harpers*, explains the environmental elitism this way.

> I think the most important thing to recognize about environmentalists is that, essentially, they don't want any solution to the energy problem. The reason is quite simple. Environmentalists are mostly people from the upper echelons of society—well-to-do, well educated professionals who are not particularly dependent on industry, and are more or less materially satisfied. They do not see any great threat in the loss of a few manufacturing jobs, the closing of a few

plants or a leveling off of the economy. In fact, in many ways they would prefer it that way. More jobs, more economic growth and more mass consumption simply mean that more people will be climbing the economic ladder and demanding what they already possess. More energy and more growth mean more people trying to move into the suburbs, more people crowding the beaches, more campers and snowmobiles. To anyone who already has the advantage of affluence and privacy, the status quo and "no-growth" economics have very positive aspects.[3]

Slower economic growth might be an attractive prospect for the materially-satisfied elitists of the environmental movement, but it would not be attractive at all for those who look to an expanding economy as a means of attaining their own slice of the pie. Perhaps this is why union leaders have become increasingly skeptical of environmentalist aims. Black leaders are equally skeptical. Vernon Jordan, former director of the Urban League has observed,

> [Environmentalists] will find in the black community absolute hostility to anything smacking of no-growth or limits-to-growth. Some people have been too cavalier in proposing policies to preserve the physical environment for themselves while other, poorer people pay the costs.[4]

The late Bayard Rustin referred to environmentalists as "self-righteous, elitist neo-Malthusians who call for slow growth or no growth…[and who] would condemn the black underclass, the slum proletariat, and rural blacks, to permanent poverty." Economist Thomas Sowell notes that "Regulatory rules have impeded people who are climbing rather than people who are already at the top. There is a fundamental conflict between the affluent people, who can afford to engage in environmental struggles, and the poor.… You don't see many black faces in the Sierra Club."[5]

When environmentalists urge an economy of "elegant frugality," the question of who gets to be frugal is rarely addressed. But as Vernon Jordan, Bayard Rustin, and Thomas Sowell were well aware, the ultimate victims of the Leisure Class Environmentalist would be the poor.

The Doomcriers. Today, the environmental movement is increasingly dominated by the political left. The ultimate evil is capitalism, and if it couldn't be buried by the proletariet, it will be consumed by the ozone hole, global cooling, global warming, population catastrophe, or whatever.

Murray Bookchin, founder of the leftist Institute of Social Ecology, declares that "the immediate source of the ecological crisis is capitalism," which he describes as "a cancer on the biosphere."[6] David Foreman, founder of the quasi-violent Earth First! declares that Western Civilization is "rotten to the core," and he seeks to build "an egalitarian, decentralized, ecologically sound" society out of "the ashes of the old industrialized empire."[7] Says Paul Ehrlich, "Most people do not recognize that, at least in rich nations, economic growth is the disease, not the cure."[8] And Al Gore wants to lead the way in changing the system: "We must all become partners in a bold effort to change the very foundation of our civilization."[9]

The genteel conservationists of the past have been elbowed aside by the savvy political activists in organizations such as Greenpeace, the Environmental Defense Fund, and the Natural Resources Defense Council. The older organizations, such as the Sierra Club and the Audubon Society, once bastions of the old-guard conservationists, have also been taken over by the political left. In 1991 the Audubon Society dumped its editor of 25 years, who says he was told that "the primary reason I had to go was my interest in nature and natural resources and that was not where the action was."[10]

These days the "action" is in lobbying and in lawsuits. And that's where the money is. In 1990 the leading environmental organizations pulled in over $400 million—ten times the total of both political parties that year.

Doomsday scenarios come and go, but the most resonant today is global warming. Not just "global warming," but a "Global Warming Catastrophe!" As Al Gore shouted in *Scientific American*, "The world is in the midst of an environmental crisis beyond anything yet experienced; unless radical steps are taken to safeguard the planet, our future on it cannot be secured."[11]

Gracious!

The great global warming scare started in earnest when climatologists came up with computer programs, known as General Circulation Models (GCM) which predicted a warming of at least 0.3 degrees Centigrade per decade due to rising levels of CO_2 in the atmosphere. CO_2, a byproduct of fossil fuel consumption, is a greenhouse gas which tends to trap the earth's heat, leading to higher temperatures. The result, we are assured, would be global catastrophe of searing heat, drought, ferocious storms, and rising sea levels wiping out thousands of square miles of coastline. The only escape from the impending catastrophe, we are told, is immediate government action. The proposed measures would be a socialist's dream come true: energy taxes, rationing, and a general top-down reordering of the entire economic system to reduce and regulate energy consumption. The immediate result would be slower economic growth and lost employment. The impact would fall most heavily, of course, upon the poor.

But how much of the global warming scenario is real?

It's true that CO_2 levels are rising—from 280 parts per million in pre-industrial times to around 350 ppm in 1990. In geologic terms, however, these levels are not high but low. Levels were about five times higher 200 million years ago, and around twenty times higher 500 million years ago. Moreover, CO_2 is only one of several greenhouse gases. In fact, 95% of these gases is water vapor. Accordingly, the actual contribution of CO_2 might be less than supposed.

Moreover, it should be understood that CO_2 is not some kind of noxious vapor, but an essential plant nutrient. Higher levels of CO_2 would mean more ample harvests—an effect which may already be taking place, judging from increased crop yields in recent years. CO_2 is not a toxic waste, but an ecological asset. Maybe we could use more of it rather than less!

Nor is there any argument that the planet has been warming. It has been warming since the "little ice age," a period of lower-than-normal temperatures in the late middle ages. But global temperatures have been fluctuating like this for hundreds of millions of years. There have been 17 glacial periods over the past two million years, the most recent about 11,000 years ago. In a more recent time frame, global temperatures increased about 0.5 degrees Centigrade from 1880 to 1940, then dropped slightly, then rose slightly. Highly accurate satellite measurements, available since 1978 (and closely confirmed by balloon measurements) indicate that there has been no warming at all over the past twenty years, and perhaps even a slight cooling.

But the real question is not whether global temperatures fluctuate, but whether they are measurably influenced by human activity. This is the question the computer models have presumed to answer.

However, the computer predictions, on which the entire global warming scenario has been based, aren't even close. Based on assumptions about the effects of CO_2, they predicted a minimum temperature rise of 0.3 degrees C per decade. Actual surface measurements, however, are indicating a trivial rise of about .013 degrees C per decade, while the more accurate[12] satellite measurements, as noted, indicate *no warming at all*, and perhaps a slight cooling!

There is an acronym employed by computer people which may be appropriate here: GIGO. Garbage In, Garbage Out. If the initial assumptions are erroneous, the answers will be equally erroneous. Climate modeling is extremely complex, and is painfully dependent upon assumptions about the underlying physical relationships. By fiddling with the assumptions, modelers can get just about any answer they desire. To base far-reaching national policies on this kind of "evidence" is foolhardy, to say the least.

The most influential voice in the global warming debate has been the United Nations Intergovernmental Panel on Climate Control (IPCC). However, it is becoming increasingly difficult to accept the IPCC as an objective scientific body.

A report in 1990 declared confidently that observed and calculated temperature changes were "broadly consistent." However, in the face of growing evidence that they were not "broadly consistent" at all, this claim was soon abandoned. But a later IPCC report in 1996 only added to the confusion—while casting doubt upon the scientific integrity of the IPCC itself.

The summary of the 1966 report, called the Summary for Policymakers, concluded that there was "a discernible human influence on global climate." This powerful statement was presented to the media and thence to the public as conclusive "proof" of the global warming theory.

To put it delicately, the report was fudged. It was soon discovered that the crucial Chapter Eight, on which the Summary was largely based, had been mysteriously re-written *after* the report had been reviewed and accepted by the full IPCC body. More than fifteen sections had been altered or deleted, completely reversing the thrust of the report. Some of the deletions:

- "None of the studies cited above has shown clear evidence that we can attribute the observed [climate] changes to the specific cause of increases in greenhouse gases."
- "No study to date has positively attributed all or part [of the climate change observed to date] to anthropogenic [man-made] causes."
- "Any claims of positive detection of significant climate change are likely to remain controversial until uncertainties in the total natural variability of the climate system are reduced."

The journal *Nature* quoted IPCC officials as stating that the report had been altered "to ensure that it conformed to a 'policymakers' summary' of the full report." Dr. Frederick Seitz, former president of the National Academy of Sciences declared, "In my more than 60 years as a member of the American scientific community…I have never witnessed a more disturbing corruption of the peer-review process than the events that led to this IPCC report."[13]

What's been going on here? The actual temperature measurements are providing no confirmation whatever to the global warming theory, and here its supporters are reduced to fudging the evidence to make their case! Maybe Philip Abelson, former editor of *Science*, had it right when he noted that if global warming "is analyzed applying the customary standards of scientific inquiry one must conclude there has been more hype than solid facts."[14]

Hype indeed. And the Doomcriers are not at all apologetic about it. Global warming guru Stephen Schneider justifies it this way:

> On the one hand, as scientists, we are ethically bound to the scientific method, in effect promising to tell the truth, the whole truth, and nothing but—which means we must include all the doubts, caveats, and ifs, ands, and buts. On the other hand, we are not just scientists but human beings as well. And like most people we'd like to see the world a better place, which in this context translates into our working to reduce the risk of potentially disastrous climatic change. To do that we need to get some broad-based support, to capture the public's imagination. That, of course, entails getting loads of media coverage. So we have to offer up scary scenarios, make simplified, dramatic statements, and make little mention of any doubts we might have. This "double ethical bind" we frequently find ourselves in cannot be solved by any formula. Each of us has to decide what the right balance is between being effective and being honest. I hope that means being both.[15]

Journalists, most of whom are politically liberal, have willingly promoted the hype. Moreover, they make little effort to disguise their bias. Charles Alexander, the science editor at *Time*, has declared, "I would freely admit that on this issue [environmentalism] we have crossed the boundary from news reporting to advocacy."[16] CNN producer Barbara Pyle proudly declares, "I switched from being an objective journalist to an advocate in July, 1980, after reading the gloomy Global 2000 presidential report. We [at CNN] didn't become the environmental network overnight."[17] Teya Ryan, producer of CNN's program "Network Earth," explains what CNN journalism is all about.

> The "balanced" report, in some cases, may no longer be the most effective, or even the most informative. Indeed, it can be debilitating. Can we afford to wait for our audience to come to its own conclusions? I think not.[18]

For years, the mainstream media have relentlessly promoted whatever doomsday scenario was in vogue. And politicians, ever-responsive to the latest fad, have been happy to jump on board. Undersecretary of State Timothy Worth has declared, "We've got to ride the global warming issue. Even if the theory of global warming is wrong, we will be doing the right thing, in terms of economic policy and environmental policy."[19] Interior Secretary Bruce Babbitt declared that openly skeptical energy companies are part of a "conspiracy" and are "un-American."[20]

Al Gore regards the issue as "settled," and sees little point in further discussion. He informed *Time* magazine in its "Planet of the Year" issue in 1988 that there is "no longer a matter of any dispute worthy of recognition." In his book *Earth in the Balance*, Gore complains that any attention paid to those who disagree "undermines the effort to build a solid base of public support for the difficult actions we must soon take." He is unhappy that opposing views are even presented, complaining that "In this case, when 98 percent of the scientists in a given field share one view and 2 percent disagree, both viewpoints are sometimes presented in a format in which each appears equally credible."

But the idea that "98 percent" of scientists share his apocalyptic views is wildly untrue. A Gallup poll conducted in 1991 for the Institute of Science, Technology and Media found that among scientists actually engaged in climate research 53% do not believe that global warming has occurred and 30% are uncertain. That leaves a paltry 17% agreeing with Al Gore!

The issue is not "settled," as Gore would have us believe. In 1996 the Science & Environmental Policy Project, a privately funded organization, addressed the global warming issue in its Leipzig Declaration, which emanated from a conference cosponsored by the European Academy for Environmental Affairs. Nearly 100 European and American climate specialists signed the Declaration, which declared in part,

As the debate unfolds, it has become increasingly clear that—contrary to conventional wisdom—there does not exist today a general scientific consensus about the importance of greenhouse warming from rising levels of carbon dioxide. On the contrary, most scientists now accept the fact that actual observations from earth satellites show no climate warming whatsoever. And to match this fact, the mathematical climate models are becoming more realistic and are forecasting temperature increases that are only 30 percent of what was considered the "best" value just four years ago.[21]

Gradually, the science is catching up with the hype, and in a year or two global warming will be recognized for the fraud that it is. And the Doomcriers will move on to some new scare. Any will do. It doesn't matter, for the environment isn't the real issue anyway; it is simply a vehicle for a political agenda of bigger government, higher taxes and more regulation.

Neo-Paganism. The extreme version of the new environmentalism, sometimes called "deep ecology," is virtually a new-age religion: a religion of asceticism which rejects material values and would return us to a more primitive way of life. Says Stewart Brand writing in *The Whole Earth Catalogue*,

> We have wished, we ecofreaks, for a disaster or for a social change to come and bomb us into the Stone Age, where we might live like indians in our valley, with our localism, our appropriate technology, our gardens, our homemade religion—guilt-free at last![22]

The Doomcriers described above do not object to technology as such; they simply want to bring it under their own political control. The Neo-Paganists, however, object to technology *in principle*. They do not seek simply to control it; they wish to abolish it in order that humankind can return to some purer state of nature. The prototype Neo-Paganist is former 1960s radical and all-around gadfly Jeremy Rifkin. He urges us

> To end our long, self-imposed exile; to rejoin the community of life. This is the task before us. It will require that we renounce our drive for sovereignty over everything that lives; that we restore the rest of creation to a place of dignity and respect. The resacralization of nature stands before us as the great mission of the coming age.[23]

Rifkin has joined every environmental bandwagon that comes down the street, but his major concern has been biotechnology, which he regards as an offense against nature. He writes in his book *Algeny* that biotech is "playing God," and is violating "species integrity." He rejects it all, urging a mystical "attainment of harmony and enlightenment; feeling a sense of oneness with the world."[24]

Stephen Jay Gould, a noted Harvard paleontologist, reviewed *Algeny* thus in the magazine *Discover*:

> I don't think I have ever read a shoddier work....If Rifkin's argument embodies an antithesis, it is not left versus right, but romanticism, in its most dangerous anti-intellectual form, versus respect for knowledge and its humane employment. In both its content and presentation, *Algeny* belongs in the sordid company of anti-science. Few campaigns are more dangerous than emotional calls for proscription rather than thought.[25]

Rifkin could be dismissed as a harmless crackpot were it not for the fact that crackpots have been empowered by federal regulation to do an immense amount of mischief. The lawsuit, filed under the terms of the National Environmental Policy Act, or the Endangered Species Act, or whatever, becomes the monkeywrench by which the crackpot gets his way.

A case in point is Rifkin's success in preventing the development of a product called Frostban which would have helped reduce the $6 billion yearly crop loss due to frost damage. But the product involved a genetically modified bacterium, and this was a red flag to Rifkin. Court challenges and community protests orchestrated by Rifkin delayed field tests for four years. With the assurance of more expensive delays to come, the company finally abandoned its efforts.

Says Albert Heier, a spokesman for the EPA, "Crackpot or not crackpot, he has the public's ear, and he has to be reckoned with."[26]

The Neo-Paganists despise technology, especially that related to energy production. Stanford professor Paul Ehrlich, for example, would oppose nuclear power simply because it is power.

> Suppose that the United States and then the world were carpeted with nuclear power plants, that they worked very economically, and all direct nuclear hazards had been reduced to the vanishing point. Assume further that the portable fuels problem were solved with a minimum of dislocation. Now mankind has available the abundant, cheap, clean power that the nuclear establishment envisions, and that power is being consumed. What happens then? Possibly the end of civilization as we know it.[27]

Ehrlich sees technology, and especially energy development, as a fundamentally disruptive force and concludes that "giving society cheap, abundant energy at this point would be the moral equivalent of giving an idiot child a machine gun."[28]

It's nice to know that Ehrlich regards us as idiot children. But someone should inform him that technology, on balance, has done far more to enhance environmental values than to degrade them.

Consider the forests. Half the world's people cook their meals over wood fires, and in some third world countries a family will spend two days searching for a one-week supply of firewood. In the cities, fuel to cook a meal can cost more than the food. In Africa vast tracts have been denuded of all vegetation under the assault of generations untroubled by the burden of technologies such as kerosene or natural gas. Similarly, South American rain forests are retreating at an alarming rate in the face of primitive slash-and-burn farming techniques. In contrast, it's the forests of the industrialized world which survive and flourish.

In Europe, forests are more extensive than at the turn of the century. In the U.S. forest areas are greater today than in the 1920s.[29] One reason is that sawmills now extract twice the useful product from a log. Another reason is that around three-quarters of U.S. forest land is under private management, which has an obvious interest in careful re-planting. Today, growth exceeds harvest by around 33%. It is the profit motive, not government, which is preserving and expanding our forests.

Another concern of the apocalyptic environmentalists has been population growth. But it is the non-industrial, non-capitalist societies in which population growth is a major concern; it is the industrialized, capitalist societies in which populations have stabilized.

Anyway, most Americans take it for granted that the primary concern of government is to improve the lot of *people*. Not the Neo-Paganists: "Man is no more important than any other species,"[30] declares the founder of "Earth First!" In this view, the top priority of government is not to look out for people, but to look out for bugs, birds, bees, and the like, even *at the expense of people*. Consider, for example, the implications of the Endangered Species Act.

In California a farmer was denied the right to plow his own land so as not to disturb the Stephens kangaroo rat. We've all heard of the spotted owl, the snail darter, the Furbish lousewort, etc. More recently, it's the Delhi Sands Flower-Loving Fly which became the subject of a lawsuit by developers, farmers and property rights advocates in California. They were joined by San Bernardino County officials who were forced to move a $487 million hospital in deference to this insect. Explained the chairman of the County Board of Commissioners,

> I think the system is out of control and something needs to be done. The Endangered Species Act was intended to save eagles and bears. Personally, I don't think we should be spending this money to save cockroaches, snails and flies.[31]

Since the creation of the planet, 99.9% of the species which ever existed have become extinct. In trying to halt an evolutionary process which has been going on for hundreds of millions of years, perhaps it is the environmentalists who are interfering with mother nature! But the Neo-Paganist is undisturbed by such thoughts, as suggested by an irate letter to the editor on the subject of the County Commissioner mentioned above.

> We are grateful for the helpful statement of San Bernardino Board Chairman Jerry Eaves that "the Endangered Species Act was intended to save eagles and bears. Personally, I don't think we should be spending this money to save cockroaches, snails and flies." The stupidity of this statement confirms our belief that developers and their minions in public office will go to any length to satisfy their corporate greed.
>   The world of insects is an integral part of the biosphere that sustains us. They make an intimate contribution to our lives and to the lives of the eagles and bears we also seek to protect. They are as sacred to us as the wind in our face and the soil under our feet.
>   In diminishing them, we are robbing ourselves and our descendants of a great treasure.[32]

We would have no quarrel with this letter-writer about protecting species which are of sentimental or cultural value to *people*—eagles, bears and the like. But here the priority is clear: we willingly protect these things because they are of value to *us*. But the Endangered Species Act turns this priority upside down. Now a species is preserved not for the *sake* of people, but *at the expense* of people. The spotted owl will be undisturbed even at the expense of people's jobs; the Stephens kangaroo rat will be undisturbed even at the expense of a farmer's right to plow his own land; the Delhi Fly will be undisturbed even at the expense of people trying to build needed housing, etc. There are nearly 1200 entries on the endangered species list, with 80 or so added each year.

The Endangered Species Act overturns one of the basic assumptions of the Judeo-Christian religion, upon which this nation's cultural and legal traditions are largely based. The Book of Genesis (1:28) makes clear that man is at the top of the food chain, not somewhere toward the bottom.

> And God blessed them, and God said unto them, Be fruitful, and multiply, and replenish the earth, and subdue it: and have dominion over the fish of the sea, and over the fowl of the air, and over every living thing that moveth upon the earth.

The new paganism, however, preaches the opposite message: that man is *subordinate* to the spotted owl, the Stephen's kangaroo rat, the Delhi Fly, and to the hundreds of other creatures now enshrined on this ever-expanding list of "endangered species."

Of course, maybe the Neo-Paganists are right about all this. Maybe we should defer to the kangaroo rat. But there is such as thing as the First Amendment: "Congress shall pass no law respecting an establishment of religion." (Where is the ACLU when we need it?) If the Neo-Paganists wish to promote a philosophy which exalts owls and rats and insects over people, that's their privilege. But they should not seek to impose this new-age religion upon the rest of us through legislation, nor should the courts permit them to do so.

The Doomcriers and the Neo-Paganists share with Diana Oughton a profound contempt for industrial capitalism. Yet, it is industrial capitalism which has permitted hundreds of millions to seek and enjoy a better life. Wrote British author C. P. Snow in 1959,

> One truth is straightforward. Industrialization is the only hope of the poor….It is all very well for us, sitting pretty, to think that material standards of living don't matter all that much. It is all very well for one…to reject industrialization—do a modern Walden, if you like, and if you go without much food, see most of your children die in infancy…then I respect you for the strength of your aesthetic revulsion. But I don't respect you in the slightest if, even passively, you try to impose the same choice on others who are not free to choose. In fact, we know what their choice would be. For, with singular unanimity, in any country where they have had the chance, the poor have walked off the land into factories as fast as the factories could take them.[33]

Thanks to hyper-regulation, the environment has become the plaything of anti-capitalist elitists and their politician allies. If they have their way, it will be the poorest among us who pay the cruelest price.

There are better ways to run things than through the clumsy machinery of political force. A few examples are presented in Part IV, "The Principles Applied."

Part Four:
The Principles Applied—
Alternatives to Political Force

18: Escape from Public Education

It is the conventional wisdom that public education is the only way the poor could receive an education. Not so. As we shall see, the children of the poor were learning to read and write long before governments became much involved.

Some years ago, in a school district just outside Los Angeles, parents found themselves with a problem which was becoming all too common across the country: an educational system strong on "life adjustment," but weak on education. Homework was replaced by such goodies as "practicing telephone techniques and the social amenities," graded report cards were eliminated, even the spelling bee was taboo because of the "emotional tension," and on and on.[1]

When three school board members sought to amend what they suspected was arrant quackery, they found themselves eyeball-to-eyeball with an indignant public school establishment. An "advisor" from the California Teachers Association was soon huddled with the district Faculty Association. Finally, amid much fanfare in the local press, the faculty group formally charged the three board members with violating the "rights of teachers" in thirty-six specific areas.

Months after this dramatic confrontation it was discovered that the thirty-six accusations had not been "obtained from teachers throughout the district" at all, as had been claimed, but had merely been copied verbatim from a convenient magazine article. But by this time the three board members had already been ousted in a bitter recall election precipitated by these fabricated charges.

While perhaps an extreme example, this episode illustrates a national trend of several decades' duration. In 1965 Congressman John Ashbrook (R., Ohio) quoted U.S. Office of Education official Carrol Hanson as declaring

> the tradition of local control has been used by certain groups to forestall increased expenditures for education; it has been used to frighten the Office of Education out of areas where the nation's interest is involved and where the Office does have a legitimate concern. The tradition of local control should no longer be permitted to inhibit Office of Education leadership.[2]

Today, the issue is settled: control rests with the teacher unions, with the state departments of education, with the U.S. Department of Education and with the courts. But not with the parents. And so public education, at one time the institution closest to the local community and most willingly supported by it, has joined the Post Office and the Pentagon in being quite beyond the effective reach of the average citizen.

Today, the public school monolith is widely perceived as being more remote, more expensive and less effective than ever, with the result that people are often less interested in "reforming" the system than in escaping it. An example of this important shift in public attitude is the tuition tax credit, a measure clearly intended as an escape hatch. A recent tax credit bill was finally gutted in Congress, but it earned a degree of bipartisan support which would have been unthinkable just a few years before. The U.S. Supreme Court has upheld a Minnesota tax credit proposal. In 1998 the Supreme Court, in a decision of major national significance, upheld Wisconsin's plan to offer vouchers to students attending private schools, including religious schools.

But even as people seek to escape the deteriorating public school system the ultimate question remains: Is there any responsible alternative to continued support of public education? Without the public schools what about the poor? Would education become exclusively the advantage of the rich? Would the nation's youth sink into ignorance, crime, and sloth?

In contemplating a society without a public school system let us first take a look at the true origins of mass education. We will find to our surprise that both in England and in the U.S. mass education was far advanced long before the State became much involved.

The origins of mass education. Contrary to popular wisdom, the first successful experiments in mass education of the poor came about not through government action but through the efforts of private individuals. In England one of the true pioneers of mass education was a Quaker schoolmaster named Joseph Lancaster, who opened his first school in London in 1798. He invited children of miners, factory workers, even of paupers. To the amazement of observers these ragged children, some barefoot and hungry, began to read, write and spell. By the time Lancaster was 21 he had outgrown one temporary accommodation after another and had finally designed and built his own school building. The sign above the entrance declared, "All that will may send their children and have them educated freely; and those who do not wish to have education for nothing may pay for it if they please."[3]

Incredibly, Lancaster by himself was able to teach a thousand pupils at one time. Lancaster would teach the fundamentals to a few of the older boys; then, as soon as one achieved proficiency in the subject he became a monitor with responsibility for teaching the rudiments to ten younger children. There were monitors for reading, writing, spelling and arithmetic. Monitors ruled paper, gave exams and promoted pupils. Pupils were promoted immediately and individually upon completion of the required work.

That the poor could be educated at all was surprising to many, but that this could be achieved quickly and inexpensively was doubly amazing. Donations from the rich and the famous began to increase, and in 1805 Lancaster was granted an audience with George III which resulted in yearly contributions from the royal family.

Lancaster's fame spread even to the United States, where his methods were adopted with equal success. DeWitt Clinton, founder of the New York Free School Society (and later governor of the state) declared,

> When I perceive that many boys in our school have been taught to read and write in two months who did not before know the alphabet, and that even one has accomplished it in three weeks—when I view all the bearings and tendencies of the system—when I contemplate the habits of order which it forms, the spirit of emulation which it excites—the rapid movements which it produces—the purity of morals which it inculcates—when I behold the extraordinary union of celerity in instruction and economy of expense—and when I perceive one great assembly of a thousand children under the eye of a single teacher, marching with unexcelled rapidity, and with perfect discipline to the goal of knowledge, I confess that I recognize in Lancaster the benefactor of the human race.[4]

Lancaster was not without detractors, however. Some church leaders, angered at his refusal to promote church doctrine, roundly attacked him as an enemy of the established religion. Yet this conflict was perhaps a blessing in disguise, for now church groups began to increase their own efforts.

Without benefit of the state, mass education was becoming a reality. One observer noted in 1813,

> From observation and inquiry assiduously directed to that object, we can ourselves speak decidedly as to the rapid progress which the love

of education is making among the lower orders in England. Even around London, in a circle of fifty miles radius, which is far from the most instructed and virtuous part of the kingdom, there is hardly a village that has not something of a school; and not many children of either sex who are not taught more or less, reading and writing. We have met with families in which, for weeks together, not an article of sustenance but potatoes had been used; yet for every child the hard-earned sum was provided to send them to school.[5]

But, unfortunately, this period of progressive, voluntary activity was soon to come to an end, for mass education was now becoming a political issue. Efforts to bring the private schools under government inspection were at first vigorously rejected, but in 1833 Parliament began to offer financial assistance and many schools eagerly accepted—and were thereafter obliged to submit to government inspection and control. Agitation continued to grow, however, for still further government activity to "fill in the gaps" in the existing system which, although subsidized, was still essentially private. The turning point came with the Education Act of 1870, which established the first government operated "board schools" supported primarily by direct taxation.

The board schools had virtually unlimited funds at their disposal, and the result was such an orgy of bureaucratic extravagance that one observer, G. R. Porter, was moved to comment,

> Unfortunately, expert knowledge of education and expert knowledge of finance are not often found in combination, and the greatest enthusiasm for educating the young is often accompanied by utter carelessness of the money of the taxpayer....At present, there is a vast amount of waste in unnecessary luxuries, in the building of ornamental palaces, in the multiplication of clerks, inspectors, and so forth.[6]

As taxes to pay for all this went higher and higher, the inevitable result of state involvement soon became apparent: when people are forced to support a government institution many can no longer afford to go elsewhere. Accordingly, scores of voluntary schools were now forced to close, while many others were taken over by the state and converted to board schools.

By 1900 the transformation to state monopoly was nearly complete. Yet, considering the amazing progress that had been achieved earlier by men like Joseph Lancaster, one cannot help but wonder what abundance in educational resources might have been developed in England had private

effort not been forced out of the market by the politician and the bureaucrat.

Mass education in nineteenth century United States. State involvement in
education had earlier origins in the United States than in England, for the
Puritan leaders of Massachusetts had passed compulsory education laws as
far back as 1642 and 1647. But in general state involvement up to the nineteenth century was limited to occasional modest subsidies to existing private schools. Of course, no two states were alike in their subsequent
approach to education, but New York State may be taken as representative
of the trend.

About the turn of the century private schools were beginning to develop
rapidly, just as in England. Church schools were commonplace. In 1805,
DeWitt Clinton founded the Free School Society whose schools, as noted
above, utilized the methods of Joseph Lancaster.

A public school system was first established in New York State in 1812.
These schools, called "common schools," were supported only in part by
state funds and local taxes, however. The largest single source of revenue
was the "rate bills," i.e., fees paid by the parents.

Even though the common schools were not free, education during this
period was virtually universal. A report in 1821 by the State Superintendent
of Education declared that of the 380,000 children in the state between the
ages of 5 and 16, 342,479 were attending school.[7] Mass education, it appears,
was already an accomplished fact.

Yet, in spite of rapid progress in this predominantly voluntary system,
agitation was increasing to abolish the rate bills, thus making support of the
public schools entirely compulsory. Spearheaded by public officials and
teachers, this campaign soon bore fruit. The rate bills were abolished in
1849, reestablished in 1851, and then abolished for good with the Free
School Act of 1867. The public schools were now 100% tax supported. Or,
to put it another way, the individual no longer retained any measure of
choice as to whether or not he wished to support a state system of education.

As noted above, voluntary schools cannot readily compete with tax subsidized public schools, and by mid-century the voluntary school population
was beginning to decline. (DeWitt Clinton's Free School Society held out
for a time, but finally merged with the New York City system in 1853.) This
trend was not viewed with any sorrow by the public school enthusiasts,

however, who had been generally hostile to the voluntary schools all along. The State Superintendent had declared in 1849,

> Private schools ought not to receive the encouragement of the state, or the support of the community. They are usually sustained by those who have the ability to employ competent teachers, and the common schools are weakened by the means applied to their support. Our district schools may be so elevated [by more public expenditure] that those who seek superior advantages for their children, can find them only in the common schools.[8]

Influential Horace Mann (an ardent admirer of the Prussian state school system) was especially irked that private schools competed for the better teachers.

> If teachers look for more liberal remuneration, they abandon the service of the public, and open private schools....While we pay so inadequately a salary at home, many of our best educated young women go south or southwest, where they readily obtain $400, $500, or $600 a year....Others of our best educated young women become assistants in academies, or open private schools on their own account.[9]

Back in 1812 the first common schools had been established merely to "fill in the gaps" in an essentially voluntary system, but by now the goal of public school leaders was not to supplement the voluntary sector, but to supplant it.

The methods of Joseph Lancaster, incidentally, were in use in some of the common schools as well as in many private schools. But opposition began to grow, especially among teachers, an increasing number of whom were products of the state teacher institutes. Some evidently regarded the monitorial systems as an affront to their own authority and resented being reduced to the supervision of "transient, ignorant and unskilled monitors."[10] Lancaster's methods gradually fell from favor, and in New York City the monitorial system was banned by the Department of Education in 1846.

And so evolved education in the state of New York: primarily a voluntary undertaking at the beginning of the century and virtually a state monopoly at the close. Yet, contrary to popular opinion, mass education was already an accomplished fact many decades before that monopoly finally became established.

What might the educational facilities of this country be today had private, voluntary effort not been preempted by state force? In considering this intriguing question one might ponder this highly significant fact: the goods and services provided today on a voluntary, free market basis—automobiles, entertainment, food, clothing, etc.—are available in abundance at steadily declining (real) cost, while the goods and services provided by the state are in chronic short supply and the taxes to pay for them go up and up. Indeed, present experience as well as past history suggest that we would have better and more abundant educational facilities today for rich and poor alike had education never become a concern of the state.

The inner city school. Although the tax-supported institution tends to crowd private effort from the field, around 13% of the school-age population (grades K through 12) is today in the non-public sector. Of particular interest is the non-public inner city school.

The principal argument in behalf of public education is that it "educates the poor," but it is in precisely this area that the public schools have failed most thoroughly. In fact, the children of the poor were receiving a better education in 1798 with Joseph Lancaster than they are receiving today in many of our public schools. At least Lancaster's students could read and write.

But where the bureaucrat performs so poorly, private effort once again shows the way. A *Los Angeles Times* article described the importance of private schools to the black community of that city:

> A number of churches run pre-school programs. The Lutheran church-Missouri Synod alone operates four elementary schools in the black community, with a significant percentage of non-Lutheran students. Black students from South Central and other areas also are bused to the Walter A. Maier Lutheran High School in Burbank, which has a 45% black enrollment. Baptists also have long been involved in the area of private schools, and the Association of Christian Schools International, run by a group of evangelical protestant denominations, operates 16 elementary schools in black areas of the city as well as Brethren High School in Paramount, with a 50% black enrollment of its 540 students.[11]

A major contributor to black education in Los Angeles is the Catholic Church, with 20 elementary and a half-dozen high schools in the heart of the black community. City-wide more than 10,000 black children attend

Catholic schools. Msgr. John Mihan, superintendent of elementary education for the Los Angeles Diocese, declared in 1980, "I think our commitment is very strong. We are so strongly committed to keeping our schools open in the inner city that we are not building any new schools in the suburbs. The whole thing was thrashed out about five years ago, even though we realize there is a large percentage of non-Catholics among our black student population."[12]

Today, in the Los Angeles archdiocese, 69% of the 70,000 elementary students, and 62.5% of the 30,000 high school students are Latino, black or Asian.

Non-church schools are also proliferating in the inner city. One of the better known efforts in Los Angeles is the Sheenway School, founded in 1972 by a Los Angeles physician and surgeon, Dr. Herbert Sheen, and his daughter, Dolores Sheen-Blunt. The school is run by his daughter, an accomplished musician who also holds a black belt in karate. With an enrollment of 70, the school has a "country store," where the children learn how to keep inventory and write bills of sale, and a darkroom where children from kindergarten through 12th grade learn photography and film processing. Aside from the basics the students are taught everything from ballet to diction. The girls wear plaid jumpers or skirts and the boys wear brown cords and white shirts. In the classroom the children rise when a visitor enters. The annual budget is around $178,000, about 65% of which is covered by tuition.

Regarding the public school system Dolores Sheen-Blunt comments,

> The public schools are designed for failure. For one thing, they are drowning in paperwork, and teachers just don't have the time to provide children with individual attention. But the more unfortunate thing about the public system is that it diminishes in people a sense of responsibility for their own lives and their own children. This huge bureaucracy is in our midst saying "We're in charge here," and as a result people are encouraged to become dependent on this outside political institution rather than on the resources within their own community. This is very unfortunate.[13]

Perhaps the best publicized inner-city effort in the nation is that of Marva Collins, whose Westside Preparatory School is located in the rundown Garfield Park area of Chicago. Her school received the sympathetic attention of *60 Minutes* and was also the subject of a made-for-TV movie, *The Marva Collins Story*.

The daughter of a black Alabama businessman, Marva Collins taught in the Chicago inner city public schools for fourteen years before leaving in disgust in 1975. She explained, "All we were doing was creating more welfare recipients." With $5000 of her own money she opened her school in one room of an old brownstone. The 200 or so black children, ages 5–12, are drilled vigorously in the basics with an emphasis on reading and writing. She starts the five-year-olds on *Aesop's Fables*, while assigning myths, novels and legends to the more advanced students. She asks, "Who can say that the classics are too hard for eight-year-olds? Why spoon-feed them until they choke on an overdose of boredom?"

Her approach seems to work. Many of her students jump from well below to well above grade level. One eight-year-old, who had been assigned while in the public schools to a class for the mentally retarded, was soon reading at the tenth-grade level.

Collins has little regard for the expensive gimmicks so dear to the hearts of the public school bureaucrats. She says, "If you gave me $20,000 worth of audio-visual equipment I'd leave it out on the sidewalk." She charges around $150 per month tuition and has a waiting list of hundreds. She does not seek federal money, declaring, "I don't want any experts telling me what's good for these kids or telling me how to teach."[14]

Marva Collins is a living rebuke to the Chicago Public School System, and a monthly newspaper published by public school teachers denounced her as a "hoax" who was "carefully constructed as a media event" aimed at "further crippling public education."[15] But through the years the public system has *always* been hostile to private effort. As the New York State Superintendent of Education declared in 1849 (quoted above), "Private schools ought not to receive the encouragement of the State or the support of the community."

But sour grapes aside, private effort is once again demonstrating its superiority over compulsory political institutions. Marva Collins and Dolores Sheen-Blunt and Msgr. John Mihan and thousands of others are doing what the public school system today is incapable of doing—they are providing inner-city children with a decent education at reasonable cost.

Home schooling. Like motherhood, public education has been for years an institution above reproach. People may have criticized some aspect of the public system but rarely the underlying principle. Today, however, the idea of state directed "unity" is no longer receiving the uncritical endorsement of just a few years ago. Indeed, to the extent that the public schools have been promoting the collective rather than the individual—and the compulsory rather than the voluntary—they have been eroding precisely the values on which a free and progressive society actually depends. In any event an increasing number of parents are removing their children from the public school system precisely *because of* its socialization aspects. To the chagrin of public school officials they are choosing instead to educate their children at home.

An article in *Reason*, appropriately entitled "Home Schooling: Up From the Underground," told the story of a couple in Amherst, Massachusetts who elected to keep their eight-year-old child out of the public schools. A warrant was issued for their arrest. But instead of running for cover, the couple went on the offensive, initiating a suit against the school authorities.

The couple could hardly be dismissed as negligent or ignorant parents. The father has a Ph.D. in biochemistry, and his wife was a student at the University of Massachusetts. Objecting to what they regarded as the public school "hidden curriculum" of conformity and anti-intellectualism, they simply believed they could do a better job of educating their own child. But school authorities argued that state law requires that educational alternatives be the equivalent of public education, and that home schooling, by its nature, could not satisfy this criterion. The judge, however, supported the couple, declaring that parents had the right to seek educational alternatives for non-religious and well as religious reasons.

> Parents need not demonstrate a formal religious reason for insisting on the right to choose other than public school education since the right of privacy, which protects the right to choose alternative forms of education, grows out of constitutional guarantees in addition to those contained in the First Amendment. Non-religious as well as religious parents have the right to choose from the full range of educational alternatives for their children.[16]

The court went on to declare that the school had no right to force its socialization upon a family.

> The question here is…not whether the socialization provided in the school is beneficial to a child, but rather, who should make that decision for any particular child.…Under our system, the parents must

be allowed to decide whether public school education, including its socialization aspects, is desirable or undesirable for their children.[17]

Courts elsewhere have been striking down the notion that "equivalent" education requires state certification of the teacher. The Kentucky Supreme Court declared in 1978, "It cannot be said as an absolute that a teacher in a non-public school who is not certified...will be unable to instruct children to become intelligent citizens." In a Michigan case the district court judge declared that "the state...has failed to produce any evidence whatsoever on the interests served by the requirements of teacher certification and the defendants' experts to the contrary demonstrated that there is no rational basis for such requirements."

Home schooling is an issue which cuts across ideological boundaries. A few years ago, when Louisiana school officials began proceedings against a couple who were educating their four children at their home-based Christian Academy, the legislature passed a bill deregulating all non-public education in that state. For once, liberals and conservatives were united. Explained the bill's author, they "agreed to disagree on many issues, but they all accept that parents have the primary right and responsibility to educate and care for their children in the manner they deem fit." After years of wrangling, home schooling finally became legal in all fifty states in 1993.

With around 1.5 million children now being taught at home, the home schooling movement can no longer be dismissed as a fringe phenomenon. Home schooling books, newsletters and mutual aid organizations abound. Groups of like-minded parents in a neighborhood can band together to share the teaching chores. In fact, families could unite to establish a church and then donate, tax exempt, up to 50% of their incomes to it. The church could then establish a well-funded private school. One home schooling newspaper, *The Link*, claims a national circulation of 25,000 and is packed with ads for hi-tech educational programs of every description, from history to math, and from the bible to anatomy.

Entire curricula are now available on VCR or CD-ROM, bringing to the home a quality of instruction competitive with the best the public schools have to offer. *National Geographic*, for example, now offers its 108 years of publication on CD-ROM. One of the fastest-growing segments of the personal computer industry is software for home schooling programs. Technology is rendering the public school system obsolete. Home schooling is not for everyone, but it is becoming an increasingly viable alternative for those parents who reject the homogenized values of a failing public school system.

Home schooling is now a significant national trend, and has even been the subject of a respectful cover article in a 1998 issue of *Newsweek*.

Conclusion. The popular notion that mass education came about through government action is simply a myth. As we have seen, mass education was an accomplished fact long before the state became much involved. Subsequent state monopoly, by squeezing private effort from the field, has undoubtedly retarded rather than advanced the cause of education. In fact, the children of the poor were receiving a better education under Joseph Lancaster 190 years ago than they are receiving today in many of our public schools.

State education has been its own worst enemy. Tax supported, it has been insulated from the public feedback by which the errors and excesses of the past might have been corrected. Current attempts at reform will be equally fruitless. Based on compulsory taxation, the public school system is inherently uncorrectable.

In a word, state education is a bad idea gone wrong. Compulsory support should be ended, and freedom of choice restored to the parent. (The tuition tax credit might be a step in the right direction.) In education as in all other areas of social concern, the key to abundance is not government, but the diverse and voluntary efforts of a free society.

If education could be returned to the marketplace, the effect would be profound. A myriad of alternatives would emerge. Proprietary schools would flourish, from pre-school to college and from trade schools to the professions. Alternatives of every description would proliferate: home schooling, private schools, industry sponsored schools, church schools, Black Muslim schools, left-wing schools, right-wing schools, storefront schools, community action schools.

Perhaps the methods of Joseph Lancaster would once again be used with success. Perhaps, like Marva Collins, many of the better teachers who now feel trapped in the public system would find in these voluntary schools a challenge, a freedom and a satisfaction which they do not presently experience. Indeed, if education could be freed from the dead hand of the State, all would benefit in the end.

19: Ending the Postal Monopoly

*Like education, postal service is not a "natural" function of government at all.
In fact, the first postal services for general use were private rather than public.*

Postal service in early England. Private carriers of freight, passengers and mail were flourishing in Elizabethan times, with private lines radiating from London to a full two hundred towns. The vigor of this free-market activity is suggested by a sort of directory of the day called the "Carriers' Cosmography" which listed the regular carriers and the inn at which they might be found. Some of the entries were exclusively letter carriers.

> There doth come from Saffron Market in Norfolk a Foot Post who Lodgeth at the *Chequer* in Holborn. There is a Foot Post that doth come every second Thursday from Nottingham. He lodgeth at the *Swan* in St. John's street. There is a Foot Post from Walsingham that doth come to the *Cross-Keys* in Holborn every second Thursday.[1]

Only later was a Royal Post finally opened to public use. James I then decreed that no private letter could be sent by any other means. His purpose was surveillance: "to meete with the dangerous and secret intelligences of ill-affected persons, both at home and abroad, by the overgreat liberty taken both in writing and riding in poste, specially in and through our countie of Kent."[2]

The Crown could perhaps tolerate a few private carriers but not in direct competition with its own lines. When John Hill sought in 1658 to establish a private post between London and York which would carry a letter for a penny compared to the Crown rate of three pence he was quickly put out of business by government edict. The major threat to the Crown monopoly, however, came from a remarkable innovator, a merchant named William Dockwra.

Dockwra's Penny Post. In 1680 a merchant named William Dockwra brought to a doubtful London its first regular mail service. In spite of the disapproval of the Duke of York (who, as the king's brother, derived the profits of the Royal Post), Dockwra set up a city pickup and delivery system that is unequaled even today. All across London Dockwra established 450 receiving stations where mail was sorted and sent on. There were 10–12 deliveries a day in the business section and 4–8 elsewhere. (In central London today there are but two deliveries a day.) Dockwra's Penny Post carried not only letters but parcels up to one pound in weight and ten pounds in value. If desired, parcels could be insured. The postage for any letter or parcel was one penny. Dockwra was the first to introduce a postmark.

In London alone, Dockwra's vigorous Penny Post employed a greater number of people than the crown post office employed in the entire kingdom. After initial skepticism the Penny Post proved to be a tremendous success, and gave promise of becoming a very profitable venture. But this was more than the Duke of York could bear, and when he became king as James II in 1685, he not only took over the Penny Post, he fined Dockwra for infringing on the royal patent![3]

It was now quite illegal for *any* private agency to carry mail, but to the dismay of postal officials the laws were still flagrantly ignored. Most of the mail service was contracted out, and many of the contractors were carrying more for themselves than for the king. One irate inspector complained,

> At Salisbury, found the postboys to have carried on vile practices in taking the bye-letters, delivering them in this cittye, especially the Andover riders. Between the 14 and 15th instant found on Richard Kent, one of the Andover riders, five bye-letters, all for this cittye. Upon examination of the fellow, he confessed that he had made it a practice and persisted to continue in it, saying he had not wages from his master.[4]

The faithful inspector had Kent whipped and reported him to his master, "but no regard was had thereto"; and the very next day "the same rider came past, ran about the cittye for letters, and was insolent."

Through the eighteenth and nineteenth centuries, burdened by archaic rules and regulations, the Royal Post floundered perpetually in the red. Service was so poor and rates so high that the major portion of mail still passed through private channels. Finally, at the instigation of a reformer named Rowland Hill, major changes were made. It was Hill's radical conviction that greater revenue would be derived not by raising the rates, but by lowering them. After a prolonged campaign his reforms were introduced in 1849, resulting in a vast increases in post office business. However, the reforms did not eliminate the increasingly troublesome private competition, as we shall see.

The Boy Messenger Service. The improved efficiency brought about by Hill did not end the threat of private competition. In 1887 an enterprising individual by the name of Richard King, noting the great number of independent messengers about the city of London, organized the Boy Messenger Service. The Post Office, however, took immediate note of the fact that the new company was providing what looked suspiciously like a postal service, and was therefore in illegal competition with the government monopoly. The company was asked to desist. King warily evaded, suggesting the possibility of a "feasible" compromise. After a number of cautious exchanges, Mr. Hunter, solicitor to the Post Office, informed the Secretary of the Post Office,

> Matters have now come to the stage at which it is necessary to determine definitely whether the Company called "The Boy Messengers Limited" is to be allowed to continue practices which are, as the Postmaster General is advised, infringements of his monopoly.[5]

The Secretary advised the Postmaster General that "the clear intention of Parliament in conferring the Postmaster General's monopoly was that there should be no organized system for the legal conveyance of letters within the United Kingdom except that of the Post Office." The matter would have reached the courts then and there had not the Postmaster, at the last minute, decided against a court test. But in the meanwhile yet another group, the District Messenger Company, had also entered the field. A worried Mr. Hunter declared, "I fear that the operation of [these concerns] are [sic] placing the Postmaster General in a position of great difficulty." A Post Office committee investigating the matter reported that "there are more serious dangers to the Revenue from the employment of private companies to deliver letters than an occasional loss of postage." Such services were

> liable to develop into a collection of letters and their delivery on prearranged rounds. It would be necessary that the Department should keep a constant watch...to see that no such development...took place, and...the Post Office might thus find itself in the position of opposing the natural extension of operations which would appear to be beneficial to the public.

The priority of Post Office comfort over public convenience thus stoutly affirmed, the committee urged that "steps should be taken to prevent further infringements of the law." The committee felt that the Boy Messengers should not be suppressed, however, "without an endeavor on the part of the Department to afford the public those advantages which it is forbidding others to afford." Accordingly, the committee concluded by approving the establishment of a "boy messenger service" run by the Post Office itself!

While the Post Office committee was hammering out its report, the Boy Messenger Service was not inactive in the halls of Parliament. The company was promoting a special bill to permit the expansion of its services. Needless to say, the bill was vigorously opposed by both the Post Office and the National Telephone Company. But matters really came to a head when the Boy Messenger Service released to the press the whole exchange of correspondence with the Post Office, which immediately initiated legal proceedings against the two private companies. At the same time the Post Office announced the establishment of its own Messenger Service.

As might be expected, the news that the government was going to suppress a popular service and then replace it with its own flimsy imitation aroused considerable interest. "Questions were asked" in Parliament, and much animated discussion appeared in the press. One letter writer found it "highly entertaining to see this sluggish and somnolent department thus goaded by private competition into clumsy and reluctant imitation." Another observed that "the role of an official…is 1) to do nothing, 2) to prevent anyone else from doing anything, and 3) to invent reasons for 1) and 2)."

The outcome was a compromise. The companies were to be granted the licenses they had sought all along, and in exchange would begin paying royalties to the Post Office on terms to be hammered out later. This appeared to be a humiliating defeat for the Post Office, but in retrospect it's clear that it had lost the battle but won the war. The companies had made a crucial strategic error in accepting any compromise at all, for having thus accepted the principle of Post Office authority, they now found themselves drawn inexorably into the web of government control. In 1891 King applied for permission to extend his service to the North, but the Post Office would not consider the question until the details of the original compromise were settled, and by that time, eight years later, interest in the northern project had evaporated. The company (the two private companies had now amalgamated) sought permission to deliver circulars, but the Post Office committee responded flatly that the companies "were not established to deliver circulars," and permission was denied.

When the company argued that inasmuch as it was providing a public service it should not be burdened by excessive royalties, the committee replied that this argument

> goes to the existence of the Postmaster General's monopoly. So long as that monopoly exists, it must be protected, and any enterprise which conflicts with the monopoly must be either altogether put down, or allowed to exist on such conditions as sufficiently safeguard the interests of the public revenue....Parliament has determined that on the whole it is for the public benefit that the carriage of letters should be the subject of a State monopoly, and that decision must be accepted with the occasional disadvantages, as well as the continual and large advantages which flow from it.

As negotiations dragged on the Post Office imposed one restriction after another. Messengers were forbidden to carry more than six letters at any one time. Soon the company found it was not making much of a profit and was in default on past royalties. The Post Office was finally agreeable to a retroactive reduction, but the Treasury was not inclined to mercy. One official, George H. Murray (later head of the Civil Service) summarized the Treasury's position in the bluntest terms.

> As to the District Messengers, the ideas which prevail here are, generally, that the sooner we kill them off the better. They seem to be on their last legs, and I should think that a demand for £2,000 down (your revised claim) would administer the coup de grace as well as anything else. But if there is really much chance of their continuing to struggle on after they had paid up, I think we should be inclined to be a little stiffer and claim our full pound of flesh. This I suppose would finish them off.

The Post Office reply to this suggestion was more circumspect: "On the contrary, I think we would avoid anything which would give the Company a pretext of saying that our royalty had extinguished it." As a result, the reduced royalties were accepted. Finally, after endless tugging and hauling, terms of the license were at last settled upon eight years after the original agreement. King finally had his license but the war was now lost. Gutted by restrictions and bled by royalties the company no longer represented much of a threat to Post Office supremacy, and the scope of the Messenger Service gradually diminished after about 1910. Today that service represents only a negligible portion of the business of the parent company. But the experience of the Boy Messenger Service provides us with an interesting lesson on how bureaucrats stay in business—a lesson as relevant today as it was a century ago in England.

The United States. In the absence of a government service people seem to manage tolerably well to get the job done. So it was with delivering mail to the colonies. At the English ports it was the custom of a ship's captain to leave a mailbag in a local tavern in which letters bound for the other side of the ocean might be deposited. The fee was a penny for a letter and two-pence for a parcel. On arrival in the Colonies letters not picked up immediately were left on a table in a nearby coffee shop to be sorted over by visitors who would obligingly pick up their neighbor's mail as well as their own. This natural and reasonably efficient free market system continued to operate for many years after official services had been established.

Gradually, colonial governments began to show an interest in postal service. The first official measure in the new world was the appointment of a postmaster by Massachusetts in 1639. In the 1650s the Dutch government of New Amsterdam imposed a fine for the private carrying of mails across the ocean, directing that all such material must go through the office of the Secretary of the Province. In time all the colonies made some kind of provision for a postal service, though none was in any way self-supporting. In the meanwhile, as always, private messengers were flourishing. Favorite carriers were Indians; they were intelligent, speedy and obviously "knew the territory."

In the early 1700s a colony-wide Royal Post was established. Predictably, the crown sought to improve business by suppressing private competition, but these laws were massively ignored—often by the postmen themselves. It was said of the faithful postman on the Boston to Portsmouth route that he carried in his bag no more than four or five letters for the Post Office, but a "tableful" for himself. An observer described the difficulty which one postmaster encountered in trying to enforce the postal monopoly.

> There's two or three vessels in constant employment between Boston and Falmouth; they are called packets, each of them makes about twenty trips yearly, and every trip they carry many hundreds of letters. Mr. Child once attempted to put the Law in force and took

the letter-bag of one of those vessels to his office, but it made such a bustle and noise in town that he dared never attempt it again.[6]

The Royal Post finally dissolved at the start of the Revolutionary War, but in 1775 the Continental Congress established the forerunner of today's U.S. Postal Service with Benjamin Franklin as its first Postmaster.

The U.S. Post Office enjoyed a rapid growth in those early years but dissatisfaction was rife even then. The complaints sound quite contemporary. A Cincinnati paper noted that oysters were being brought from Baltimore in five days while the mail took seven. A greater cause of concern, however, was the wholesale corruption during President Jackson's administration. Much of the mail was let out on contract, with a degree of corruption and patronage and waste which was truly awe-inspiring. One company won a contract for thirty routes on a bid of $37,000 a year—and was then permitted to increase the bill to $107,000. This common practice was delicately known as "improving the bid." In 1835 Congressman William Cort Johnson charged that the Post Office was "corrupt from head to heels."

As always, high rates minimized Post Office revenue while encouraging private competition. *Hunts Merchant's Magazine* observed, "Government enterprise is wholly unable, under its most advantageous promptings, to compare with private enterprise." Others concluded at the time that "the transmission of correspondence is no more a national concern than the construction of railways or telegraphs or the transit of passengers and goods." Overall, a majority of the most lucrative traffic, private letters, was still carried by private means, and in 1843 twenty mail-carrying express companies flourished in the Boston area alone.

The most notable private carrier was the American Letter Mail Company, established by the famous American anarchist, Lysander Spooner. Operating originally between Boston and New York (at 5 cents per letter compared to the Post Office rate of 18¾ cents), Spooner soon extended his operations to include Philadelphia and Baltimore. The fact that private carriers were providing superior service at lower cost, however, was a source of continuing embarrassment to the political leadership, and legislation was obviously called for. Senator William Merrick of Maryland declared flatly that there would be no attempt to compete with the private firms; they would be put out of business by "penal enactment."[7] Spooner pointed out in a fiery pamphlet that "The Constitution expresses, neither by terms nor by necessary implication any prohibition upon the establishment of mails, post offices, and post roads by the states or individuals," but his objections were to no avail, and in 1845 legislation imposed stiff penalties on private carriers. Spooner fought back for another seven months before finally exhausting his resources.

Although Spooner was out of the way, other companies, especially in the cities, continued to deliver mail. In 1852 a puff in something called *Goddey's Ladies Book* declared,

> Bloods Dispatch: We are gratified to learn that the proprietor of this great public convenience has greatly increased its facilities, and that it is now making five post-office and four city deliveries daily. We are assured, also, that responsible and intelligent men only are employed as carriers, and upon each letter is stamped the date and hour of delivery.[8]

So, in 1868, Postmaster General Hold tightened the screws still further by declaring (by virtue of an act of 1851) that all streets, lanes, avenues, etc. within Boston, New York and Philadelphia were post roads, and that all persons engaged in the private transport of letters thereon were subject to prosecution. Most of the local companies thereupon ceased their postal business.

The Post Office has continued through the years to guard with the utmost jealousy its lucrative monopoly over first class mail. In the 1930s the A&P grocery chain was accused of using a private mail service between its stores and offices and was obliged in an out-of-court settlement to hand over a whopping $900,000 in penalties. Some years ago the CF&I Steel Company of Denver, Colorado was unhappy with the mail service to its Pueblo plant 120 miles away, so the company stopped using the mails and instead hired an armored car to make the 2½ hour trip. A CF&I executive declared, "We were incurring substantially less cost and getting better service." The Denver Post Office, however, learned of the practice, and promptly warned the company of the possible $500 fine and six months in jail. The company dropped the new service, and "at the Post Office's suggestion" paid a $2000 penalty to cover postage the company had not used during that period. Another Colorado concern, Public Service Company, started in 1964 to use a bus company to transport billing material among its various branches; the Post Office demanded that the company either use the U.S. Mails or pay the Post Office an equivalent fee. The company chose the latter course, and thus was obliged to pay the Post Office $9000 a year in tribute for postage it never used. A company official guardedly explained, "Let's just say the buses have a schedule that more closely parallels our needs."[9]

Years later, in 1973, the Postal Service agreed to reconsider the ban on private delivery of such inter-plant mail. But in September of 1974 that dangerous thought was firmly put aside. Postal officials, confirming once again the priority of bureaucratic security over public convenience, declared soberly that the Postal Service's financial condition requires "that the most careful consideration be given to any proposal that might cut postal revenue."[10]

Postal interests manage to look increasingly foolish with each new crackdown. In 1971 Independent Postal Services of America (IPSA), a company which specializes in 2nd, 3rd and 4th class mail, offered to deliver Christmas cards for five cents each as compared to the government rate (at that time) of eight cents. But the National Association of Letter Carriers, joined by the Postal Service, gained a court injunction against the company, claiming its activity would threaten the jobs of union members and cut into Christmas overtime!

But Postal authorities weren't kidding about those Christmas cards. In December of 1974 the six children of the Gibson family of Mountain Lakes, New Jersey were warned by postal inspectors that their yule-time enterprise of delivering Christmas cards for five cents each was a federal offense which could earn them a $500 fine. The Feds backed off only in the face of scornful local publicity.

In 1976 Mr. and Mrs. J. Paul Brennan of Rochester, New York started a mail service catering primarily to lawyers and small businessmen in the central district of the city. For ten cents per letter they guaranteed same-day delivery, and their enterprise soon grew to 500–600 letters a day. Said 23-year-old Patricia Brennan, "We've never lost a customer and never had a complaint, and that's something the Postal Service can't say."

But Postal Service official George A. Freeman was not amused. "If all the elements are there," he opined, "it could be prosecuted in federal court." To which Mrs. Brennan retorted,

> Under the law I can have an abortion or open a massage parlor, but I cannot deliver letters. The government has a monopoly on first class mail and a law that protects that monopoly. Someone is going to beat that statute. I may wind up in the can, but maybe I'm young enough and stupid enough to win....You know, the Postal Service

should hire me. I'd show them how to deliver letters. The Pony Express was faster than they are.[11]

But Mrs. Brennan's spirit was to no avail, and in December of 1977 a federal judge ordered the Brennans to cease and desist. They appealed the ruling but finally lost in January of 1979 when the Supreme Court refused to review.

While the Postal Service so jealously guards the first class turf, it is rapidly losing the race elsewhere. In 1967 the United Parcel Service handled only about half as many packages as did the Post Office; today the volume is around ten times that of the Post Office. Over two hundred private companies are in the mail business in one way or another in every city in the country, and business is booming. In New York City the M. J. Santulli Mail Service carries 30 million letters *a day* to and from the Post Office for businesses which cannot wait for the plodding mailman. Purolator Services, the largest private courier in the U.S., has its own private mail terminals in over 100 major cities throughout the world. Federal Express and DHL are two more heavyweights in the overnight courier business. Increases in second class rates over the last few years have provoked cries of anguish from hard-pressed magazine and newspaper publishers, many of whom are now taking a serious look at private delivery systems. Experimenters have included *Time*, *Newsweek*, *Good Housekeeping*, *Wall Street Journal*, *Better Homes and Gardens*, *Reader's Digest*, and others. The *Wall Street Journal* already uses private delivery for around 75% of its 1.5 million circulation. *Reader's Digest* uses private delivery for 150,000 of its California subscribers. This is more than just an experiment, said *Digest* vice president Coleman Hoyt some years ago, "We are committed to alternative delivery on a permanent basis."[12]

The U.S. Post Office was reorganized into the Postal Service back in 1968, but the new service remains as solicitous as ever of political and postal union interests. With postal wages representing 85% of operating costs the influence of the powerful unions has been especially perverse. When the President's Council of Wage and Price Stability suggested in 1976 that competition "could lead to greater economic efficiency including less rapidly rising postal labor costs," the president of the American Postal Workers Union was outraged. He charged angrily that such proposals are "apparently part of a conspiracy by members of the Administration, certain members of Congress, and people in the private sector to take over the U.S. Postal Service and turn it over to private entrepreneurs."[13]

Postal Service *management* is equally adamant in defending the turf. When a 1996 GAO report asked whether the Postal Service could continue to justify its monopoly, Postmaster General Marvin T. Runyon responded,

> The Private Express Statutes provide the financial underpinning that allows the Postal Service to provide universal mail delivery at a uniform postage rate for letter mail. The unintended consequence of removing the statutes may well mean the end of universal and affordable mail service as the American people have known it.[14]

Runyon's objection is that private concerns would "skim off the cream" in the lucrative urban areas and leave the rural areas without adequate coverage. But all of our contemporary experience suggests that the free market accommodates very well all who wish to be accommodated. For example, daily newspapers are privately delivered to the remotest households, while United Parcel already delivers any place in the U.S. with no extraordinary charge for rural delivery. The free market manages to work things out. But most ironic about the cream-skimming charge is that the most outrageous cream-skimmer all these years has been the postal bureaucracy itself, maintaining by obstinate decree its coercive monopoly over first class mail!

However, time may be running out for the Postal Service dinosaur. That comet in the sky is technology. Fax and e-mail now constitute a $19 billion a year industry, all of it bypassing the post office. At the same time electronic money transfers take another massive chunk out of Postal Service business. The Checkfree Corporation in Norcross, Georgia, handles computerized billing for 1.5 million people, and 47% of its transfers are electronic—at one to four cents per transaction—rather than by mailing a check. Banks and other businesses are actively promoting the faster and less expensive electronic transfers. As the trend accelerates, the impact upon shakey Postal Service finances will be profound.

The Postal Service is a dinosaur, and its days are numbered.

From the preceding survey of postal history it should be abundantly clear that postal service is not a "natural" function of government at all. On the contrary, bureaucrats have maintained their position in the field only by the most obstinate suppression of private competition.

The Postal Service monopoly over first class mail should be ended. Subsidies of any description should be halted. Private firms should be free to compete on an equal basis. If the Postal Service then goes bankrupt, so be it.

20: Farewell To City Hall

The proprietary community is, quite literally, an alternative to municipal government.

T*he Art of Community* by social anthropologist Spencer Heath MacCallum is a genuinely original book, presenting perhaps the first integrated discussion of the proprietary community: a community in which ownership is not dispersed among a number of occupants but is retained by a single managing group. The proprietary community has been in evidence for decades, of course, in the form of shopping centers, mobile home parks, industrial parks, etc., but MacCallum has broken new ground in his interpretation of this concept as a major step in the evolution of social organization. Building on the ideas of his grandfather, Spencer Heath,[1] MacCallum explains,

> Recently, however, an interesting development has occurred which parallels in some respects the history of the natural sciences. In the Middle Ages, before there was any science of chemistry or physics, there was nevertheless some very successful empirical chemistry and physics in the arts of tanning and dyeing and metallurgy. In a like way, an empirical art of community has developed within Western society since mid-century, in a span of barely twenty years. It has appeared in the real-estate field, outside of the cognizance of the social sciences and without appreciation of its significance within the real-estate industry. Rudimentary as it yet is, this empirical art may provide models of healthy social functioning from which to infer much more than we know of the structure and function of communities and so move us closer to an authentic natural science of society.[2]

A proprietary community is a residential, commercial or industrial development in which site ownership is retained by a single managing group which thereafter performs many of those functions customarily delegated to city hall. A shopping mall, for example, which includes scores of independently-run stores, is a mini-city in which many of the services usually associated with government—security, pedestrian thoroughfares, roads (the parking areas), trash collection, etc., are provided instead by the proprietary authority. Housing developers have been promoting the proprietary community idea for years, of course, offering as part of the "package" such things as private security and private recreational facilities—lakes, golf courses, tennis courts, clubhouses, etc. Laguna Niguel, a 7000-acre residential development south of Los Angeles, includes planned commercial and industrial areas as well. Century City, a 180-acre private development in the heart of Los Angeles, includes around 800 high rise apartment units with recreational facilities, scores of commercial establishments, a 1600-room hotel and a dozen multi-story office buildings. It provides its own private security patrol and trash pickup, and maintains its own park areas, pedestrian malls and parking areas. Century City is indeed a city—but unlike any other: no city hall, no city bureaucracy, and no corrupt political machine. In short, Century City is an entire mini-metropolis organized and run by private rather than political means.

Perhaps the most extensive proprietary community in the world is Disney World in Florida, a 27,000-acre recreation and business complex which will eventually include a residential community of 20,000. Because Disney World has a municipal charter from the state, it is exempt from political interference in the form of local taxes, zoning laws, building codes, etc. Freed from the hand of city hall, the result is indeed a "city of the future." In an article in *New York* appropriately entitled "Mickey Mouse for Mayor," Peter Blake wrote some years ago,

> Only the Disney people (of all the daring New Town planners in the United States) have constructed entirely new mass-transit systems. Only the Disney people have built lakes and lagoons, artificial surf and waterfalls; only they are building, at Disney World, four miles of new beaches...and only they have built, also, housing, stores, golf courses, stables, nature trails and camping grounds—while not at all bankrupting themselves or the taxpayers (whoever they may be) but getting richer and richer, and making people of Florida and southern California and the world happier and happier.
>
> All the extraordinary technical innovations introduced in Disney World as a matter of course have been known to every U.S. urban designer for decades; unhappily, however, nothing can ever get done in New York because there are too many people gainfully employed in the city bureaucracy whose function it is to figure out why something unprecedented will never work....But at Disney World there was no such gainfully-employed bureaucracy, and so they installed (for example) a city-wide underground vacuum-cleaner system with

ducts that run under the streets, surfacing now and then to become garbage chutes which suck in all garbage to a central compacting and garbage disposal plant.[3]

Disney World and the thousands of other thriving proprietary communities across the country represent, quite literally, the free-market alternative to municipal government.

The concept of the proprietary community does not sit well with those on the political left, however. Private property includes the right to exclude, and this threatens the most cherished desire of the liberal: to elbow his way into other people's lives. Unfortunately, court decisions are constantly limiting the right of shopping malls to exclude political activists picketing, protesting, handing out leaflets, and otherwise annoying people who came to shop, not be lectured at. Just one example: a few years ago a group of 70 Queer Nation activists overran a shopping mall in southern California, handing out condoms to teenagers and plastering stickers proclaiming "Promote Lesbianism," and "Queers Bash Back." For the sake of their customers, management should certainly have been entitled to run these people off—but the result these days would be instant lawsuit accompanied by loud noises about the First Amendment.

The First Amendment, of course, should not oblige someone else to provide the soap box. But in spite of such aggravations, the trend toward the proprietary community has been emerging for the past eighty years. The essential ingredient is unified ownership. MacCallum explains,

> The first was the phase of "turning over" properties—of acquiring land for resale in a rising market, subdividing it, and then disposing of it in as many small pieces as possible through a public promotion. The second phase was like the first, except that the land was improved before it was "turned over." This was modified speculation, for it entailed some positive production of value and so brought some stability to real estate. This is the phase we are still in; the era of the developer-builder and the planned subdivision. But there are strong signs [of] a third and more mature phase, a phase that had its beginnings quite early and is characterized by retention of land ownership in whole title for continuing administration for income. Here the reverse of subdivision occurs. As the desirability of larger sites for effective land planning and management is recognized, land assembly instead of subdivision becomes the goal.[4]

The proprietary community overcomes the often insurmountable difficulty which arises from fragmented ownership. Once the lots have been sold off into individual ownership, even a few of them, replanning and resubdividing become virtually impossible. Nowhere is the problem of fragmented ownership more severe than in cities, where the difficulty is appropriately described as urban blight. MacCallum describes the dilemma of merchants trying to get together on something as simple as widening a street.

> All went well until the day they considered which side of the street to widen. At that point, enlightened as they were, and with the best of intentions, they found themselves poised for combat. The interest of each and every one was threatened. Because of the structuring of their interests, each had to insist that the widening take place on the other side of the street. When it came to parking lots, on the other hand, each wanted them on his side of the street and as close to his property as possible—but without taking any of his property....
>
> This exemplifies the difficulty attendant on any community development program when the land is held in divided ownership. It is the longstanding dilemma of traditional communities that has resulted in virtual paralysis of the heartland of every major city....So long as individuals have ownership in parts less than the whole, their interests will collide with the interests of others....The habitual course is to continue in stalemate until a crisis forces a solution that is at best short term and achieved only at questionable social cost through the forcible intervention of an agency outside the system of contract and exchange.[5]

In a leasehold community, however, whether residential or commercial or industrial, the problem of fragmented ownership is resolved as the private interests of the lease holders are reconciled in the complementary interest of the managing organization. Because coercive and arbitrary intrusion by government is no longer a "necessity," the individual rights of lease holders are, in fact, more secure than if they owned the property outright.[6]

Although the proprietary community is more often associated with a new development, its most promising application may be the revitalization of areas of urban decay. MacCallum explains,

> A novel proposal for a private approach to urban redevelopment might also one day prove its worth and augment these beginnings. Architect Arthur C. Holden of New York suggested in the 1930s

that instead of outside interests assembling blighted properties in downtown areas by purchase, which requires almost prohibitive amounts of capital when it can be done at all, the existing multiple land owners within an area might form an owning and managing corporation for that area and pool their separate titles at appraised values in exchange for equivalent undivided shares in the whole. The resulting corporation would find itself owning an extremely valuable piece of property which could be pledged to secure funds for its redevelopment. With financing available from conventional sources, no money investment would be required for the owners, nor any expenditure of taxes by the public, for the replanning and redevelopment of the assembled area. Because the value of the assembled property would exceed the sum value of the parts before pooling (being now of an economic size for redevelopment), each owner's equity would be correspondingly greater. In addition, it would be more liquid. Each would have traded an uncertain interest in a blighted area for a secure share in a productive enterprise.[7]

For example, a group of adjacent homeowners in Watts, let us say, could pool their properties in a corporation from which each would lease back his own home. With the properties thus under unified rather than fragmented control, the neighborhood could be forcefully regained from the gangs and drug pushers by measures such as traffic control (turning streets into cul-de-sacs), private security, fences, or whatever. With unified control over a stabilized neighborhood, property values would increase sharply.

Private management, even apart from the idea of unifying fragmented ownership, can reverse urban decay. Consider the transformation of seven-acre Bryant Park[8] in the center of New York City.

For decades, Bryant Park was a trash-filled and dangerous hangout for gangs and drug dealers, and the scene of around 150 robberies and ten rapes per year. Finally, a far-sighted group of property owners and neighbors formed the Bryant Park Restoration Corporation. It then took seven years to get the Parks Department to relax its grip and grant the organization a fifteen-year lease. Over a five year period the park was totally rebuilt, and re-opened in 1992.

Today, *GQ* magazine describes Bryant Park as "the most urbane setting in America." The park is monitored by firm but unarmed guards, and the drug dealers are gone. The rest rooms, which had been out of commission for 35 years, are now spotless. Kiosks provide amenities and pay rent. The popular Bryant Park Grill pays rent of $750,000 per year. The park attracts visitors with 380 or so special events per year. Transferring public property to private management has transformed a public eyesore into a neighborhood delight.

But there is a cloud on the horizon. The reader will recall the history of early educational efforts (Chapter Eighteen) and early postal services (Chapter Nineteen). Private individuals showed the way, and then government, seeing a good thing, moved in. Ominously, the city Department of Business Services has discovered that it should have more to say about Bryant Park operations and is imposing new oversight and reporting requirements. If history is any teacher, bureaucracy will gradually tighten its grip and Bryant Park will slowly revert to its previous sad state.

The people of New York City would obviously be better served if ownership of Bryant Park were transferred completely to private hands. It is not likely, however, that the political class—politicians, bureaucrats and liberal activists—would ever contemplate such a reduction in their own authority.

Perhaps the most original part of MacCallum's book is his interpretation of the proprietary community in terms of social anthropology. The general literature of social science, he observes, suggests two principal modes of social organization, kinship and sovereignty (i.e. government). MacCallum suggests, however, that the evolution of social organization could more properly be divided into kinship and *contract* with government merely an "unstable transition" between the two. Government, he declares,

> can better be understood, not as an alternative principle of association, but as a condition that manifests itself where there is a default or insufficiency of proprietary community administration. Communities with weak or fractionated property in land are least capable of adapting to change and lack appropriate means of responding to crisis. Force here gains a foothold as a response to a crisis which a community is unprepared to meet. If the crisis continues for long, then the community manifests the pathological condition of sovereignty, a condition in which the force response has become institutionalized, or habitual.[9]

Force, the principal product of government,

> is not an organizing principle in its own right—a basis for association—but a natural and primitive expedient in crisis. Force arises in

situations where action is called for but we do not know what kind—where we are impelled to action but do not know what is appropriate to accomplish our objective, if indeed we are clear what the objective is. It arises in those situations where any kind of action seems preferable to no action. The exercise of force in community affairs indicates a lack of understanding of alternatives, an insufficiency of social technology. It represents not a kind of social organization, but the lack of it.[10]

In short, political force is not a solution, but rather a crisis response to the fact that optimum modes of property organization are not being employed. In the case of the merchants trying to widen the street, the result would be stalemate and decay until finally, in desperation, the merchants themselves would turn to government to "settle" the problem by decree. MacCallum suggests a higher plateau of social organization, the proprietary community—the community of contract—in which problems of property organization can be harmoniously resolved without resort to political intervention.

The proprietary community is not merely a novel variation in real estate development. The significance of the concept cannot be overstated, for it represents nothing less than a proven, workable and expanding alternative to political government itself.

21: Protection: Crime; Fire

Protection, like any other needed service, seems to be more reliably provided by the marketplace than by government.

In the U.S. the evolution of justice has been largely the transition from private to public retribution—from the vigilante to the court room. But perhaps true justice does not lie in retribution at all, but rather in protection, to prevent the harm from occurring to begin with.

Retribution—private. An excited cowboy brought word into Bridges Wells that rustlers had struck Drew's ranch and killed a hired hand, Kincaid. A crowd gathered, and bitter, angry men saddled up. The rustling had gone on long enough; the law had not stopped it—it was time for decent men to stop it themselves. Osgood, the ineffectual preacher, and old Davies urged restraint, but Bartlett, the one with the yellow, gappy teeth, spoke for the majority.

> "For that matter," he called, raising his voice still higher, "What is justice? Is it justice that we sweat ourselves sick and old every damned day in the year to make a handful of honest dollars, and then lose it all in one night to some miserable greaser because Judge Tyler, whatever God made him, says we have to fold our hands and wait for his eternal justice? Waiting for Tyler's kind of justice, we'd all be beggars in a year.
>
> "What led rustlers into this valley in the first place?" he bellowed. "This is no kind of a place for rustlers. I'll tell you what did it. Judge Tyler's kind of justice, that's what did it. They don't wait for that kind of justice in Texas any more, do they? No, they don't....I say stretch the bastards...stretch them."
>
> Farnley, a friend of the slain ranch hand, snarled at Judge Tyler, "The bastard that shot Larry Kincaid ain't commin here for you to fuddle with your damned lawyer's tricks for six months and then let him off because Osgood or Davies, or some other whining women, claim he ain't bad at heart. He ain't commin' anywhere. Kincaid didn't have six months to decide if he wanted to die, did he?"

And so the stage was set for the classic tale of lynch-law, *The Ox-Bow Incident*, by Walter Van Tilberg Clark.

The posse, dominated by the iron-willed ex-confederate officer Tetley, soon overtook the three men who had been seen driving cattle out of the far end of the valley. The evidence against them—young Donald Martin, the old man and the Mexican—was overwhelming: the ranch Martin claimed to own in the neighboring county had been abandoned for years; moreover, the Mexican had a gun which had belonged to Kincaid. Above all, they had Drew's cattle and no bill of sale.

Martin pleaded, "I'm no rustler, though. I didn't steal them. I bought them and paid for them." Then suddenly he wanted to talk a lot. "I bought them this morning; paid cash for them. My own were so bad I didn't dare try to risk bringing them up. I didn't know what the Mono Lake country was like. I sold them off in Salinas. I had to stock up again."

He could see nobody believed him.

"You can wait, can't you?" he pleaded. "I'm not likely to escape from an army like this, am I? You can wait till you see Drew, till you ask about me in Pike's. It's not too much to ask a wait like that, is it, before you hang men?"

Everybody was still just looking at him or at the ground.

"My God," he yelled out suddenly, "you aren't going to hang innocent men without a shred of proof, are you?"

The inquisition went on, far into the night. Davies begged them to wait, but prodded on by Tetley the men were in no mood for further delay.

"My God," Martin said huskily, "you aren't going to, really! You can't do it!"

They gave him time to write a letter to his wife. It was nearly dawn. Tetley ordered the three placed on horses. Ropes were thrown over a limb, and nooses were fixed about the men's necks. Finally,

Napes fired the shot, and we heard it echo in the mountain as Ma and Farnley cut their horses sharply across the haunches and the holders let go and jumped away. The horses jumped away too, and the branch creaked under the jerk. The old man and the Mex were dead at the fall, and just swung and spun slowly. But young Gerald Tetley didn't cut. His horse just walked out from under, letting Martin slide off and dangle, choking to death, squirming up and down like an impaled worm, his face bursting with compressed blood. Gerald didn't move even then, but stood there shaking all over and looking up at Martin fighting the rope.

After a second Tetley struck the boy with the butt of his pistol, a back-handed blow that dropped him where he stood.

"Shoot him," he ordered Farnley, pointing at Martin. Farnley shot. Martin's body gave a little leap in the air, then hung slack, spinning slowly around and back, and finally settling into the slowing pendulum swing of the others.

Within the hour Tetley and the rest found they had killed the wrong men.

The Ox-Bow Incident, perhaps the most artistically compelling argument in all of American literature against vigilantism, has contributed much—perhaps too much—to the contemporary abhorrence of private action. Today, the mere thought of "taking the law into one's own hands" invites instant opprobrium. For example, consider the outraged critical response to the 1974 Charles Bronson movie, *Death Wish*. Benumbed by the savage assault upon his wife and daughter, Bronson arms himself with a .44 and procedes to extinguish a wide assortment of New York City muggers. In no instance does he provoke an assault; in each case—in a deserted subway, in an alley, on a lonely street—he is the intended victim. But Charles Champlin, writing in the *Los Angeles Times*, complained that the movie's "incitement to every-man-his-own-executioner vigilante action against street crime was vile and demagogic pandering to an audience's fears." The *New Yorker* described it as a "death-wishing, irresponsible film." To the *Wall Street Journal*, this was an example of film makers "busily marketing hate."

To the audience, the sight of someone striking back at street crime was highly refreshing, but to *Time* such a response was incomprehensible; the reviewer was outraged that one preview audience "actually cheered."

And so, rejecting private action as "vigilantism" we have turned the matter of justice over to the state where it presumably belongs. But it is not clear that the cause of justice has been much advanced thereby.

Retribution—public. Because private retribution was dangerous, crude and inadequate, we have turned to the state. So today we have trial by jury, innocent until proven guilty, jury of one's peers, due process, etc.—all the trappings of the modern system. One wonders, however, if the innocent are really any safer. Paradoxically, the individual may be more vulnerable to arbitrary force today than he was 100 years ago in the old west. Consider, for example, the true story of William DePalma.

In 1968, in spite of testimony by 15 witnesses that he was miles away at the time, DePalma was convicted of robbing a bank in Buena Park, California. The principal evidence against him was a set of his fingerprints supposedly lifted from the bank counter. DePalma served 2½ years in prison on McNeil Island before it was finally proven that the fingerprint evidence had been forged by a Buena Park police sergeant. In 1975 DePalma finally received a $750,000 settlement but declared, "They could give me this building and McNeil Island subdivided into condominiums and no way will it turn my hair black again or take the wrinkles from my face....I haven't been able to smile for damned near 8½ years....We'll never forget what happened, but we're going to try."[1]

Thirty years have passed since the DePalma case, but people are no less subject to arbitrary injustice. Consider the case of former Dade County, Florida, policeman Grant Snowden, one of the many caught up in the child molestation frenzy of the 1980s. The principal witness against him was represented to the jury as being a psychologist and an "expert" in these matters. In fact, her only credential was a degree in speech. The usual scenario in these cases, seen dozens of times across the country, was repeated: halting testimony extracted from small children by prolonged sessions of cajolery, wheedling and leading questions. Any parent with an ounce of sense knows that small children, anxious to please the adult, can be induced to say just about anything. Many clinical studies confirm this phenomenon. No matter. And no matter that there was not a shred of credible evidence that any of these children had actually been molested. The prosecution, headed by politically-ambitious Janet Reno, was implacable, and Snowden was tried and convicted in 1984. Not until February of 1998 was this outrageous conviction overturned. Fourteen years out of this man's life.

DePalma and Snowden lost years out of their lives, caught up in the awesome meatgrinder of state "justice." One wonders how many hundreds, thousands or tens of thousands of innocent people have suffered just that fate at the hands of state justice, the principal alleged virtue of which is that it protects the rights of the innocent!

The Old West was a walk in the park compared to life today in Cook County, Illinois. Ask gambler Ken Eto. Eto was invited to the house of a mob boss for dinner, but a few hours after leaving home someone shot him three times in the head. But Eto lived—and talked. More shocking than his angry revelations about local crime figures was his identification of the hit-man: a deputy sheriff.

For decades the Cook County Sheriffs Department has been little more than a protection racket shielded by the law and subsidized by the taxpayer. In the ensuing months sheriffs were implicated in schemes to sell city jobs, manipulate sheriff's auctions and take bribes from criminals in exchange for dropping charges.[2]

More recently, during an FBI sting operation in New Orleans, agents overheard a policeman using his patrol car phone to direct another officer to execute someone who had lodged a brutality complaint against him. Within ten minutes, before the agents had time to intervene, the woman had been shot to death. An FBI memo noted that the sting operation was terminated "because of the extreme violence exhibited by the officers, which included threats to kill the undercover FBI agents acting as couriers and also to steal the cocaine being shipped." Eleven officers and one civilian were finally convicted of corruption and about 200 officers were fired.[3]

But none of this is new in places like Cook County, New Orleans, New York City and elsewhere. Dozens of cities across the country have been pestholes of police corruption for literally over a century. Periodically a reform group will clean things up for a while, but in a few years the corruption will be back to normal.

The major argument for public rather than private justice is that the rights of the innocent are more secure, but in real life this assumption may be just one more popular myth. Indeed, as the random examples listed above suggest, there is little evidence that the individual is any more secure from miscarriages of state justice than he was from miscarriages of private justice a century ago in the Old West. In fact, he may be less secure. The very size, complexity and impersonality of the "failsafe" legal system of today has rendered it more awesomely dangerous than its simpler, and therefore more visible Western counterpart. In *The Ox-Bow Incident* it was at least possible to identify the villains, but who is really accountable for what happened to DePalma or Snowden? Or for the institutionalized corruption in Cook County or New Orleans? No one. Just that vast, amorphous, and utterly unaccountable blob known as "government."

Our pursuit of justice, it appears, has propelled us out of the frying pan and into the fire. Private retribution was inadequate—but its acknowledged shortcomings pale into insignificance beside the waste, cruelty, indifference and stupidity now massively institutionalized by the state. So where do we go from here? Finally, one is driven in another direction entirely. Perhaps the real issue is not private versus public retribution at all. Perhaps the real issue is retribution itself.

Retribution versus protection. Only the indelibly naive still suppose that our courts and prisons either protect the innocent or rehabilitate the guilty. If anything, the aggressor comes out of prison more dangerous to us all than when he went in. But if the system does not protect or rehabilitate, what does it do? Its only real function, just as in the western movie, is retribution—to see that the bad guy "gets what he deserves." But is the cause of justice really advanced thereby? It depends on one's definition of justice.

Retribution is justice only in the sense of reciprocity—an eye for an eye, a tooth for a tooth. True justice, however, is hopefully something more than the exchange of harm for harm. True justice is—or should be—the *upholding of rights*. Retribution does not serve this end at all. It may be better than nothing, but by definition it comes too late. The rights have already been violated and retribution does not undo the harm. Even if the aggressor is apprehended the murdered man cannot be brought back to life; the stolen property will probably never be recovered, etc. One's view of retribution, then, is ambivalent: gut satisfaction that the villain "gets what he deserves"—tempered by the realization that justice has not triumphed; as far as the victim's rights are concerned it has already failed.

From the standpoint of upholding rights retribution accomplishes little. Moreover, considering the vast expense associated with the clanking machinery of of state "justice," retribution merely adds to the heavy price of crime. The total cost of public law enforcement is around $30 billion a year, most of which is devoted to the tasks of apprehension, trial and imprisonment. But when hundreds of thousands of dollars can be spent seeking retribution for a thousand dollar or hundred dollar or ten dollar crime, one wonders what the point really is. Vast amounts are taken from us in taxation to support a system of state retribution which does not work anyway and which may, in fact, aggravate the problem.[4] Crime has gotten so out of hand, and conventional police departments are so incapable of handling it, that former Los Angeles Police Chief Edward Davis once advised worried citizens "to bar their doors, buy a police dog, call us when we are available and pray."[5]

The time-honored system of retribution is simply not working today—if indeed it ever worked.[6] Far better to divert the vast sums squandered in its support to that which people really want and need: not retribution after the harm has been done, but *protection* to prevent the harm from occurring to begin with.

Because the state is utterly preoccupied with retribution people must look for protection elsewhere. And in greater and greater numbers they are doing precisely that, looking to the free market for everything from better door locks to entire walled and guarded communities. Today, private protection has suddenly become a $20 billion a year industry. Today, two out of every three uniformed policemen work for *private* companies. In a typical block of corporate offices in Manhattan perhaps 20 different private police forces may be working at one time. Burns International Security, Wells Fargo, Pinkerton and Wackenhut are the four largest security companies in the nation, each directing forces of over 30,000. Nation-wide around 10,000 firms provide protection in one form or another. And protection is the business, not retribution. Says the Los Angeles area manager for Wackenhut, "Our primary function is to protect property and persons, not to make arrests."

The trend in private protection is toward technology, not firepower. The *Wall Street Journal* observed a while ago,

> Meanwhile, more and more guards are relinquishing their weapons....A Memphis-based company with 5000 employees, Guardsmark Inc., has 99% unarmed guards and uses the fact as a marketing device.
>
> "Guards don't need weapons. They are more a threat and menace to society by having a gun," says Ira Lipman, the president of Guardsmark. "We have walkie-talkies, closed-circuit cameras, electronic fences, bullet-proof glass, card-key systems. We really don't need to be armed."[7]

Private, guarded communities, industrial and residential, have been springing up all over the country for years. Genesec Development Corp. of Cleveland developed a "total security" industrial park in Hinkley, Ohio, in which, according to the developers, an electronic detection system would "prevent the theft of even a needle." Sugar Creek, a 1000-acre residential community outside of Houston, is an electrically fortified city surrounded by a six foot brick wall, and patrolled by private guards. The homes were snapped up as soon as they went on sale. In Southern California The Island portion of Westlake Village, the country portion of Diamond Bar, The Cays in Coronado, and Rolling Hills just south of Los Angeles, are all fenced and guarded communities. Evelyn DeWolfe, writing in the *Los Angeles Times* 25 years ago, sniffed that the unspoken word in these places is "prestige," but to the residents it is quite another matter. A resident of Westlake declared, "The snobbish connotations of this place, if any, is from those who don't live here about those who do....Where we lived before we were broken into three times."[8]

In the ensuing years private residential protection has become a major growth industry. More than 1100 security companies operate in Southern California today (1998) with more than half in Los Angeles where "Protected By ..." signs have sprouted like mushrooms on more than 120,000 well-manicured lawns. Nationally, according to *Security Sales*, a trade magazine, around 20% of residences have security monitoring systems of some kind, about double the percentage of 1987. The typical installation costs around $1200 plus a $20 per month monitoring fee.

Most home security companies will simply report an alarm to the police department, which may repond in 50 minutes or so. (Most alarms are false.) Some companies, such as Westec, offer an armed response within around five minutes, depending on the location.

But perhaps the greatest virtue of the private protection agency is that it can be fired on the spot. In contrast, the corrupt or incompetent police department, with all of the majesty of the law behind it, can remain solidly entrenched at the public trough for decades.

The ultimate private protection, of course, is to buy a gun. Thirty-one states now have "shall issue" laws allowing people (except those with a felony conviction) to carry a concealed weapon. The result appears to be a *lower* crime rate where more people are armed. In his book *More Guns, Less Crime*,[9] John R. Lott, formerly chief economist for the U.S. Sentencing Commission, studied the correlation between crime and gun ownership broken down by county since 1977. Lott calculates that if the remaining 19 states "had adopted right-to-carry provisions in 1992, about 1500 murders and 4000 rapes would have been avoided."

Lott concludes that "of all the methods studied so far by economists, the carrying of concealed handguns appears to be the most cost-effective method for reducing crime."

However, gun control advocates point out that crimes are often committed with guns. True enough. It is not clear, however, how crime would be reduced by disarming the law-abiding. But the bottom line in this debate is not over whose study to believe. If someone weighs the risks and chooses to own a gun, that's his (or her) decision. In a free society this choice should not be infringed upon.

In any event, private protection works. A 1992 study by the National Center for Policy Analysis found that people acting in self-defense kill three times as many criminals each year as do the police.

Protection and the role of the state. "Suppose private protection were to fail," one might ask. "Suppose a robbery or murder or whatever were to take place anyway. What then? Would it not be necessary then to turn to a system of state retribution to pursue, apprehend, convict and imprison the aggressor?" The late Robert LeFevre, founder and past-president of Rampart College, answered with an unequivocal "No." Once the injustice has occurred, LeFevre emphasized, it is already too late. The costs and dangers associated with state retribution simply compound the original harm. Better to divert that wealth and effort to better protective measures so that the misfortune is not repeated.

"Well, must not there be a 'limited government' of some kind to at least oversee these private measures and serve as a final arbiter in the event of a dispute?" Again, it depends on what kind of private justice it was: private *retribution* would indeed require a government to supervise it. For example, suppose Smith's TV set were stolen and he suspected Jones had taken it; Smith would call upon his private retribution agency to retrieve his set and punish Jones. Jones, however, especially if he were innocent, would indignantly protest, calling on his own private force to defend him and retaliate against Smith's aggression. A state of war would exist between two armed camps and some kind of government structure would no doubt be required to impose a settlement. As long as justice is centered on the idea of retribution, the state will indeed be around to "supervise."

As LeFevre pointed out, it is the element of *retribution* which makes the state a seemingly essential fixture in the field of justice. Replace retribution by protection, however, and the role of government could be greatly reduced. (The author is greatly indebted to Mr. LeFevre for his seminal observations on the subject of justice, the individual and the state.)

The problems of crime and violence will not be solved by hiring more police, judges, and lawyers, or by building more prisons. That approach has reached a dead end. The surer approach to justice does not lie in retribution, but in protection. And in numberless ways people are turning away from government and toward the marketplace to gain that protection. The increasing resort to private measures should not be deplored, but welcomed as a hopeful trend toward a safer—and freer—society.

Fire Protection

Visitors to Scottsdale, Arizona, may see an unusual sight: lime-green fire engines. This would be the equipment of Rural/Metro, a hugely successful private fire department.

Rural/Metro got its start 50 years ago in 1948, when Louis L. Witzeman became concerned about the lack of fire protection in his community. He collected some capital and bought a used truck, got some neighbors to subscribe to his service, and he was in business.

As a private company, Rural/Metro was not burdened by the hide-bound traditions of municipal departments. His trucks were essentially home-made—short on chrome but long on utility. Some of his fire fighters were full-time, but others were part-time, on call when needed.

By the early 1960s Witzeman's company was serving 200,000 persons in the Scottsdale and surrounding areas for about one-sixth the per capita cost in comparable-sized communities served by conventional municipal departments. In 1969 the company began to provide ambulance service as well.

By 1998 Rural/Metro had annual revenues of $440 million and more than 9000 employee/owners in 450 communities, who provide emergency health services or fire protection to more than 12 million people throughout North and South America. Overall, the per capita charge for fire coverage is still about half the rate for traditional municipal coverage. A six-month comparison study conducted for Scottsdale by a management consultant firm found that Rural/Metro provided "one of the best fire departments we have had the opportunity to review."[10]

Rural/Metro is now traded on NASDAQ, and has been described by *Forbes* as one of the 200 best-run small companies in the nation.

In a brochure directed to city officials, Rural/Metro asks, "If we get our surgeon or our airline pilot from the private sector, why not our paramedic or our firefighter?" The brochure goes on to list some of the advantages of out-sourcing these services.

> Financial and performance accountability are actually easier to enforce with a private contractor than with your own department. If your own fire or emergency ambulance department goes over budget, what are you going to do: tell them to quit responding? But a private sector provider with a fixed fee contract takes the financial risk as a cost of doing business; the taxpayers are protected. And if your own department isn't meeting performance standards, improving performance can be difficult and time consuming. With a private sector provider, it's either improve or get fired. In terms of management time and commitment, it's clearly easier to manage a contract than a department, particularly when it comes to personnel issues. And if you can provide ambulance and fire services more effectively and at less cost, you can free up tax dollars to go to other pressing community needs, such as increased police protection.

Would that the issue were that simple. Rural/Metro ran into a buzz-saw when it sought to establish itself in the heavily-unionized Northeast.

When the town of Rye Brook, New York decided it was paying too much to the neighboring town of Port Chester for coverage, it contracted with Rural/Metro to provide the service. But Rye Brook is an upscale community while Port Chester is blue-collar and heavily unionized. The two communities were not on good terms to begin with, and the contract was bitterly resented by union sympathizers. The mayor of Rye Brook found messages on his answering machine, "We know your routine. Don't be surprised if you're run off the road."[11]

Rural/Metro found itself caught in the middle. Says spokesman Jeff McQueen, "They threw bottles at our trucks and spit on our people."[12] It became increasingly difficult to retain on-call reservists, who kept resigning under the pressure. Explained Rural Metro's regional president for the Northeast, "The fact is that we are a for-profit company, and that was just not well-received in the communities surrounding Rye Brook."[13]

When neighboring departments would call for assistance in the event of a major fire, Rural/Metro was studiously ignored. One of the fire chiefs was quoted as declaring "We don't want what they got. Simple as that."[14]

More ominous, the nearby Port Chester department made it clear that it would not respond to a call for help from Rye Brook. The fire chief acknowledged that he was so ordered by Port Chester city officials—who later declined comment.[15]

The conflict came to a head in December of 1997 when a million-dollar house caught fire. The 911 call was tardy, and the house was soon fully engaged. A call for assistance went out to the Port Chester department. It did not respond. The house burned to the ground.

This was more than Rye Brook had bargained for, and when Rural Metro later acknowledged that it would be unable to assure a sufficient number of on-call reserve firefighters, the contract was terminated by mutual agreement. The town elected to create its own municipal fire department—independent of the union hard-liners of Port Chester.

Says the Mayor with some bitterness, "[The experiment] was not a success.…We thought it was the best for Rye Brook. Other jurisdictions said, 'No way,' and they tried to undermine it and make sure it failed. That's what we were up against."[16]

For Rural/Metro, the Rye Brook experience was a serious setback. But only one in a 50-year history of outstanding success. The overall trend is unmistakable: the company continues to flourish, and continues to demonstrate that private enterprise, where permitted to do so, can do the job cheaper and better.

Whatever the task—education, postal service, protection—the marketplace can clearly out-perform government. But what about national defense? This, of course, is the toughest nut of all, and will be the subject of the following chapter.

22: National Defense

Government does not always protect the people; more often, the people are called upon to protect the government. Of all the failures of the coercive state, none has been more profound than "national defense."

After Gideon had freed them from the Midianites, the men of Israel said to him, "Rule thou over us, both thou, and thy son, and thy son's son also: for thou has delivered us from the hand of Midian."

The Israelites had been loosely organized on a tribal basis—but they wanted a king just as other people had. But Gideon replied, "I will not rule over you, neither shall my son rule over you. The Lord shall rule over you."

One hundred years later the Israelites were still seeking a king to lead them in battle, and this time it was Samuel who gave them a similar warning.

> This will be the manner of the king that shall reign over you: He will take your sons, and appoint them for himself, for his chariots, and to be his horsemen; and some shall run before his chariots. And he will appoint him captains over thousands, and captains over fifties; and will set them to ear his ground, and to reap his harvest, and to make his instruments of war....And he will take your fields, and your vineyards, and your olive yards, even the best of them, and give them to his servants. And he will take the tenth of your seed, and of your vineyards....And he will take your men servants, and your maid servants, and your goodliest young men...and put them to his work....And ye shall cry out in that day because of your king which ye shall have chosen you.[1]

But the Israelites finally got their king. A whole line of kings. And the kings built magnificent palaces and maintained great armies—and the taxes to pay for it all rose higher and higher. But as the state became greater the people became somehow diminished. The Israelites were finally defeated in war, their cities destroyed and the people dispersed.

History abounds with examples of societies which have been strongest and most cohesive *in the absence* of central political rule, only to decline later as political control increased. In 479 B.C. the mighty Persian Empire was repulsed by the Peloponnesian League, a loose confederation of free and independent Greek city states. The political fragmentation was not a weakness, but a strength resulting in a unity which was far more significant—the unity of people fighting to maintain their own independence. Later, however, this independence was snuffed out. Under Pericles, Athens finally imposed on much of Greece the dubious blessing of strong, central "democratic," bureaucratic government. Greece belonged less and less to the people and more and more to the state. The result was not strength, order and peace, but civil war, disintegration and disaster.

Military strength does not lie merely in the power of the state to regiment the individual, but more profoundly in the determination of free people to defend what is theirs. This is not to say that those fighting for their own freedom will always win; the Irish were massacred by Cromwell, the Indians by the U.S. Cavalry, the Biafrans by Nigeria, etc. History does suggest, however, that free men fighting for their own way of life can often out-fight and outlast and out-think much greater forces fighting only in obedience to the state. This is a lesson which the mighty Soviet Union learned to its dismay in Afghanistan. Moreover, as society becomes more complex, it becomes even more difficult for the state to maintain control over a restive population.

Private individuals in defense of their own rights can often accomplish military success with an efficiency and dispatch far beyond the capacity of any state. Consider, for example, the story of a daring Englishman named John Philipot.

In 1377 England had lost the initiative in the 100-year war with France. A particularly galling blow fell when a Scot named Mercer, in command of a fleet of French, Scottish and Spanish ships, sailed into Scarborough and captured a number of English ships at anchor. The people waited for government to act—but nothing happened. Finally, John Philipot, a wealthy London grocer, "took the law into his own hands." At his own expense he outfitted a small squadron of ships, recruited a thousand men, and set sail. He overtook Mercer's fleet and decimated it. He recovered all the captured British ships, captured 15 Spanish ships as well, and returned to England a hero. The haughty marcher barons who ruled the country, however, were not at all pleased, declaring that a commoner, and a civilian at that, had no business meddling in affairs of state. But as Philipot replied to one noble critic, "My Lord Earl, if the nobles of England had not left the country open to invasion it would not have been necessary for me to interfere."[2]

A few years after Philipot's exploit, Jean Angot (1480–1551), a ship-builder in Dieppe, France, accomplished a similar feat. Incensed because two of his vessels had been harassed by the Portuguese, he collected a private navy of 17 ships. He attacked Lisbon, captured the harbor and a number of ships and maintained a blockade until the city sued for peace.[3]

If you have trouble believing that story, consider that the mighty Spanish Armada (a typical product of state planning, it should be noted) was defeated by the *private* forces of Sir Francis Drake and others. They had a crucial assist from the weather—but no material help at all from Queen Elizabeth, who did not even supply the powder and shot.

During the American Revolution some two thousand Colonial privateers took to sea, and in 1776 alone this "free enterprise" navy captured 250 British merchantmen, causing the insurance rates from the West Indies to England to rise 23%. While the British Navy had to get its manpower via the press gang, privateering was so popular among the Colonials (prize money was split 50-50 between owner and crew) that Rhode Island even passed a law trying to limit the size of crews. Says Jameson, "probably as many as 90,000 Americans were first and last engaged in these voyages, a number of men almost as great as served in the army and greater than that of the army in any single year save one."[4] Silas Deane wrote Robert Morris in 1777 that American cruisers "sailed quite around Ireland and took or destroyed seventeen or eighteen sail of vessels, they most effectively alarmed England, prevented the great fair at Chester, occasioned insurance to rise, and even deterred the English merchants from shipping goods in English vessels at any rate, so that in a few weeks forty sail of French ships were loading in the Thames on freight, an instance never before known." Deane added that "even the packet boats from Dover to Calais were for some time insured." A witness before Parliament lamented that the losses suffered "could not be less than two million two hundred thousand pounds."[5] Privateering brought the revolution home to England in a most painful way, contributing greatly to the unpopularity of British policies. And the aggressive and highly effective "free enterprise" navy was maintained without impressment and without one cent of tax support.

In defense of their own homes, their own families, their own honor, people do not need a bureaucrat to tell them what to do or how to do it. On the contrary, history is strewn with the wreckage of societies which have relied on their government to defend them, and time and again, the result has been to exhaust the nation of its resources, drain the people of their spirit and so erode their freedoms that when a genuine crisis did occur there was little left to defend and little with which to defend it.

The greatest saboteur of a society's will and strength is government itself. In discussing the British Navy after World War I Parkinson[6] notes in his wry manner the inverse relationship between the number of bureaucrats and the number of seaworthy ships, while France in the 1930s was left utterly defenseless by its own myopic defense establishment. We have in the U.S. today a massively expensive government establishment which, in the name of "national defense," drew us into an illegitimate war in Vietnam—and then was unable to win it. At the same time, in the name of "defense," government has wasted untold billions on weaponry which was utterly superfluous. Our hugely expensive missile detection and interception efforts, for example, were as useless as the Maginot Line. There was nothing—absolutely nothing—to prevent a potential enemy from bringing H-bombs into this country piece by piece and assembling them in every major city to be set off on command. Easier still, H-bombs could have been secreted in the holds of freighters to be docked at every major port.

In spite of the billions spent on defense we are in many respects weaker because of government, not stronger. The greatest loss, however, is that in relying on government we rely less on ourselves. Consider, for example, the periodic seizure of American tuna fishing ships on the high seas by various South and Central American navies a few years back. The fishermen, out of habit, turned to government for protection, which, of course, was not forthcoming.[7] But suppose it were not the custom to turn to Washington in such matters? Suppose it were the custom instead that people handle these problems themselves? A half-dozen skin divers hired by the Tuna Association could no doubt dispose of most of the Ecuadorian Navy—including the destroyers provided it by the U.S. Government—if they set their minds to it. This is not to say that such action should necessarily be undertaken, but it *could* be done. And whether in ancient Greece or in modern America, this is where the ultimate strength of a society lies. Not in the extent to which people turn to government, but in the extent to which they are willing to act, as individuals, in defense of their own property, their own rights and their own independence.

Now and then Americans do "take the law into their own hands," and the results are highly refreshing. In 1979, Tehran was boiling with anti-American sentiment and industrialist Ross Perot was becoming increasingly concerned about the welfare of 131 of his employees plus their 220 dependents. Most slipped out of the country, but two of his top aides, plus a half-dozen other employees, were arrested and imprisoned. The Iranians demanded a $13 million ransom. With the U.S. State Department displaying its customary hand-wringing impotence, Perot organized a crew of rank amateurs to attempt a rescue. In marked contrast to the later failure of the U.S. Government to rescue the sixty embassy hostages, Perot's free-enterprise plan, complete with a careening escape through a hostile countryside, was a rousing success.

Private groups, acting in their own private capacity, are at least not in a position to legally coerce an entire nation into pursuit of some foolish commitment or adventure. Governments, however, do precisely this. History abounds with instances in which governments have acted not in legitimate defense at all, but in furtherance of the pride, avarice or folly of political leaders and those about them. Said Teddy Roosevelt in 1898 as Assistant Secretary of the Navy, "No triumph of peace is quite so great as the supreme triumph of war....The diplomat is the servant, not the master, of the soldier." Roosevelt did everything within his considerable power to promote a national war with Spain over Cuba. He got what he wanted.

In 1900 Albert Beveridge spelled out on the floor of the Senate the mission he had in mind for the American people.

> The times call for candor. The Philippines are ours forever...and just beyond the Philippines are China's illimitable markets. We will not retreat from either. We will not repudiate our duty in the archipelago. We will not abandon one opportunity in the Orient. We will not renounce our part in the mission of our race, trustee under God, of the civilization of the world. And we will move forward to our work, not howling out our regrets, like slaves whipped to their burdens, but with gratitude for a task worthy of our strength and thanksgiving to Almighty God that He has marked us as His chosen people to lead in the regeneration of the world....This question is elemental. It is racial. God has not been preparing the English- speaking and Teutonic people for a thousand years for nothing but vain and idle contemplation and self-administration. No! He has made us the master organizers of this world to establish system where chaos reigns....This is the divine mission of America.[8]

The tradition of imperialism ushered in by Roosevelt, Beveridge, and many others in political life left us a heritage to be paid for in American blood. Cuba, the Philippines, China. Our military expansion into the Far East led ultimately to Pearl Harbor and Korea.

When all power rests with the state the population is dragged into whatever venture happens to thrill the breast of the politician. In 1961 J. F. Kennedy was blowing the same old trumpet in committing the American people to "pay any price, bear any burden, meet any hardship, support any friend, oppose any foe to assure the survival and the success of liberty." The result was a blind march into Vietnam with 50,000 more sacrifices on the alter of what we continue ingenuously to describe as "national defense."

Of course, the military expansionism of this country over the past century has not been solely the work of political leaders. Business groups, intellectuals, and church groups have all at one time or another eagerly encouraged the extension of U.S. influence through the mechanism of the armed state. Where the major blame lies, however, is not the important point, for politicians will cater to the loudest hue-and-cry whatever its source.

Whether in Cuba in 1898 or in Vietnam or in Israel or in El Salvador, the principle is—or should be—the same: *private* individuals and groups should be free to take (or reject) any measures they wish, in the form of donating money or arms or manpower or whatever. To throw the issue into the political arena, however, to harness all of the American people to policies which may prove disastrous (but which, given the political nature of things, will be virtually irreversible), and to induce in others an enervating dependence on those policies, is to invite disaster for all concerned.

That mindless juggernaut, the state, is a mischievous weapon in whatever hands it happens to be. The solution, then, is not merely to place some new politician or group in charge, but rather to look elsewhere for safer means of defending ourselves.

Invariably we assume that national defense above all else must be supported and maintained by government—i.e. by force. But as MacCallum put it, force is not really an organizing principle at all, but rather "A natural and primitive expedient in crisis....The exercise of force in community affairs indicates a lack of understanding of alternatives, an insufficiency of social technology. It represents not a kind of social organization but the lack of it."[9] Perhaps we resort to taxation and the draft not because we must, but because voluntary alternatives have been preempted. It is of interest, then, to speculate as to the form that national defense might have taken in this country had defense never become a monopoly of the state.

For a time, volunteer militia and privateers would have sufficed, and, in fact, did suffice. In the twentieth century, however, a more sophisticated structure would presumably have been required. The emergent structure might, for example, have been in the form of a nation-wide consortium of insurance companies—companies which would have had a vested interest in protecting the physical property of those whom they had insured. In principle, this concept is not without precedent. A few decades ago it was not uncommon to see in some of the larger cities *yellow* fire engines—engines from private fire departments owned and operated by insurance companies for the purpose of protecting their clients' property from fire and themselves from loss.[10] What might have evolved, then, is the identical principle with respect to national defense: profit-motivated insurance companies, in filling the demand for war damage insurance (assuming a threat of some kind really existed) would at the same time have established those private agencies of national defense which would have minimized the degree of their own risk.

It is instructive to contrast the motivation of a free-market defense with that of the government-operated variety. As the *Pentagon Papers* and the LBJ tapes disclosed so vividly, the motivation behind our involvement in Vietnam was not self-interest at all, nor was it even an altruist desire to make things better for the Vietnamese. The only real reason for our being there, it seems, was a desire on the part of successive political administrations to maintain their own dubious credibility. A free-market defense agency, on the other hand, would have no incentive whatever for wasting its resources in someone else's back yard. It would be concerned with one thing and one thing only: to protect the lives and properties for which it was responsible. And this, of course, is what national defense is supposed to be all about.

Of course, what *might* have happened in the absence of a state monopoly on defense is mere conjecture, for the Pentagon is not going to move over for Hartford Fire and Casualty. A gradual, evolutionary approach to free-market defense, however, is not out of the question, and may, in fact, be taking place today. Nor would some kind of "national consensus" be required to implement such a trend. On the contrary, the essence of a free-market approach to things is small, independent, isolated and unremarkable beginnings, expanding and growing in number. Every American business at home and abroad, from the Tuna Association to Getty Oil to New York Life, has the potential for defending its own interests—and, by extension, the interests of us all. Added together, these influences could evolve into a tough, subtle and viable fabric of defense quite beyond the capacity of foreign states even to comprehend, let alone combat.

A gradual separation of government from defense is no less feasible than its separation from religion or economics. Lacking is only the awareness that a realistic alternative does exist, that true security does not rest with the blind and foolish state but with the voluntary institutions of a free society.

The role of the multinational. Nothing in the stars decrees that nations must forever be at swords-point. Perhaps the most far-sighted national defense rests not in the accumulation of greater mountains of weaponry at all, but rather in the encouragement of those developments which draw people together rather than drive them apart. One such trend is the multinational corporation; companies like IBM, Philips Petroleum, GE, GM, Ford, Exxon—global giants with subdivisions the world over—whose far-flung operations are unrestrained by national boundaries or loyalties. Yearly sales of the 4000 or so multinationals have mushroomed from $200 billion in 1960 to over a trillion dollars today, representing 15% of the world's product. The multinationals, whose treasuries often exceed those of the countries in which they operate, wield a quiet but increasingly significant influence in international affairs.

To the growing annoyance of national leaders, the multinational company enjoys a high degree of immunity from political control. The multinational can calmly shift billions of dollars across national borders with hardly a trace, can move profits to the subsidiary in the country with the lowest taxes, can direct capital and resources in accordance with economic reality rather than political caprice, and can in general frustrate the designs of political leaders. As the late Salvadore Allende complained before the UN, "the multinationals are not accountable to or regulated by any parliament or institution representing the collective interest." Professor Perlmutter of the Wharton School of Finance and Commerce voiced a similar worry. "What guarantees are there that the key executives of the 300 geocentric super-giants will show a social responsibility to the world community of consumer and citizens?" And Perlmutter concluded, as do many others, that there is "a need for rules and laws at the world level."[11]

To the dismay of many, the multinational is indeed relatively immune from political control—but this is precisely its principal virtue! The ability of the multinational to base its decisions on economic rather than political considerations represents a thoroughly hopeful step toward world peace. Throughout all of history a major cause of international conflict has been the attempt by one group or another to gain commercial advantage by political means—if not by imperialist military control, then more subtlety, by tariffs, quotas, discriminatory taxation, restrictive currency controls and the like. Accordingly, if the multinational can keep the world's economic affairs out of the political arena, so much the better.

Ironically, one of the principal claims of Marxism over the years is that world socialism would overcome national boundaries. But today, it is not Marxism but capitalism that is surmounting national boundaries and bringing people together in peaceful commerce.

Indeed, hope for peace and progress does not lie with political control, but with voluntary exchange on the widest possible basis. Where the politician has little to offer but force, the businessman in the free market, if he wishes to make a profit, must provide the jobs which others are willing to fill, and the goods and services which others wish to buy. Accordingly, if the multinationals can frustrate the designs of political leaders, if they can overcome the barriers of narrow political interest, then so much the better. The global capitalists are achieving precisely that degree of peaceful international cooperation at which political leaders have been so conspicuously inept.

Governments do not prevent wars; they start wars. History is littered with the debris of nations which, in the name of "national defense," have either been led to destruction by their own political leaders, or have been crushed from within by the overwhelming tax burden of their own defense establishment. But there are better ways to do things. It is just as true of national defense as of education or postal service or municipal government—in all areas, real progress is not the product of political force, but of the voluntary institutions of a free society.

There are better ways to run things than through the clanking machinery of political force. So, where do we go from here? This question will be the subject of Part V, "What Now?"

Part Five:
What Now?

23: The Proper Role of Government

The proper concern of government is not "compassion," but liberty. When government, in the name of "compassion," initiates force against the individual, it has become the agent of despotism.

The preceding chapters have sought to illustrate the excesses of government. Government does have a legitimate role, however: to protect the individual against force and fraud. It's when government becomes the aggressor that the trouble begins.

Well then, how do we draw the line between what government should and should not do?

The proper role of government. Throughout 6000 years of recorded history people have gone through contortions trying to discover the proper *structure* of government without defining the proper *role* of government. Accordingly, the search has been endless. As Rose Wilder Lane described it some years ago,

> From Nebuchadnezzar to Hitler, history is one long record of revolts against certain living rulers, and revolt against kinds of living authority.
>
> When these revolts succeed, they are called revolutions. But they are revolutions only in the sense that a wheel's turning is a revolution. An Old World revolution is only a movement around a motionless center; it never breaks out of the circle. Firm in the center is belief in Authority. No more than the Communist or the National Socialist (Nazi) today, has any Old World revolutionist ever questioned that belief; they all take it for granted that some Authority controls individuals.
>
> They replace the priest by a king, the king by an oligarchy, the oligarchs by a despot, the despot by an aristocracy, the aristocrats by a majority, the majority by a tyrant, the tyrant by oligarchs, the oligarchs by aristocrats, the aristocrats by a king, the king by a parliament, the parliament by a dictator, the dictator by a king, the king by—there's six thousand years of it, in every language.[1]

For 6000 years people have sought to devise the optimum *structure* of government, but the important issue is its *role*.

Government is the agency of legalized physical force. It can use that force to protect individual rights (as when the policeman subdues the criminal) or to violate them (as when the dictator imprisons his opposition). It is the manner in which government uses the legalized force at its disposal that distinguishes a free society from a tyranny. This crucial distinction can be described as follows: in a free society government uses force only in *retaliation* against those who violate individual rights, while under tyranny the state *initiates* the use of force against those who have violated the rights of no one.

Government should respond only when rights have been violated by some act of force or fraud. *Failure* to act (except in violation of some prior agreement) does not constitute a violation of rights. To illustrate: if a person murders another, it is clear that he has violated rights by a positive act of force. On the other hand, if a person chooses not to rescue a drowning person, no right has been violated. This nonaction might be morally reprehensible, but (in the absence of some contractual obligation) it does not properly constitute a violation of rights in any legal sense.[2] Other examples of nonaction: it is not a violation of rights to refuse to contribute to a worthy charity. It is not a violation of rights to refuse to hire someone. It is not a violation of rights to refuse to donate blood to a dying man. It is not a violation of rights to refuse to sell a house to a particular party. It is not violation of rights to refuse to give a quarter to a hungry beggar. It is not a violation of rights to decline to subsidize an artist. A pacifist violates the rights of no one when he refuses to fight. Rights can be violated only by some positive act, not by refusal to act.

Government in a free society must not *initiate* the use of force. Accordingly, freedom cannot mean such things as "freedom from want" or "freedom from hunger," for if government were to guarantee such "freedoms" it could do so only by initiating force against those who would be compelled to pay the bill.

"Compassion" is not the proper concern of government. *Liberty* is the proper concern of government—to maintain that climate of freedom in which people can decide for themselves the extent to which they wish to serve the interests of others.

If we are concerned, as we should be, about the welfare of those less fortunate, let us consider that it has been in the freer societies, in which the individual is secure from state aggression, that rich and poor alike have fared best. Accordingly, let us first uphold the principles of freedom on which this genuine progress depends, then perhaps we can dispense with government-enforced "compassion."

Government in a free society will use force only in *retaliation* against those who have violated rights by some positive act of force or fraud. It will not *initiate* the use of force. Let us apply this straightforward rule to the following situation: suppose the majority in a community considers a particular book to be pornographic; does it have the right to pass a law forbidding the sale of that book? A private community, of course, such as those described previously, could make any rule it chose. In the public arena, however, government would have no business banning the sale. In fact, government interference in such a case would itself constitute a violation of rights, for government censorship is ultimately imposed by initiating (or by threatening to initiate) physical force against the bookseller. He must comply or his property will be confiscated; if he resists he could be jailed; if he resists too strenuously, he could conceivably be shot. Another example: Suppose a television station refuses to grant free time to an individual to air his views. Has a right been violated? Should government intervene? No, for neither his life nor his property have been taken from him by any positive act of force or fraud. It is certainly not a violation of someone's rights to refuse to listen to him, or to provide him with a soap box.

Would government seek to subsidize the arts? It can do so only by taking from us the means by which we might support our own preferences. And when government seeks to "do good" by force, it invariably corrupts everything it touches. Including the arts. Louis XIV of France sought to be the patron saint of writers, but as nineteenth century British historian Thomas Buckle observed,

> In no age have literary men been rewarded with such profuseness as in the reign of Louis XIV; and in no age have they been so mean-spirited, so servile, so utterly unfit to fulfil their great vocation as the apostles of knowledge and the missionaries of truth....To gain the favour of the king, they sacrificed that independent spirit which should have been dearer to them than life. They gave away the inheritance of genius; they sold their birthright for a mess of pottage.

As Buckle concluded, "What happened then would, under the same circumstances, happen now."[3]

Would the SEC and antitrust seek to assure "fairness" or a "level playing field"? But when the armed bureaucrat seeks to enforce such totems of ideological law, he must resort to force. Would government seek to neutralize bigotry by passing compulsory housing legislation? But when it attempts to wrest from the individual the control of his own property, government has again become the initiator of force; it has again become the master rather than the servant. Would government seek to educate our children? It does so by forcibly confiscating from us the means by which we might support our own choice of school. When government supports abortion services, it does so by forcing many Americans to support programs they regard as morally repugnant. Again government has become the initiator of force, and instead of upholding liberty, it is eroding it.

Would government pursue "social justice" by redistributing the wealth? But government cannot give to some what it has not first taken from others, and so for all its good intentions it has become the initiator of force—it has become the agent of legalized theft. Ex-Marxist David Horowitz understands the process well.

> The unequal distribution of wealth flows from the free choices of individuals in the economic market. The only practical meaning that complaints about social injustice have, therefore, is that a system exists in which individuals are free to choose their occupations, to succeed and to fail, and there is no power to make the results "correspond to our wishes." In other words, the only remedy for "social injustice" is for a state to abrogate individual freedoms, eliminate such choices, and organize the social order to correspond to *its* conception of what is morally right. The demand for "social justice," consistently advanced, is really the demand for a command economy organized by a totalitarian state.[4] [Emphasis in the original.]

The initiation of legalized force against the individual is the distinguishing characteristic of tyranny. When Hitler declared that it was the duty of the individual to serve the Fatherland, he imposed that duty upon dissenters by initiating force against them. When Mussolini seized ultimate control of all private property, his decrees were backed up by the threat of physical force. Lenin seized control of the means of production by initiating the use of force. To the extent that government—any government—initiates the use of force against the individual, it has become a tyranny.

And the nature of tyranny is not altered by good intentions. Throughout history much blood has been shed by those who meant harm, but a great deal more has been shed by those who meant only to do "good." Over the centuries "unselfish" men of burning conviction have held the vision of a better society. "We know what is needed," they told themselves. "For the sake of humanity, must we not act?" (*Liberté!*) "Can we let a selfish few stand in the way of a better life for all?" (*Egalité!*) "And if it is necessary to use stern measures, is it not justifiable?" (*Fraternité!*)

It is at this point that the humanitarian sets up the guillotine. Some of the worst tyrannies in history have been imposed by "unselfish" men who felt they had the right to do good—by force.

It is the proper role of government to protect people from force or fraud. It is *not* the proper role of government to force them to be "compassionate," or "fair," or "moral," or "progressive." Whether force is initiated for the sake of the rich or the poor, for the black or the white, for the Catholic or the Protestant, for business or for labor, for women or for men, the result is the same: tyranny emerges from the shadows, step by step. Nor does "legality" or "majority rule" alter its features, for Nazism was legal, and a lynch mob is majority rule.

Of course, it's easy enough to say what government should or should not be doing. But how can our hyper-intrusive government be restrained? Is political action the answer? The limits of political action will be the subject of the following chapter.

> "If one needs what others earn
> No longer need one steal it!
> Government now does the job,
> And people hardly feel it!"
> —from *Tom Smith and His Incredible Bread Machine*

24: The Limits of Political Action

Government is force, and politics is the process of deciding who gets to use it on whom. This is not the best way to solve problems.

By and large, the American people really are better than their political leaders. Here's why: Most people live and work in a marketplace of voluntary transactions based on persuasion and cooperative behavior. That is, the shopkeeper cannot force the customer to put down his money; he can only persuade. The politician, however, lives in a different ethical universe where the ultimate currency is not persuasion but force. From this point on, the values are totally different. In the marketplace the person who panders and demagogues and dissembles will probably remain on the lower rungs of success, but in politics the person who panders and demagogues and dissembles will be praised for his political skill and may end up in the White House.

The ethical standards of the professional politician are simply different from those by which the rest of us try to live. Based ultimately on force, politics is an arena in which the least principled will often rise to the top. Perhaps this is why the professional politician is viewed with such contempt by so many Americans.

During each political campaign season a Los Angeles lawyer named Linda Abrams, a Phi Beta Kappa from UCLA, places a sticker on all her personal correspondence urging, "Don't vote—it only encourages them." But her objection goes beyond a mere distaste for the general tackiness of political behavior. "Political control," she explains, "whether applied to education, energy, business or whatever, is the most disruptive single influence in our society today. But the ballot doesn't permit us to oppose the *concept* of political control; all we can do is choose which group is to exercise it. Better to boycott the polls entirely than to sanction such a meaningless process."

Abrams has identified a basic problem with political action: the voter may choose between ruler A and ruler B, but he cannot choose that there be *no* ruler.

Small wonder that politicians appear to be "all the same." Essentially, they *are* all the same. The ultimate issue is the individual versus the state, but the politician, as confirmed by his oath of office, has already cast his lot with the state. Each would use the state in a different way, but each, with a few honorable exceptions, would use the state, if not for this noble cause then for that one. A Clinton does not reverse a Bush; he merely shifts the emphasis. Administrations may come and go, but the net thrust of political action will always be in the direction of higher and higher levels of government activity. Accordingly, no matter who wins the election the individual loses; only the state gains, nourished every two years by the bewildered affirmation of the voter.

The divisive nature of political action. The political process creates more problems than it solves. Consider again the contrast between the political and the marketplace transaction. When the shopkeeper sells his product to the customer, each party enjoys a net gain. The shopkeeper values the customer's money more highly than the item (otherwise, he would not sell). The customer, on the other hand, values the item more highly than the money (otherwise, he would not buy). In any voluntary transaction *both* parties experience a net gain. Government action, however, is quite a different matter, for government can give to some only what it has first taken forcibly from others. Unlike the free-market, for every beneficiary of government action there is a victim. Accordingly, government "compassion" will inevitably set group against group.

The divisive nature of political action is most obvious, of course, during a political campaign, with its rampant appeal to bloc voting. Where the marketplace brings people together in mutually profitable exchange, political action drives them apart. The politician must emphasize differences, not common ground. He must stress the advantages which he can gain for this or that group—thus arousing the resentment of the rest who know quite well that it will be taken out of *their* hides, one way or another. The rich resent the poor because of welfare; the poor resent the rich because of fat government contracts and subsidies. Whites resent blacks because of affirmative action, while blacks resent whites because of white values forced upon them in white-dominated public schools. Farmers resent subsidized aerospace engineers, while aerospace engineers resent subsidized farmers, and on and on. Political action does not resolve these antagonisms—it causes them.

The extent to which diverse races and cultures and interests are able to live together in relative harmony is the extent to which each poses no threat to the other. When life is dominated by government, however, each faction in its own defense is turned against the rest. In Northern Ireland, for example, because housing, education, jobs, money, health care, etc., are all controlled by the state, Catholics must struggle for political power—and fearful Protestants must struggle to prevent them from getting it. In his book *The Economics and Politics of Race*, Thomas Sowell notes the dangers inherent in the politically-run society.

> The politicization of economic and social life increases the costs of intergroup differences, and tends to heighten mutual hostility....Politics offers "free" benefits for people to fight over. Markets put prices on benefits, forcing each group to limit its own use of them, thereby in effect sharing with others. A society with both Buddhist and Islamic citizens must somehow allocate its available building materials in such a way as to have these materials shared in the building of temples and mosques. If the building materials are shared through economic processes, each set of religious followers weighs costs against benefits and limits its demand accordingly. But if these same building materials are provided free or are otherwise shared through political processes, each group has an incentive to demand the lion's share—or all—of the materials for building its own place of worship, which is always more urgently needed, in more grandiose proportions, than the other.
>
> Groups that hate each other often transact peacefully in the market place but erupt into violence when their conflicting interests are at stake in political decisions.[1]

Wherever one looks, the principle is the same: political control aggravates every difference, heightens every suspicion and intensifies every hatred. The greatest generator of social discord is government—the institution of legalized force. Only in a free-market, non-political society can the spirit of live-and-let-live prevail.

The myth of political reform. The state is force. Nothing else. Not persuasion or cooperation or brotherhood; just force. But an institution based on force will be virtually immune to reform.

The political mechanism will work inexorably to the advantage of those who seek the favors of the state, and to the disadvantage of those who pay the ever-mounting bill. For example, consider the unequal contest over (let us say) a proposed subsidy for this or that industry.

Because those in favor of the proposal have much at stake, their lobbying efforts will be intensive and well-financed. To the individual taxpayer, however, the impact will be at most a few pennies per year. Accordingly, opposition will be muted and dispersed. Only on April 15 will the accumulated impact of such handouts be brought to the attention of the victimized taxpayer. Yet, even then (especially then!) he has no real choice in the matter: he must pay or go to jail. And so, year by year and decade by decade, the handouts multiply in number and the tax burden builds higher and higher. The political process is not a means of solving this problem; based on force, the political process *is* the problem.

Imposed ultimately by the tax collector and the jail cell, the beneficiaries of government largess are insulated from the counterbalances by which the rest of us are automatically restrained. For example, the businessman might indeed wish to raise his prices again and again, but he is limited ultimately by the willingness of the customer to buy his product. The laborer would be equally glad to receive a thousand dollars an hour for his efforts, but he too is limited by the willingness of others to support his desires. Government, however, based on force, is undeterred by "consumer resistance." Because the out-voted taxpayer must pay his taxes or go to jail, those on the receiving end of government "compassion" can vote for more and more of the same without limit. The long-term danger is obvious.

> A democracy…can only exist until the voters discover they can vote themselves largess out of the public treasury. From that moment on the majority always votes for the candidate promising the most benefits from the public treasury with the result that Democracy always collapses over a loose fiscal policy, always to be followed by a Dictatorship.

Does this sound as though it might apply today? This statement was written 200 years go by Professor Alexander Fraser Tytler as he described the collapse of the Athenian Republic over 2000 years before.[2]

The interests of the politician and of the private citizen conflict not only in means but in ends. The private citizen (at least the one who is not himself the beneficiary of government favor) seeks minimum interference with his life, but the politician has good reason to push in precisely the opposite direction—being human, he does not pursue insignificance; like the rest of us, he seeks a measure of importance, prestige and influence. His interests, then, are not served by minimizing the role of government, but by maximizing the role of the institution of which he is a part.

To seek reform by political means, then, is an exercise in futility. This or that scoundrel might be turned out of office, but a fundamental change in direction is unlikely. Based on force, the relentless state is inherently immune to reform—at least from within.

The myth of majority rule. The state is force, and politics is simply the means of determining who is in charge; the game of deciding who coerces whom for whose benefit. In itself, this is not a productive process. But another reason government seems so strangely, congenitally incapable of running things sensibly arises from the very nature of representative government.

We do not wish an *un*representative government, of course. So we try very hard to make it as representative as possible. Hence the ultimate political ideal of majority rule. But here the problem emerges, for where an issue is in doubt, *the majority is always wrong*. Consider that any major breakthrough in the understanding of things will *always* be greeted with indifference or opposition by the majority. (Otherwise it would not be a breakthrough at all, but an already accepted truth!) When Copernicus suggested that the earth went around the sun, the majority believed otherwise. When private individuals in eighteenth century England introduced the "barbaric" practice of inoculating against smallpox, the majority, including virtually the entire medical profession, was appalled. The majority laughed at the Wright Brothers and ignored Bell. A breakthrough, by definition, concerns something previously undiscovered and unaccepted. Advances are then made by individuals or by small groups of cooperating people who *overcome* majority opinion or indifference. Later, of course, when the innovators are finally proven right, the majority comes along. At the outset, however, when the issue is in doubt, the majority is always wrong.

The fact that the majority is always wrong has interesting implications for the concept of democracy—a system which, to many, means state control of the individual and his property in accordance with the supposed wishes of the majority. But if the majority is invariably wrong, how fare those areas under state domination? Science? Industry? The arts? Clearly, the thrust of any state-directed effort, in accordance with majority rule, will always be in the direction of the safe, the sure, the average, the uninspired, the mediocre. What does this mean, then, to our treasured concept of "progress" via political means? It means that any "progress" which comes about through political action will not be progress at all; it will be either a prevention of something better or a regression to something worse. In a word, where majority rules, progress stops.

And so one is drawn to the conclusion that majority rule is a false god; that the goal of free people should not be majority rule at all but self-rule, not political action but individual action, not the "public interest" but private interest. The Bill of Rights does not tell the majority what it *may* do, but what it may *not* do. When the individual is free to pursue his own self-interest (limited only by the equal right of others to do the same), the public weal will take care of itself.

The limits of political action. Government is force, and politics is simply the means of deciding who gets to use it at whose expense. By its nature, then, politics will inexorably represent the interests of those who seek the favors of government. Hence the bewilderment of voters who find that no matter who wins the election, government continues to grow bigger and more intrusive. At best, transient reforms can be accomplished, but the underlying dynamic of politics is constantly to expand the role of the state.

Accordingly, those seeking to limit the role of political force in our society are quite literally disenfranchised. Linda Abrams was mostly right: you can vote for ruler A or ruler B, but you can't vote for *no* ruler. Political action can possibly be helpful for educational purposes, or as a rear-guard effort, but its effectiveness as an influence for less government is limited. It is simply the wrong instrument.

So, is history implacably against us? Is Tytler's grim scenario written in our stars?

History does not make people; people make history, and they can change its course when they choose to do so. In fact, people have within their grasp a weapon far more effective than the ballot: they have the ability to say "no"—to withhold the sanction without which government is powerless. Attitudes are changing, and that sanction is gradually being withdrawn as people turn away from government and toward the voluntary alternatives of the marketplace. Political government as we know it may already be in its twilight, as we shall see in the final chapter.

"Well, I vote in all elections, and in any way I can,
I support the politician with the very noblest plan.
So, I do my civic duty, and although I clearly see
That we are *all* being robbed—*well you can't blame me!*"
—from *Tom Smith and His Incredible Bread Machine*

25: Twilight of the State

People have at their disposal a weapon more powerful than the ballot: their refusal to cooperate.

Coincident with the age-old quest for perfect authority has been the age-old conflict between authority and conscience. Was Antigone justified in defying Creon, the lawful king?

At Nuremberg, of course, the decision was clear—the obligation to "do one's duty" has its limits. But the choice between civic duty and private conscience is rarely so obvious. What about draft resistance during the Vietnam War? What about a tax strike? What about pot laws? Should the responsible citizen always obey the law? Or is the individual justified in referring ultimately to his own conscience?

On balance, the American people take a dim view of civil disobedience. As long as the bad laws can be changed by orderly means, so the consensus goes, we have an obligation to obey all laws, bad as well as good. And so the law-abiding American citizen cooperates with IRS, assists Antitrust, and makes sure that the OSHA forms are submitted on time. He may grit his teeth, but as a public-spirited citizen he feels the obligation to obey.

But suppose bad laws cannot really be changed after all? Indeed, as major elements of society become increasingly dependent upon state privilege, their interest is less in reform than in preventing it. Nor can the political leadership itself be relied upon to set matters straight, for those in positions of comfortable prestige have equally little reason to challenge the status quo. In reality, the idea of "changing bad laws by orderly means" may be just a convenient myth. More likely (and as confirmed by the unending growth of government) the fate of bad legislation is simply to be buried under more of the same.

The public-spirited citizen, then, is truly caught in a no-win situation. Trapped by his sense of civic responsibility, he supports an irreversible process by which his earnings are expropriated, his property confiscated and his freedoms systematically eroded. So, what does he do? Does he continue to obey? Or, finally, does he resist?

The temptation, of course, is to resist. And yet...

At this point our conventional wisdom sounds the warning: "Only respect for authority stands between us and ruin. Obey the law, or lapse into chaos." And so our public-spirited citizen vacillates, wondering if indeed we would "rather bear the ills we have than fly to others we know not of."

But are we really so sure that order depends on reverence for political authority? Indeed, a look at history suggests otherwise, for those societies which have lapsed into chaos have generally done so not because people questioned political authority but because they didn't. And as people rely on the compulsory state to solve their problems the subtle fabric of voluntary loyalties—family, economic, community, religious—gradually atrophy. Then, when the state finally collapses (as it inevitably does) the descent into barbarism is assured. Czarist Russia comes to mind, or Bourbon France.

So, perhaps political authority does not hold a society together, but rather sets the stage for subsequent collapse. In any event, a compelling empirical argument can be made that the healthiest societies have been those with the least reverence for political rule. After all, the Magna Carta was not the product of orderly and obedient subjects, nor was the Declaration of Independence.

Still, a prescription for selective obedience to the law is disturbing. For example, what do we do about a Charles Manson? His conscience tells him that murder is perfectly acceptable. Do we say to Manson, "Let your conscience be your guide; obey the rules which please you and ignore the rest"?

But the question misses the point, for we are not trying to prescribe a society amenable to Charles Manson but to the rest of us. We are interested in the kind of free, non-authoritarian society in which the rest of us can best uphold our own non-Manson values. (In this case, for example, perhaps by means of the private, guarded communities mentioned in Chapter Twenty-One.)

What it all comes down to is this: if we believe in individual rights, then that's precisely what we mean—the right of the individual to decide for himself what to do with his own life. He does not have a "civic duty" to play the game by someone else's self-serving rules. The true responsibility is not to "the law" but to one's own values,[1] and if the law is contrary to those values the individual has no obligation to obey.

In his famous essay "Civil Disobedience," Henry David Thoreau put it this way: "I think that we should be men first and subjects afterward. It is not desirable to cultivate a respect for the law, so much as for the right." In

1846 he spent a night in jail because of his refusal to pay a tax, a portion of which might have supported the U.S. invasion of Mexico.

Mahandis Gandhi, a disciple of Thoreau, carried the idea of non-cooperation much further. Thoreau's stand was personal, an expression of private conscience, but Gandhi forged a spirit of civil disobedience into a powerful weapon of national liberation. Gandhi recognized the monumentally important fact that state authority cannot prevail, or even function very well, without the cooperation of those under its control. British authorities were painfully aware of their ultimate helplessness in the face of widespread passive resistance.

The more complex the society, the less likely that it can be run simply by force. Even in Nazi Germany authorities needed the cooperation of the German people. Albert Speer, Minister of Armaments, noted in his memoirs that "Just issuing an order proved insufficient even in the Third Reich, even in wartime. We, too, were at the mercy of the willingness of the people involved."[2] Even in the mighty Soviet Empire the rulers were ultimately at the mercy of the ruled. In Poland, for example, the Soviets could extract only the meagerest cooperation from the people, and as a result Poland was as great a burden to the Soviets as India was to Great Britain.

Philosopher-novelist Ayn Rand added a new dimension to the idea of non-cooperation, noting the crucial importance of one segment of society in particular, the producers—those who provide the services, man the machines and create the wealth. Yet, the productive element of society permits itself to be taxed, regulated and hectored by a growing army of politicians, bureaucrats and assorted social parasites. Rand described this sheep-like compliance as the "sanction of the victim." And, like Gandhi, she recognized that if this sanction were withdrawn the omnivorous state would at last be brought under control.

There are two groups of people whose non-cooperation could be a real threat to government authority: the taxpayer and the businessman.

The taxpayer. As IRS officials acknowledge, the system is largely dependent upon voluntary compliance. Only around 2% of returns receive even a cursory audit, and the chances that a tax-evader will get caught are minuscule. Yet the patriotic and law-abiding American citizen continues to cooperate with the tax collector. Why is this?

There are two reasons for this voluntary compliance: people feel it is their "civic duty," and they suppose that government is the only way to run things. So they cooperate. As suggested throughout this book, however, they are mistaken on both counts.

1) *Civic duty*. People accept the altruist premise that civic virtue lies in service to the "greater good." The virtuous taxpayer should be willing to serve the poor, the old, the young, the arts, the collective, the public interest, the whatever, as directed by government. "Our duty to the (fill in the blank) takes precedence over private greed," so the altruist argument goes. Or as the Nazis put it, *Gemeinnutz vor Eigennutz* (common interest before self).

People may not agree with these altruist sentiments, but they feel they *should* agree. Hence, while taxes for all the noble-sounding crusades are often bitterly resented, opposition to them is muted and uncertain, and underlying public sanction, however grudging, continues.

Here, however, the altruist position is rejected at the outset. In a free society it is not the duty of the individual to serve "others," it is his right to live his own life for his own sake.

2) *No alternative*. The second reason people cooperate with the tax collector is the assumption that there is no other way to run things. Police protection, postal service, education, defense, etc., are services from which the taxpayer himself derives some direct benefit. Accordingly, as a "good citizen" and in his own assumed self-interest, he feels the obligation to cooperate in "paying his share,"—and he expects others to do the same.

Suppose, however, he found (as suggested in the previous chapters) that these are not "natural" functions of government at all, but could be accomplished in a superior manner by other means? In this event, the impulse to cooperate would vanish.

Writer Rose Wilder Lane had no doubts about her "civic duty" to pay her taxes. In her correspondence she embraced tax resistance with downright enthusiasm.

> I do not think that any honesty is involved in paying taxes. Taxation is plain armed robbery; tax-collectors are armed robbers. I will save my property from them in any way that I think I can get away with. If you wake in the night with a flashlight shining in your face and a masked man with a gun ordering you to tell him where your money is do you feel that you're morally obliged to tell him the truth, the whole truth, and nothing but the truth? I think you might. I don't. I will try to get out of that predicament with as little loss as possible. In regard to taxes, this means taking advantage of every legality that

any attorney can find in the tax "laws" so called, and regulations. I have no scruples about this whatever, anything that I want to do with my money, and that I can in any way slip under any legality so that the robbers won't find it and rob me of some of it, I do. They make the legalities, trying to be smart about who gets how much of my property; and to keep as much as possible of my own, I'll outsmart them if I can.[3]

Rose Wilder Lane could have eased her resentment had she done what many others are doing today: she could have established her own church, to which she could then have contributed up to 50% of her income, tax exempt, thus diverting a significant portion of her money to *her* interests rather than to those of the government. A church need not be theistic in nature. A church is presumptively tax exempt, and the First Amendment, as confirmed by the courts, assures that the IRS cannot pick-and-choose between "acceptable" and "not acceptable" churches. Those who have tried to use their church as an obvious tax scam have run into problems with the IRS, but if people engage in genuine church activities such as charity, education, and the propogation of a coherent ethical doctrine, the IRS has little basis for complaint.

The authority of the IRS depends ultimately on the cooperation of the taxpayer, and that cooperation is dwindling as people become increasingly angry with the arrogance, ineptitude and corruption of the political class. The do-it-yourself church is a peaceful and legal means by which people can "withdraw their sanction" if they choose to do so.

Tax resistance takes many forms, legal and not-so-legal. Across the country, tax resistance is truly getting into the big numbers as an estimated 20 million Americans operate to some degree "off the books." Estimates in 1993 placed the size of the underground economy at $500–$700 billion dollars, with a loss in taxes of around $127 billion.

Tax resistance measures are without number and as varied as the individuals engaged in it. Those whose defiance is loud and blatant will occasionally end up in jail, but for every resister apprehended thousands of others, one can be sure, go quietly on their way.

Of course, the implications of the growing tax resistance movement have not been lost upon officialdom. Back in May of 1972 former IRS chief Johnnie M. Walters chose to define the issue in moral terms. In deploring what he described as an "increased public tolerance of tax cheating," he asserted that "When a taxpayer cheats on his taxes he is stealing. And this, in my opinion, is worse than just stealing from an individual or a merchant, because it is stealing from the public—from 200 million Americans. We can never afford to let that sort of philosophy become acceptable."[4]

Well, let us clarify the ethical issue: It's not the person who defends his own property who is stealing, but the person trying to take it from him. Moreover, there are few needed functions of society which cannot be performed in a superior manner by private, voluntary means. Accordingly, any measure which reduces the revenue and the power of the omnivorous state is a step toward a freer and a better society. So, who knows? Perhaps the real "public spirited citizen" is not the one who obediently pays his taxes but the one who, like Thoreau, does not.

> "I revere the Constitution, and obey our many laws,
> And I promptly pay my taxes which support each foolish cause.
> Though our leaders will destroy us (as I point out constantly),
> Still I've done my civic duty, *so you can't blame me!*"
> —from *Tom Smith and His Incredible Bread Machine*

The Businessman. As agencies such as Antitrust, SEC, OSHA and the rest become increasingly burdonsome, perhaps the business community will also consider the merits of civil disobedience. Thoreau observed,

> Trade and commerce, if they were not made of India-rubber, would never manage to bounce over the obstacles which legislators are continually putting in their way; and, if one were to judge these men wholly by the effects of their actions and not partly by their intentions, they would deserve to be classed and punished with those mischievous persons who put obstructions on the railroads.

The cost in dollars is bad enough, but more subtle and more destructive in the long run is the steady erosion of the productive and innovative vigor of this country. Many businessmen (at least, those who are not themselves dependent on political favors such as subsidies, tariffs, antitrust harassment of competitors, etc.) are well aware of the suffocating influence of bureaucracy and are saddened and frustrated by the trend. Yet, ironically (just as with the individual taxpayer described above) the business community itself continues to provide the vital cooperation without which bureaucracy could not function.

Again, the regulator is painfully dependent upon the regulated. For example, the first step in an antitrust suit will often be a demand for a mountain of company records on which the government can build its case. And the company, ever desiring to be the "good citizen," will dig them out. During the height of the first energy crisis government agencies were so bereft of information they had to turn to the private companies for the data on which subsequent regulations could be based. From the caverns of bureaucracy pours forth a continuous flood of questionaires which businessmen obediently answer, forms which they obediently fill out, and commandments to which they obediently adhere.

Why does the businessman cooperate so readily with the bureaucrat? Not merely because of the law; as the experience of Prohibition indicated, obnoxious laws can be evaded easily enough if people choose to evade. The businessman's remarkable compliance may be due largely to his uncertain conscience on the subject of the profit motive. In our current intellectual climate profit-seeking is "greed," and the least the guilt-ridden businessman can do to expiate the sin is to cooperate with his "selfless" antagonist, the bureaucrat.

But in spite of what our intellectual betters tell us, self-interest is what freedom is all about. And the individual, whether businessman or hippie, egghead or hardhat, should not be shy about saying so.

Nor should the businessman hesitate to contrast his own function with that of the bureaucrat. The businessman (most of them, anyway) deals in persuasion, cooperation and productive skill, while the bureaucrat, in contrast, deals exclusively in force. To suppose that a Bill Gates has a "moral obligation" to cooperate with the armed bureaucrats of Antitrust is humbug. If anything, the obligation is not to cooperate, but to resist.

Henry G. Manne, Professor of Law and Political Science at the University of Rochester, is unequivocal in urging businessmen to reconsider their compliant attitude toward bureaucracy. Twenty-five years ago, addressing the 78th Annual Congress of American Industry, he declared,

> The threats of controls and higher taxes, the vilifications by politicians and the media, and the calls to patriotism and social responsibility are but the carrots and sticks of political bullies who can ultimately rationalize the last ounce of control over our private lives.
>
> If you have any faith in the economic and social miracle that is the free market system, use every legal means at your command to vex, confuse, delay, undermine and avoid every regulation adopted

or proposed by Congress, the administration, and the bureaucracy. Instruct your lawyers and your accountants to stay as narrowly within the letter of the law as they possibly can while still keeping you out of jail. You are not *legally* obliged to follow the spirit of the law and not *morally* obliged to follow the spirit of a law that is without any redeeming economic or social justification.

Force the government into litigation at every turn. Whenever possible, on constitutional or other colorable grounds, seek individually or in a class action to enjoin the enforcement of price controls and allocation regulations. Force the government to prove the constitutionality of every one of these intrusions, and seek declaratory judgments when there is the slightest possibility of confusion in the interpretation of regulations.[5]

A spirit of noncooperation was starting to emerge in the late 1970s. When OSHA inspectors paid a surprise visit to F. G. Barlow's plumbing shop in Pocatello, Idaho, they received a nasty shock: Barlow refused to admit them without a search warrant. The case went all the way to the Supreme Court which, in May of 1978, sided with Barlow. This was a landmark case which sent ripples of dismay through all of bureaucracy. Stung by the adverse publicity, OSHA went so far as to retract a few of its sillier rules. (For example, it's no longer a matter of federal law that toilet seats be open at the front.) In the meanwhile, the American Conservative Union, which had helped finance Barlow's case, went on to contact 170,000 employers previously inspected by OSHA, suggesting that in the future they should also reject OSHA inspectors who lacked a search warrant.

The spate of non-cooperation was not limited to smaller companies. General Motors, Chrysler and American Motors tied up the FTC in separate lawsuits to prevent fishing expeditions through company records; Polaroid sued the EPA over invasion of privacy; Dow Chemical did the same. When Sears, Roebuck canceled its government contracts rather than contend further with a hodge-podge of contradictory "fair employment" regulations, bureaucracy was stunned. The Labor Department affirmative action enforcement chief declared angrily that "Sears has told us to shove our contracts," but that he was determined to bring about an era of enforcement "tougher than ever." But this was just the shouting of a petty bully whose bluff had been called.

By withholding its cooperation the business community could, if it chose to, reverse the tide of bureaucratic encroachment. But if self-interest alone were not sufficient reason to withhold that cooperation, the businessman might consider as well that the tremendous costs of regulation are ultimately passed on to consumers, and the burden falls most heavily upon the poor. In this light, resistance to the state might be, in fact, the truest expression of "social conscience." As Thoreau put it,

> If the injustice is part of the necessary friction of the machine of government, let it go, let it go: perchance it will wear smooth—certainly the machine will wear out...but if it is of such a nature that it requires you to be the agent of injustice to another, then, I say break the law. Let your life be a counter friction to stop the machine. What I have to do is to see, at any rate, that I do not lend myself to the wrong which I condemn.

The real power of the state does not lie in its guns or jail cells but in the confused willingness of individuals to subordinate their legitimate rights to some alleged "greater good." And when this sanction is withdrawn, the state is in trouble.

Twilight of the state: The public school system may be taken as a microcosm of the failure of political force as an effective way to run things. Insulated from the feedback of the marketplace, mistakes are not corrected; they metastasize. A few decades ago we had the infamous "look-and-say" reading instruction, with phonics pushed to the background. A disaster. Then we had the "life adjustment" fad. Another fiasco. Then the bewildering "new math." Another failure. Most recently, we are treated to the utter silliness of the "self esteem" movement. Over the years, informed people have cried out, "stop this nonsense," but the juggernaut of public school quackery, undeterred by the displeasure of mere parents, and nourished by an ever-increasing torrent of tax money, has plowed onward and downward.

And so it will be with any institution maintained by force: immune from the feedback of the marketplace, it will inexorably deliver less and less while costing more and more, all the while spiraling slowly into decay and stagnation.

Political force is simply not the way to run things, and maybe the message is starting to be absorbed. Across the spectrum of human activity, people are turning away from government as the all-purpose problem-solver. As noted in previous chapters, alternatives proliferate: private schools, private protection, private mail, private communities. The motives are not so much ideological as practical: the private sector works better.

Movement toward the marketplace is accelerating, and a major factor is technology. Technology has always been a liberating influence. The invention of the printing press meant that people were no longer so dependent on the authority of the Catholic Church. The telegraph, telephone and automobile have all tended to emancipate the individual from traditional restraints.

The electronics age accelerates the process at a furious pace. The broadcast media no longer consist of three major networks centered in New York City and sharing a common world-view with Washington, D.C.; there now exists a wide variety of cable channels and satellite networks along with thousands of independent TV and radio stations, all of which have the capacity for independent action and editorial opinion. The Internet also provides an information source quite apart from traditional avenues. As the information age becomes more diverse it simply outruns the ability of the bureaucrat to regulate it. At the same time the economic structure becomes ever-more widely dispersed. As Smokestack America declines, with its immense concentrations of labor and capital, the trend is toward smaller companies and more of them. At the extreme is the so-called "electronic cottage," whose occupant used to work at an office in the city but who now stays at home with his or her computer, beyond the reach of the union organizer—and perhaps beyond the reach of the IRS as well.

Aided by technology, people are "voting with their feet" by pulling away from the traditional government institutions. Television and computer classrooms offer viable alternatives to the centralized public schools; electronic protection measures linked to a central office reduce our reliance on the municipal police department; electronic mail cuts deeply into the postal monopoly. To the consternation of the IRS a dispersed and complex economy provides the cover for a huge and growing underground economy, working "off the books." And an off-shore bank account is only a computer-click away.

The "sanction of the victim" is gradually being withdrawn, and the impact upon state authority is profound. In the past, those who have protested the ever-expanding claims of government have been routinely trashed as "selfish," or "mean spirited," but the time-worn tactic of *moral intimidation* is wearing thin. World War II is ended, the Cold War is over, and the wartime acceptance of top-down political authority has largely evaporated. Some deplore the trend, seeing in it a loss of "national purpose," or "brotherhood," or "compassion," but they are mistaken. The trend away from government should not be deplored, but welcomed. Government is not "national purpose," or "brotherhood," or "compassion"; it is simply force, and the less of it the better.

Historian Will Durant observed that "Civilization begins with the first voluntary act—and ends with the last." Through most of the twentieth century we have relied increasingly on the compulsory state to solve our problems—and the result is a society increasingly corrupted and demeaned by politics.

There are better ways to run things. It is time to abandon the institutions of political force and move on. The political state is in its twilight. It has served its limited historical purpose. As MacCallum put it, government is merely the "unstable transition" between the society of kinship and the society of contract. The next plateau in social evolution—if we can achieve it—is a society based not on political force but on the voluntary alternatives of the marketplace.

And this, finally, is what a free society is all about.

Appendix:
Tom Smith and His
Incredible Bread Machine

Tom Smith
and His Incredible Bread Machine

Part I

This is the legend of a man whose name
Was a household word: a man whose fame
Burst on the world like an atom bomb.
Smith was his last name; first name: Tom.

The argument goes on today.
"He was a villain," some will say.
"No! A hero!" others declare.
Or was he both? Well, I despair;
The fight will last 'til kingdom come;
Was Smith a hero? Or was Smith a bum?
So, listen to the story and it's up to you
To decide for *yourself* as to which is true!

Now, Smith, an inventor, had specialized
In toys. So people were surprised
When they found that he instead
Of making toys, was *baking bread!*
The news was flashed by CBS
Of his incredible success.
Then NBC jumped in in force,
Followed by the *Times*, of course.
The reason for their rapt attention,
The nature of his new invention,
The way to make bread he'd conceived
Cost less than people could believe!
And not just make it! This device
Could in addition *wrap and slice!*
The price per loaf, one loaf or many:
The miniscule sum of under one penny!

Can you imagine what this meant?
Can you comprehend the consequent?
The first time yet the world well fed!
And all because of Tom Smith's bread!

Not the last to see the repercussions
Were the Red Chinese, and, of course, the Rusians,
For Capitalist bread in such array
Threw the whole red block into black dismay!
Nonetheless, the world soon found
That bread was plentiful the world around.
Thanks to Smith and all that bread,
A grateful world was at last well fed!

But isn't it a wondrous thing
How quickly fame is flown?
Smith, the hero of today
Tomorrow, scarcely known!
Yes, the fickle years passed by.
Smith was a billionaire.
But Smith himself was now forgot,
Though bread was everywhere.
People, asked from where it came,
Would very seldom know.
They would simply eat and ask,
"Was not it always so?"

However, Smith cared not a bit,
For millions ate his bread,
And "Everything is fine," thought he.
"I'm rich and they are fed!"

Everything was fine, he thought?
He reckoned not with fate.
Note the sequence of events
Starting on the date
On which inflation took its toll,
And to a slight extent,

The price on every loaf increased:
It went to one full cent!

A sharp reaction quickly came.
People were concerned.
A White House aide expressed dismay.
Then the nation learned
That Russia lodged a sharp protest.
India did the same.
"Exploitation of the Poor!"
Yet, who was there to blame?

And though the clamor ebbed and flowed,
All that Tom would say
Was that it was but foolish talk
Which soon would die away.
And it appeared that he was right.
Though on and on it ran,
The argument went 'round and 'round
But stopped where it began.

> There it stopped, and people cried,
> "For heaven's sake, we can't decide!
> It's relative! Beyond dispute,
> There's no such thing as 'absolute'!
> And though we try with all our might,
> Since nothing's ever black or white,
> All that we can finally say is
> 'Everything one shade of grey is'!"
> So people cried out, "Give us light!
> We can't tell what's wrong from right!"

To comprehend confusion,
We seek wisdom at its source.
To whom, then did the people turn?
The Intellectuals, of course!

And what could be a better time
For them to take the lead,

Than at their International Conference
On Inhumanity and Greed.
For at this weighty conference,
Once each year we face
The moral conscience of the world—
Concentrated in one place.

At that mighty conference were
A thousand, more or less,
Of intellectuals and bureaucrats,
And those who write the press.
And from Yale and Harvard
The professors; all aware
The fate of Smith would now be known.
Excitement filled the air!

"The time has come," the chairman said,
"To speak of many things:
Of duty, bread and selfishness,
And the evil that it brings.
For, speaking thus we can amend
That irony of fate
That gives to unenlightened minds
The power to create.

"Since reason tells us that it can't,
Therefore let us start
Not by thinking with the mind,
But only with the heart!
Since we believe in *people*, then,"
At last the chairman said,
"We must meet our obligation
To see that they are fed!"

And so it went, one by one,
Denouncing *private greed*;
Denouncing those who'd profit thus
From other people's need!

Then, suddenly each breath was held,
For there was none more wise
Than the nation's foremost Pundit
Who now rose to summarize:

"My friends," he said, (they all exhaled)
"We see in these events
The flouting of the Higher Law—
And its consequence.
We must again remind ourselves
Just why mankind is cursed:
Because we fail to realize
Society comes first!

"Smith placed himself above the group
To profit from his brothers.
He failed to see the Greater Good,
Is Service, friends, to Others!"

With boldness and with vision, then,
They ratified the motion
To dedicate to all mankind
Smith's bread—and their devotion!

The conference finally ended.
It had been a huge success.
The intellectuals had spoken.
Now others did the rest.

The professors joined in all the fuss,
And one was heard to lecture thus:
(For clarity, he spoke in terms
Of Mother Nature, birds and worms):

"That early birds should get the worm
Is clearly quite unfair.
Wouldn't it much nicer be
If all of them would share?
But selfishness and private greed

Seem part of nature's plan,
Which Mother Nature has decreed
For bird. But also Man?
The system which I question now,
As you are well aware,
(I'm sure you've heard the term before),
Is *Business, Laissez-Faire!*

"So students, let me finally say
That we must find a nobler way.
So, let us fix the race that all
May finish side-by-side;
The playing field forever flat,
The score forever tied.
To achieve this end, of course,
We turn to government—and force.
So, if we have to bring Smith down,
As indeed we should,
I'm sure you will agree with me,
It's for the Greater Good!"

Comments in the nation's press
Now scorned Smith and his plunder:
"What right had he to get so rich
On other people's hunger?"
A prize cartoon depicted Smith
With fat and drooping jowls
Snatching bread from hungry babes,
Indifferent to their howls.

One night, a TV star cried out,
"Forgive me if I stumble,
But I don't think, I kid you not,
That Smith is very humble!"
Growing bolder, he leaped up,
(Silencing the cheers)
"Humility!" he cried to all—
And then collapsed in tears!

The clamor rises all about;
Now hear the politician shout:
"What's Smith done, so rich to be?
Why should Smith have more than thee?
So, down with Smith and all his greed;
I'll protect your right to *need!*"

Then Tom found to his dismay
That certain businessmen would say,
"The people now should realize
It's time to cut Smith down to size,
For he's betrayed his public trust
(And taken all that bread from us!)"

Well, since the Public does come first,
It could not be denied
That in matters such as this,
The public must decide.
So, SEC became concerned,
And told the press what *it* had learned:
"It's obvious that he's guilty
—Of what we're not aware—
Though actually and factually
We're sure there's *something* there!"

And Antitrust now took a hand.
Of course it was appalled
At what it found was going on.
The "bread trust" it was called.

"Smith has too much crust," they said.
"A deplorable condition
That Robber Barons profit thus
From cutthroat competition!"

WELL!

This was getting serious!
So Smith felt that he must

Have a friendly interview
With SEC and 'Trust.
So, hat in hand, he went to them.
They'd surely been misled;
No rule of law had he defied.
But then their lawyer said:

"The rule of law, in complex times,
Has proved itself deficient.
We much prefer the rule of men.
It's vastly more efficient.

"So, nutshell-wise, the way it is,
The law is what we *say* it is!

"So, let me state the present rules,"
The lawyer then went on,
"These very simple guidelines
You can rely upon:
You're *gouging on your prices*
If you charge more than the rest.
But it's *unfair competition*
If you think you can charge less!

"A second point that we would make,
To help avoid confusion:
Don't try to charge the *same* amount,
For that would be *collusion*!

"You must compete—but not too much,
For if you do, you see,
Then the market would be yours—
And that's monopoly!
Oh, don't dare monopolize!
We'd raise an awful fuss,
For that's the greatest crime of all!
(Unless it's done by us!)"

"I think I understand," said Tom.
"And yet, before I go,
How does one get a job like yours?
I'd really like to know!"

The lawyer rose then with a smile;
"I'm glad you asked," said he.
"I'll tell you how I got my start
And how it came to be."

(His secretaries gathered 'round
As their boss did thus expound:)

"When I was a lad going off to school,
I was always guided by this golden rule:
Let others take the lead in things, for heaven's sake,
So if things go wrong—why, then it's *their* mistake!"
    (So if things go wrong—why, then it's *their* mistake!)

"Following this precept it came to pass
I became the president of my senior class.
Then on to college where my profs extolled
The very same theory from the very same mold!"
    (The very same theory from the very same mold!)

"Let others take the chances, and I would go along.
Then I would let them know where they all went wrong!
So successful was my system that then indeed,
I was voted most likely in my class to succeed!"
    (He was voted most likely in his class to succeed!)

"Then out into the world I went, along with all the rest,
Where I put my golden rule to the ultimate test.
I avoided all of commerce at whatever the cost—
And because I never ventured, then I also never lost!"
    (And because he never ventured, then he also never lost!)

"With this unblemished record then, I quickly caught the eye
Of some influential people 'mongst the powers on high.

And so these many years among the mighty I have sat,
Having found my niche as a bureaucrat!"
   (Having found his niche as a bureaucrat!)

"To be a merchant prince has never been my goal,
For I'm qualified to play a more important role:
Since I've never failed in business, this of course assures
That I'm qualified beyond dispute *to now run yours!*"
   (That he's qualified beyond dispute to *now run yours!*)

"Thanks; that clears it up," said Tom.

     The lawyer said, "I'm glad!
     We try to serve the public good.
     We're really not so bad!

     "Now, in disposing of this case,
     If you wish to know just how,
     Go up to the seventh floor;
     We're finalizing now!"

So, Tom went to the conference room
Up on the seventh floor.
He raised his hand, about to knock,
He raised it—but no more—
For what he overheard within
Kept him outside the door!
A sentence here, a sentence there—
Every other word—
He couldn't make it out (he hoped),
For this is what he heard:

     "Mumble, mumble, let's not fumble!
     Mumble, mumble, what's the charge?
     Grumble, grumble, he's not humble?
     Private greed? Or good of all?

     "Public Interest, Rah! Rah! Rah!
     Business, Business, Bah! Bah! Bah!

"Say, now this now we confess
That now this now is a mess!
Well now, what now do we guess?
Discharge? Which charge would be best?

"How 'bout 'Greed and Selfishness'?
Oh, wouldn't *that* be fun?
It's vague enough to trip him up
No matter *what* he's done!

"We don't produce or build a thing!
But before we're through,
We allow that now we'll show Smith how
We handle those who do!

"We serve the public interest;
We make up our own laws;
Oh, golly gee, how selflessly
We serve the public cause!

"For we're the ones who make the rules
At 'Trust and SEC,
So bye and bye we'll get that guy;
Now, what charge will it be?

"Price too high? Or price too low?
Now, which charge will we make?
Well, we're not loath to charging both
When public good's at stake!

"But can we go one better?
How 'bout monopoly?
No muss, no fuss, oh clever us!
Right-O! Let's charge all three!

"But why stop here? We have one more!
Insider Trading! Number four!
We've not troubled to define
This crime in any way so,

This allows the courts to find
Him guilty 'cause we say so!"

So, that was the indictment.
Smith's trial soon began.
It was a *cause célèbre*
Which was followed 'cross the land.
In his defense Tom only said,
"I'm rich, but all of you are fed!
Is that bargain so unjust
That I should now be punished thus?"

Tom fought it hard all the way.
But it didn't help him win.
The jury took but half an hour
To bring this verdict in:

"Guilty! Guilty! We agree!
He's guilty of this plunder!
He had no right to get so rich
On other people's hunger!"

"Five years in jail!" the judge then said.
"You're lucky it's not worse!
Robber Barons must be taught
Society Comes First!
As flies to wanton boys," he leered,
"Are we to men like these!
They exploit us for their sport!
Exploit us as they please!"

The sentence seemed a bit severe,
But mercy was extended.
In deference to his mother's pleas,
One year was suspended.
And what about the Bread Machine?
Tom Smith's little friend?
Broken up and sold for scrap.
Some win. Some lose. **The end.**

EPILOGUE

Now, bread is baked by government.
And as might be expected,
Everything is well controlled—
The public well protected.

True, loaves cost ten dollars each.
But our leaders do their best.
The selling price is half a cent.
Taxes pay the rest!

end of part I

In Part II, not included here, the narrator debates the issues of capitalism with his excitable friend, Jack. As Jack sees it, the status quo is pretty much OK:

> "If one needs what others earn,
> No longer need one steal it!
> Government now does the job,
> And people hardly feel it!"

But in the end, Jack is mugged by reality.

Parts I & II from R. W. Grant's *Tom Smith and His Incredible Bread Machine* (Manhattan Beach, Calif.: Quandary House, 1978). The Quandary House website is at http://www.quandaryhouse.com/. Illustrations by Richard Stein.

Notes

Notes to Chapter 1: The Robber Barons

1. Matthew Josephson, *The Robber Barons* (New York: Harcourt, Brace and World, 1962), foreword, p. vi.
2. Ibid, p. 126.
3. Ibid, p. 66.
4. Ibid, pp. 18–19.
5. Ibid, p. 131.
6. Ibid, p. 78.
7. Ibid, pp. 92–93.
8. Ibid, p. 165.
9. Ibid, p. 111.
10. Ibid, p. 112.
11. Ibid, pp. 112–113.
12. Ibid, 162–163.
13. Dominick T. Armentano, *Antitrust and Monopoly* (Oakland, Calif: Independent Institute, second edition, 1990), p. 67.
14. John K. Winkler, *Morgan the Magnificent* (Garden City, N.Y.: Doubleday, Doran and Co., 1932), p. 198.

Notes to Chapter 2: The Progressive Era

1. Gabriel Kolko, *The Triumph of Conservatism* (1963. Reprint. Chicago: University of Chicago Press, 1967), p. 13.
2. Ibid, p. 35.
3. Ibid, p. 36.
4. Ibid, p. 59.
5. Ibid, p. 135.
6. Cited by John K. Winkler, *Morgan the Magnificent* (Garden City, N.Y.: Doubleday, Doran & Co., 1932) p. 284.
7. Kolko, op. cit, p. 259.
8. Ibid, p. 259.
9. Ibid, pp. 274–275.
10. Ibid. p. 277.

11. Harold Fleming, *Ten Thousand Commandments* (Irvington-on-Hudson, N.Y.: Foundation for Economic Education, 1951).
12. *FTC v Morton Salt Co.*, 334 U.S. (1948).
13. John Kenneth Galbraith, *American Capitalism* (New York: Houghton Mifflin Company, 1956) p. 143.
14. After three years of stalling Antitrust finally dropped the suit.
15. See the *Wall Street Journal*, April 29, 1965. The Consolidated Food Corporation, a large food processor, distributor and chain store operator, had merged with the Gentry Company, a small manufacturer of food seasoning. The FTC claimed that Consolidated encouraged its suppliers to patronize Gentry.
16. "Justice Agency Bids for Stiffer Penalties Including Jail on Corporate Price Fixers," *Wall Street Journal*, October 20, 1976.
17. Cited by D. T. Armentano, "The Great Electrical Equipment Conspiracy," *Reason*, March, 1972.
18. "A Talk With Antitrust Chief William Baxter," *Wall Street Journal*, March 4, 1982. Baxter is now professor emeritus at Stanford Law School.
19. Mason is referring to the Moog Industries Case, which he cites in his book.
20. Lowell Mason, *Language of Dissent* (New Canaan, Conn.: Long House, 1950), p. 68.

Notes to Chapter 3: Boom and Bust

1. The *Encyclopedia Britannica* lists the nation's "long, severe depressions" as starting in the years 1837, 1873, 1882, and 1929. (The 1882 relapse is often regarded as a continuation of the depression of 1873.)
2. This does not mean that interest rates would necessarily be low in an absolute sense, down to 5% or 4% or 3%. Depending on other conditions during the inflationary boom they might even appear to be "high" at 10% or 15%. Whatever the rate, however, it is lower than it would have been in the absence of government intervention. Accordingly, the interest rate is no longer reflecting the true economic picture. The feedback loop has been disrupted.
3. But suppose the inflation is not halted? Suppose the inflation is continued year after year and decade after decade? Like a narcotic, the dosage must become greater and greater, and there will result ulti-

mately a period of hyper-inflation such as that experienced by the German Weimar Republic of the early twenties. The outcome in this case is far worse than any depression: it means the dislocation of the entire economic structure.

4. *The Federal Reserve System: Purposes and Functions*, Fiftieth Anniversary Edition (Washington, D.C.: Board of Governors of the Federal Reserve System, 1963), pp. 69, 75.

5. Murray N. Rothbard, *America's Great Depression* (Princeton, N.J.: D. Van Nostrand, 1963).

6. Ibid, pp. 117, 119.

7. Ibid, p. 113.

8. Ibid, p. 134.

9. Benjamin M. Anderson, *Economics and the Public Welfare* (Princeton, N.J.: D. Van Nostrand, 1949). pp. 182–183.

10. By comparison, over the eight-year period between 1988 and 1996 the M2 money supply increased by about 28%.

11. Rothbard, op. cit., p. 152.

12. In his book *The Great Crash*, John Kenneth Galbraith dismisses this thesis as "a tribute only to recurrent preference in economic matters for formidable nonsense." He explains that "the explanation [that the Federal Reserve System was responsible for the speculation and the ultimate collapse] assumes that people will always speculate if only they can get the money to finance it. Nothing could be farther from the case. There were times before and there have been long periods since when credit was plentiful and cheap—far cheaper than in 1927–29—and when speculation was negligible."

But Galbraith misses the point in saying only that low interest rates do not necessarily cause overspeculation. Indeed, in a free market the interest rates would no longer be low! If borrowing became excessive credit would tighten and interest rates would move higher, thus damping out the boom before it got out of hand. In the '20s, however, government-inspired credit expansion eliminated this restraint.

Notes to Chapter 4: The Great Depression

1. Murray N. Rothbard, *America's Great Depression* (Princeton, N.J.: D. Van Nostrand, 1963), p. 179.

2. Ibid, p. 218.

3. Benjamin M. Anderson, *Economics and the Public Welfare* (Princeton, N.J.: D. Van Nostrand, 1949), p. 222.

4. Rothbard, op. cit., p. 271.

5. Ibid, p. 295.

6. Anderson, op. cit., p. 280n.

7. Garet Garrett, *The People's Pottage* (Caldwell, Idaho: Caxton Press, 1958) p. 38.

8. An amendment to an agricultural act passed on April 20, 1933.

9. Anderson, op. cit., p. 317.

10. Ibid, p. 319. Gore was later purged from office by Roosevelt.

11. Ibid, pp. 348–349.

12. Garrett, op. cit., p. 35.

13. *Collier's*, October 25, 1947.

14. Garrett, op. cit., p. 36.

15. Fireside Chat, October 22, 1933.

16. *A. L. A. Schecter v U.S.*, 295 U.S. 495 (1935).

17. John Maynard Keynes, "National Self-Sufficiency," *Yale Review*, Summer, 1933, pp. 760–761.

18. James Strachey Barnes, *Universal Aspects of Fascism* (London: Williams and Norgate, 1929), pp. 113–114.

19. There are those who argue, however, that pump priming "gets things moving" by spending money that would otherwise be hoarded were it left in private hands. But one reason people hoard their money rather than invest it is that economic conditions are uncertain. And the principal reason for the uneasiness of the 1930s was the disposition of New Dealers to engage in interventionist measures such as pump priming!

20. Quoted by Katie Louchheim in *The Making of the New Deal* (Cambridge, Mass.: Harvard University Press, 1984).

Notes to Chapter 5: Capitalism and the Intellectuals

1. Bertrand Russell, *The Impact of Science on Society* (New York: Columbia University Press, 1951), pp. 19–20. This and several of the following citations are taken from an outstanding little book called *Capitalism and the Historians* (Chicago: University of Chicago Press, 1954; "Phoenix" paperback edition, 1963) edited by F. A. Hayek. Essays were contributed by historians T. S. Ashton, Hayek, Louis Hacker, W. H. Hutt,

and Bertrand de Jouvenal. Page numbers refer to the "Phoenix" edition.

2. *Capitalism and the Historians*, pp. 171–172.

3. Ibid, p. 176.

4. Ludwig von Mises, *Human Action*, (New Haven, Conn.: Yale University Press, 1949), p. 615.

5. Perhaps the reformers should have inquired into the fate of those children put out of work by the child labor laws.

6. Hayek, et. al., op. cit. p. 50.

7. Ibid., op. cit., p. 157.

8. Ibid., op. cit., p. 117.

9. The *Rocky Mountain News* noted recently that at the University of Colorado at Boulder, Democrats on the faculty outnumber Republicans by a ratio of 31-to-1. There's not a single Republican in the Journalism Department. Reported by Vincent Carrol, "Republican Professors? Sure, There's One," *The Wall Street Journal*, May 11, 1998, editorial page.

10. Arthur Schlesinger, *The Vital Center* (Boston: Houghton Mifflin Company, 1941), pp. 33 & 28.

11. Joseph A. Schumpeter, *Capitalism, Socialism and Democracy* (New York: Harper and Row, Colophon Edition, 1975), p. 145. In describing the intellectual Schumpeter notes "the absence of direct responsibility for practical affairs," and adds that "his main chance of asserting himself lies in his actual or potential nuisance value."

12. Arthur Schlesinger, Jr. in his report to the Democratic National Committee in 1959.

13. Ibid.

14. Cited by Bastiat in *The Law* (Irvington-on-Hudson, N.Y.: The Foundation for Economic Education, 1962).

15. Paul Johnson, "The Heartless Lovers of Mankind," *Wall Street Journal*, January 5, 1987.

Notes to Chapter 6: Regulation Today

1. Henry G. Manne, *Insider Trading and the Stock Market* (New York: The Free Press, 1966).

2. Henry G. Manne, "Insider Trading and the Law Professors," *Vanderbilt Law Review*, April, 1970.

3. "Stock Trading Before the Announcement of Tender Offers: Insider Trading or Market Anticipation?" The Office of the Chief Economist, SEC, Feb. 24, 1987; footnote 4.

4. Thomas Ricks, "Dingell Opposes Bill Defining Insider Trading," *Wall Street Journal*, March 9, 1988, p. 2.

5. *Washington Post*, April 3, 1985.

6. Felix Rohatyn, "Junk Bonds and Other Securities Swill," *Wall Street Journal*, April 18, 1985, p. 30.

7. Mark Hosnaball, "Money-Mad Mike," *Playboy*, January 1991. Ironically, there appeared in the same issue an article lauding the vision of Ted Turner in creating his new TV network. This venture had been financed by Milken's junk bonds.

8. Parking refers to the temporary placement of stock with an associate for the purpose of disguising ownership. The stock is reclaimed later at the original price regardless of any change in the market price. Because the "beneficial ownership" has really not changed, the government regards such a transaction as spurious. One purpose of stock parking might be to get around capitalization requirements: by having cash in hand rather than the sequestered stock, net capitalization could be overstated.

9. One of the conditions of the plea bargain was that Milken provide damaging information about others. The information he provided was close to worthless, but the sentence was finally reduced to two years.

10. The full passage: "[F]orcing PC manufacturers to take one Microsoft product as a condition of buying a monopoly product like Windows 95 is not only a violation of the court order, it's plain wrong." Quoted in "Microsoft Under Attack, But Who Is It Hurting?" *USA Today*, October 23, 1997.

11. Debora Vrana and Thomas S. Mulligan, "Intel Violates Antitrust Law, FTC Suit Alleges," *Los Angeles Times*, June 9, 1998.

12. Alan Greenspan, "Antitrust," in *Capitalism; The Unknown Ideal*, by Ayn Rand (New York: New American Library, 1967).

13. Glen Yago, "The Regulatory Reign Of Terror," *Wall Street Journal* editorial page, March 4, 1992.

14. George Gilder, "The War Against Wealth," *Wall Street Journal*, September 27, 1990, editorial page.

Notes to Chapter 7: Why Principles Matter

1. Richard S. Wheeler, "Lead Us Not into Temptation," *Insight and Outlook* (around 1962).
2. The terms "forestalling" and "regrating" referred to economic practices somewhat similar to today's wholesaling, i.e., buying a large quantity of produce with the expectation of selling at a profit later on.

Notes to Chapter 8: Individualism

1. Still, Smith knew perfectly well that self-interest was not exclusively a matter of material gain. As he noted in his first book, *The Theory of Moral Sentiments*, a person may value the happiness of another "though he derives nothing from it, except the pleasure of seeing it."
2. Robert Whiting, *You Gotta Have Wa* (New York: MacMillan, 1989), p. 70.
3. Definitions are from the *Webster* unabridged, Second Edition.
4. *Webster* defines sacrifice as "To suffer loss of, give up, renounce, injure or destroy for an end (specified or implied) regarded as superior." The question, of course, is who makes the decision.
5. It's interesting to note that modern feminism, at least in its early days, represented a rejection of altruism: of the notion that the woman's highest moral duty was selfless devotion to the whims and demands of husband and children. The feminist message was one of individualism: that the woman had the right to live her own life in accordance with her own values. (Of course, what feminism stands for today is another matter.)
6. Cited by Arthur Schlesinger, *The Vital Center* (Boston: Houghton Mifflin Company, 1962), p. 54.
7. Ibid., p. 56.

Notes to Chapter 9: Private Property

1. The term private property refers not merely to one's home or bank account or business. One's skills, one's convictions, one's person, etc., are equally one's private property. In short, private property includes all of the products of one's life acquired or maintained through one's own productive effort and/or through voluntary transaction with others.

2. From William Bradford's *History of Plymouth Plantation* (circa 1630), and from Captain John Smith's *The Generall Historie of Virginia, New England, and the Summer Isles* (1624).

3. Garrett Hardin, "The Tragedy of the Commons," *Science*, December 13, 1968.

4. Oscar W. Cooley, "Pollution and Property," *The Freeman*, June, 1972.

5. See Jane S. Shaw and Richard Stroup's article "Gone Fishin' " in *Reason*, August-September, 1988.

6. William Tucker, "Conservation in Deed," *Reason*, May, 1983.

7. Herbert L. Matthews, *Fruits of Fascism* (New York: Harcourt, Brace and Co., 1943), pp. 144–145. Matthews was head of the *New York Times* Rome bureau during the greater part of Mussolini's reign.

8. *USA Today*, December 29, 1995, editorial page.

9. Linnet Myers, "Forfeiture Laws, Fair or Foul?" *Chicago Tribune*, March 12, 1996.

10. Ibid.

11. "Private Property vs. Public Rights," *USA Today*, February 6, 1995.

12. "EPA v. Private Property," *Wall Street Journal*, August 27, 1990, editorial page.

13. James S. Burling, "Don't Let Pro-Zoners California-ize Houston," *Houston Chronicle*, February 24, 1995, A:39.

14. True, the State pays for the property it seizes. But if eminent domain is justified by this fact, then there is nothing to prevent the State from nationalizing every scrap of private property merely by paying for it with the property owners' own tax money.

15. Martin Anderson, *The Federal Bulldozer* (Boston: M.I.T. Press, 1965).

Notes to Chapter 10: The Market Economy

1. Screenplay by Alvin Sargent, based on a play by Jerry Sterner.

2. This case is described by Dominick Armentano in *Antitrust and Monopoly* (Oakland, Calif.: The Independent Institute, 1996) pp. 112–118.

3. Quoted by Bruce Bartlet in "The Old Politics of a New Industrial Policy," *Wall Street Journal*, April 19, 1983, editorial page.

4. Charles Lane, TRB column, *The New Republic*, April 27, 1998.

Notes to Chapter 11: The Origin of Cooperation

1. Robert Axelrod, *The Evolution of Cooperation* (New York: Basic Books, 1984).

2. Claudia Rosett, "How Peru Got a Free Market Without Really Trying," *Wall Street Journal*, January 27, 1984.

Notes to Chapter 12: The Death of Diana

1. Peter Collier and David Horowitz, *Destructive Generation* (Los Angeles: Second Thoughts Books, 1995), p. 275.
2. Interestingly, the headmistress at the Madeira School was Jean Harris, now in prison for the murder of her lover.
3. Lucinda Franks and Thomas Powers, "The Destruction of Diana," *Readers Digest*, November, 1970.
4. Thomas Powers, *Diana: The Making of a Terrorist* (Boston: Houghton Mifflin Co., Boston, 1971; Bantam paperback edition 1971), pp. 111–112.

Notes to Chapter 13: The War Against the Poor

1. Myrna Oliver, "Unlicensed Contractor Fined $500 for Defying Court Order," *Los Angeles Times*, April 24, 1977.
2. "Get Out of Her Hair," *Wall Street Journal*, Sept. 4, 1998, op-ed page.
3. Walter E. Williams, *The State Against Blacks* (New York: New Press, 1982), ch. 6. Also Williams' "Put the Brakes on Taxicab Monopolies," *Wall Street Journal*, June 11, 1984, op-ed page.

Notes to Chapter 14: Rent Control versus the Poor

1. Senator Thomas F. Eagleton, "Why Rent Controls Don't Work," *Reader's Digest*, August, 1977.
2. "Report on the New York City Loan Program," Committee on Banking, Housing and Urban Affairs, U.S. Senate, Report 94–900, May 17, 1976. Cited by Ted Diensfrey in *Rent Control Myths and Realities* (Vancouver, BC: Fraser Institute, 1981), p. 11.
3. "End Rent Control," *New Amsterdam News*, May 1, 1976. Cited by Diensfrey.
4. Cary Lowe and Richard Blumberg, "Modern Regulations Protect Landlords as Well as Tenants," *Los Angeles Times*, November 20, 1977.
5. Interestingly, a program of direct assistance to those in need, the burden of which would have fallen on the entire community rather than on the apartment owners alone, seems not to have been considered.
6. These comments were taped, and the tape was later widely circulated, much to the chagrin of SMRR officials. Related by Mark E. Kann, *Middle Class Radicalism in Santa Monica* (Philadelphia: Temple University Press, 1986), p. 203.

7. For example, in 1988 Apt. #3 at 422 Hill St. rented for $332 per month while the virtually identical #6 rented for $519 per month. The discrepancy arose during the 1970s when the owner refrained for years from raising the rent of the elderly tenant in Apt. #3. "She was a dear old lady, and she just couldn't afford an increase," explained the owner. But the old lady finally moved away, and rent control prevented any significant adjustment. As a result, this apartment was kept permanently off the market, reserved for friends or left vacant.

8. Statement at the board meeting of October 27, 1988. An angry "tenants' rights" attorney later declared, "That's disgusting! I'd be delighted to sue her in behalf of her sub-tenant!" The response of the board, however, appeared to be a collective shrug.

9. Dave Larson, "Quest for Shelter Where the Mountains Meet No-Vacancies-by-the-Sea," *Los Angeles Times*, May 4, 1986, Part VI, p. 1.

10. Mark E. Kann, op. cit., p. 176.

11. For a while the permitted rent increases were a flat two-thirds of the CPI. Later, the system reverted to a more complex formula which came out to about the same figure.

12. Saul Rubin, "Rent Law Revisions Proposed," *Santa Monica Evening Outlook*, December 1, 1987, p. A1.

13. *Rent Control, Undermaintenance, and Housing Deterioration*, (Santa Monica, Calif.: Rand Corporation, 1982), #P-6779.

14. Tracy Wilkinson, "Owner Calls Dilapidated Building Product of Rent Control," *Los Angeles Times*, October 29, 1987.

15. Ibid.

16. A revealing expression used by supporters of a proposed ballot initiative to eliminate this exemption. Mentioned by Tracy Wilkinson, "Santa Monica to Weigh Slow-Growth, Rent Control Initiatives," *Los Angeles Times*, April 21, 1988.

17. Statement by Commissioner Penny Nagler, quoted by Louise Yarnell in "Sides Back Rent Plan in Theory," *Santa Monica Evening Outlook*, July 12, 1987, p. A1.

18. "We have lots of building going on for luxury hotels for rich people." Complaint by Commissioner Bauer at the board meeting of October 27, 1988.

19. Robert Lypsyte, "Waging the Rent Wars on the Far West Side," *New York Times*, June 22, 1997.

20. David Shulman, "SM City Council: Conservatives Posing as Radicals," *Santa Monica Evening Outlook*, July 23, 1981. Cited by Kann, op. cit, p. 176.

21. Mark Carnoy and Derek Shearer, *Economic Democracy: The Challenge of the 1980s* (Armonk, N. Y.: M.E. Sharpe, Inc., 1980) p. 402. Economic democracy, a term coined by Tom Hayden, describes the political movement founded by him in 1977, the Campaign for Economic Democracy.

22. Kann, op. cit., p. 130.

23. Ibid.

24. Frederic Bastiat, *The Law* (Irvington-on-Hudson, N.Y.: Foundation for Economic Education, 1962), p. 21.

Notes to Chapter 15: Big Labor

1. F. A. Harper, *Why Wages Rise* (Irvington-on-Hudson, N.Y.: Foundation for Economic Education, 1957).

2. See Burton W. Folsom, Jr., "The Minimum Wage's Disreputable Origins," *Wall Street Journal*, June 27, 1998, editorial page.

3. The NRA, a New Deal measure, already included minimum wage codes. As noted in Chapter Four, the former Director of Research for the NRA estimated that these codes forced about one-half million blacks onto relief in 1934.

4. "Let's Not Raise the Minimum Wage," *Fortune*, July, 1972.

5. Ibid.

6. Thomas Sowell, "Racism, Quotas and the Front Door," *Wall Street Journal*, July 29, 1978.

7. *Fortune*, December, 1968.

8. It was often claimed that the injunction was frequently used to forbid legitimate strikes. Where (and if) this was the case the labor injunction was indeed abused. However, where the injunction was used to forbid illegal acts, such as massed picketing or goon-squad violence, it was a legitimate measure and should not have been curtailed.

9. An episode described by Sylvester Petro in *The Kohler Strike* (Regency, 1961), pp. 84–85.

10. Indianapolis Wire Bound Box Co., 89 NLRB 617 (1950); *NLRB v Hopes Mfg. Co.*, 170 F.2d 962 (6th Cir. 1948); Winona Textile Mills, Inc., 160 F.2d 201 (8th Cir. 1947). Cited by Sylvester Petro, *The Labor Policy of the Free Society* (New York: Ronald, 1957), p. 246.

11. The Wagner Act itself does not oblige the employer to make any concessions at all. The NLRB, however, has evidently decreed otherwise.

12. E.g., AS. Beck Shoe Corp., 92 NLRB 1457 (1951); *NLRB v Winona Textile Mills, Inc.*, 160 F.2d 201 (8th Cir. 1947). Cited by Petro. op. cit., p. 242.

13. *Hickory Chair Mfg. Co. v NLRB*, 131 F.2d 549 (4th Cir. 1942); Cook Auto Machine Co., 84 NLRB 688 (1949), 184 F.2d 841 (6th Cir. 1910). Ibid.

14. *NLRB v Morris Kirk & Sons*, 151 F.2d 490 (9th Cir. 1941); *NLRB v Sun Tent-Luebbort Co.*, 151 F.2d 481 (9th Cir. 1945); Blue Ridge Shirt Mfg. Co., 70 NLRB 741 (1946). Ibid.

15. Sue McAllister, "U.S. Accuses Hotel of Awarding Unfair Raises," *Los Angeles Times*, June 10, 1998.

16. *Chicago Tribune*, December 27, 1996, 3, 3:5.

17. Diane Lewis, "Fired Worker Will Get Back Pay from Somerville Firm," *Boston Globe*, March 6, 1998, E, 3:2.

18. When in 1994 the United Steel Workers lost a close election at the Cambell Chain plant in York, Pennsylvania, it charged that the company had unfairly influenced the outcome. The company vigorously denied the charges, but an NLRB administrative judge recommended to the full board that the company be forced to bargain with the union anyway—without benefit of another election to decide the issue. The case is still pending. The parent company, Cooper Industries, vows to appeal the expected adverse ruling to the courts. See also, L. M. Sixel, "Cooper Ordered to Recognize Union," *Houston Chronicle*, April 14, 1995, C, 2:1.

19. Jim Barlow, "Board Labors at Killing Teamwork," *Houston Chronicle*, April 18, 1996.

20. D. Diane Hatch, "Employer-Established Employee Council Is Held Unlawful," *Workforce*, June 1998, v. 77, no. 6, p. 120.

21. In the *union shop* the employee must join the union within a certain time from the date of employment. In the *closed shop* the employee must belong to the union before he can be hired.

22. Arch Puddington, "Is Labor Back?," *Commentary*, July, 1998.

Notes to Chapter 16: The War on Drugs

1. Figures reported by Surgeon General Koop in 1988 were: drug abuse, 6000 deaths per year; alcohol, 125,000; cigarettes, 350,000.

2. Herbert Hill, "Anti-Oriental Agitation and the Rise of Working-Class Racism," *Society*, January-February, 1973; p. 52. Cited by Thomas Szasz in *Ceremonial Chemistry* (Holmes Beach, Fl.: Learning Publications, 1985) p. 78.

3. Ibid.

4. Quoted by David Musto, *The American Disease* (New Haven, Conn.: Yale University Press, 1973), p. 44.

5. *Literary Digest*, March 28, 1914, p. 687. Cited by Musto, op. cit., p. 255.

6. Dr. Edward Huntington Williams, "Negro Cocaine Fiends Are a New Southern Menace," *New York Times*, February 8, 1914, Part V, p. 12.

7. Jack Nelson and Ronald Ostrow, "Illegal Drug Scene Spurs Rise in Police Corruption," *Los Angeles Times*, June 13, 1998.

8. Joel Brinkley, "Shultz, in First Major Drug Speech, Says Control has Top Priority," *New York Times*, September 15, 1984, Part I, p. 5.

9. Marlene Simons, "Peruvian Rebels Halt U.S. Drive Against Cocaine," *New York Times*, August 13, 1984, Part I, p. 1.

10. On the other hand, perhaps it wouldn't. Ethan Nadelman points out that when a dozen states decriminalized possession of marijuana during the 1970s consumption declined just as it was declining elsewhere. (*Reason*, October, 1988, pp. 27–28).

11. Government policy makes no distinction between use and abuse, as evident from the foolish and short-lived "zero tolerance" program in which the Coast Guard was confiscating yachts upon discovery on board of minute amounts of marijuana. To the anti-drug warrior use and abuse are the same thing. But the public knows better, and these unrealistic policies simply dilute the credibility of all government efforts, even those which might deserve support.

12. Ronald Hamowy, et. al., *Dealing with Drugs* (San Francisco: Pacific Research Institute for Public Policy, 1987) p. 7.

13. Robert Scheer, "The Drug War Can't Abide Honest Stats," *Los Angeles Times*, July 21, 1998, editorial page.

Notes to Chapter 17: Environmentalism

1. When *60 Minutes* did a segment on the Kaiparowits controversy they did their filming in a more picturesque area 70 miles away, and the proposed site was never seen. Explained the producer, in a classic display of media chutzpah, "It's not interesting at all. There's nothing there."

2. "A Replay of Kaiparowits?" *Wall Street Journal*, October 20, 1977.

3. William G. Tucker, "The Environmentalists' Great Illusion," *Los Angeles Times*, May 26, 1979.

4. Cited by William G. Tucker in *Progress and Privilege* (Garden City, N.Y.: Anchor Press/Doubleday, 1982), p. 37.

5. Ibid.

6. Steve Chase, ed., *Defending the Earth: A Dialogue between Murray Bookchin and Dave Foreman* (Boston: South End Press, 1991), pp. 57–59. Cited by Ronald Bailey, *Eco-Scam* (New York: St. Martin's Press, 1993).

7. Ibid., pp. 73–75.

8. Paul Ehrlich and Anne Ehrlich, *The Population Explosion* (New York: Simon & Shuster, 1990), p. 175. (Cited by Bailey.)

9. Al Gore, *Earth in the Balance* (New York: Houghton Mifflin Company, 1992) p. 14.

10. Sharon Begley, "Audubon's Empty Nest," *Newsweek*, June 24, 1991, p. 57. Cited by Michael Fumento, *Science under Seige* (New York: William Morrow and Company, Inc., 1993).

11. Al Gore, "A New Initiative to Save the Planet," *Scientific American*, April, 1990, p. 124. Cited by Fumento.

12. Surface monitors are often located in populated areas which are influenced by the "urban heat island" effect. That is, these locations are slightly warmer due to the localized human activity: automobiles and the like. Moreover, as the population increases, the upward bias increases, giving the illusion of "global warming." Satellite and balloon measurements, of course, are not subject to these local inaccuracies.

13. Frederick Seitz, "A Major Deception on 'Global Warming'," *Wall Street Journal*, June 12, 1996, editorial page. Benjamin Santer, who was evidently responsible for the rewrite, responded in a letter to the editor (June 25, 1998) that "IPCC procedures *required* changes in response to [comments]." (Emphasis in the original.) To which Seitz replied (July 11, 1998), "Of course they do, but not after the governments have accepted the final draft."

14. Philip Abelson, "Uncertainties about Global Warming," *Science*, March 30, 1990, p. 1529. (Cited by Bailey.)

15. Quoted by Jonathan Schell, "Our Fragile Earth," *Discover*, October, 1989, p. 47. (Cited by Bailey and Fumento.)

16. David Brooks, "Journalists and Others for Saving the Planet," *Wall Street Journal*, October 5, 1989, A 28. (Cited by Fumento.)

17. From transcript of a speech by Barbara Pyle to the 1990 "Early Warnings" conference sponsored by the *Utne Reader* in Minneapolis. (Cited by Bailey.)

18. Teya Ryan, "Network Earth: Advocacy, Journalism and the Environment," *Gannett Center Journal*, Summer, 1990, p. 71. (Cited by Bailey.)

19. Robert James Bidinotto, "Environmentalism: Freedom's Foe for the 90's," *The Freeman*, November 1990, p. 418. (Cited by Fumento.)

20. "Babbit's Conspiracy," *Wall Street Journal*, August 8, 1997, op-ed page.

21. S. Fred Singer, *Hot Talk, Cold Science* (Oakland, Calif.: The Independent Institute, 1997) p. 41.

22. Stewart Brand, writing in the *Whole Earth Catalogue*. (Cited by Fumento.)

23. Jeremy Rifkin, *Algeny: A New Word—A New World* (New York: Penguin Books, 1984), p. 188. (Cited by Bailey.)

24. Ibid., p. 233.

25. Stephen Jay Gould, "Review of *Algeny*," *Discover*, January, 1985, 34–35. (Cited by Bailey.)

26. Interview by Bailey, op. cit., p. 103.

27. Paul R. Ehrlich, "Machine Guns and Idiot Children," *Not Man Apart* (a publication of Friends of the Earth), Vol. 5, #18, mid-September, 1975.

28. Ibid.

29. According to the USDA Forest Service, the forest coverage was 1100 million acres (46% of the total land area) in 1600, 675 million acres (30%) in 1920, and 737 million acres (33%) in 1992.

30. Quoted by John Fayhee, "Earth First and Foremost," *Backpacker*, September, 1988. (Cited by Bailey.)

31. David Savage, "Buzz Over a Fly Presents Challenge to Species Act," *Los Angeles Times*, June 15, 1998.

32. Letter to the editor from William H. DuBay, Costa Mesa, Calif., *Los Angeles Times*, June 20, 1998.

33. C. P. Snow, *The Two Cultures, and a Second Look* (London: Cambridge University Press, 1964.) pp. 25–26. (Cited by Fumento.)

Notes to Chapter 18: Escape from Public Education

1. From *Guidance Handbook for Teachers*, Wiseburn Schoool District, around 1960.
2. Cited in *National Review Bulletin*, March 2, 1965.
3. See Erica Carle's "Education without Taxation," *The Freeman*, March, 1962.
4. *The Life and Writings of Dewitt Clinton* (Baker and Scribner, 1849), p. 318; cited by Carle.
5. James Mill in *Westminster Review*, October, 1813. Cited by E.G. West, *Education and the State* (London: Institute of Economic Affairs, 1965), p. 136.
6. Ibid, p. 154.
7. E. G. West, "The Political Economy of American Public School Legislation," *Journal of Law and Economics*, Vol. X, October 1967, p. 105.
8. Ibid, p. 121 (from the 1849 Annual Report of the New York Superintendent of the Common Schools).
9. Ibid, p. 115 (from the 1846 Annual Report of the Secretary of the Massachusetts Board of Education).
10. Quoted by Carle, op. cit.
11. William Overend, "Alternatives to Public Education," *Los Angeles Times*, June 26, 1980.
12. Ibid.
13. From discussions with Ms. Blunt.
14. "Westside Story, An Inner-City School That Works," *Time*, December 26, 1977.
15. Paul Gigot, "The Effort to Tear Down a Teaching Hero," *Wall Street Journal*, March 15, 1982.
16. Gerald King, "Home Schooling: Up from the Underground," *Reason*, April, 1983.
17. Ibid.

Notes to Chapter 19: Ending the Postal Monopoly

1. Alvin F. Harlow, *Old Post Bags* (D. Appleton and Co., 1928) pp. 122–123.
2. Ibid, p. 117.
3. When James was driven from the throne three years later Dockwra was granted a pension of £500, and in 1697 was appointed controller of the

nationalized Penny Post. In 1700, however, the victim of bureaucratic jealousies, he was forced out of the enterprise which he had created.

4. Harlow, op. cit., pp. 122–123.
5. From a study by Ronald H. Coase, "The British Post Office and the Messenger Companies," *Journal of Law and Economics*, 1961, pp. 12–65.
6. Harlow, op. cit., p. 259.
7. Cited by James J. Martin in *Men Against the State* (Colorado Springs, Co.: Ralph Myles Publishing Co. , 1970), p. 170.
8. Harlow, op. cit., pp. 400–401.
9. Wayne E. Green, "Playing Post Office—Firms Find They Cannot Circumvent U.S. Mails," *Wall Street Journal*, June 5, 1967.
10. "Plan to Let Firms Deliver Some Mail for Business Ended," *Wall Street Journal*, September 17, 1974.
11. Fred Ferretti, "Private Mail Delivery and the Letter of the Law," *New York Times*, September 25, 1971.
12. "Magazines Desert U.S. Postal System," *Los Angeles Times*, November 23, 1978.
13. "Unions Charge Conspiracy on Postal Service," *Los Angeles Times*, March 31, 1976.
14. Bill McAllister, "Postal Service Vulnerable to Increased Competition, GAO Says," *Washington Post*, September 23, 1996.

Notes to Chapter 20: Farewell to City Hall

1. The rationale of the proprietary community was first investigated by the late industrialist/philosopher Spencer Heath in *Politics Versus Proprietorship* (mimeographed by him in 1935), in which he forecast proprietary administration of public services for profit as the social (market) alternative to political government. He elaborated upon this theme in the early 1940s in a major manuscript, *Citadel, Market and Altar*, which, upon the urging of his grandson, he privately published in 1957. From the 1950s Heath's predictions began to be supported by trends in the real estate field. MacCallum has examined this growing evidence in the light of modern anthropology and has published his findings in several articles and in his present book.
2. Spencer Heath MacCallum, *The Art of Community* (Palo Alto, Calif.: Institute for Humane Studies, 1970).
3. Peter Blake, "Mickey Mouse for Mayor!" *New York*, February 7, 1972, p. 41; excerpted in *Reason*, April, 1972, p. 10.

4. MacCallum, op. cit., p. 39.

5. MacCallum, op. cit., pp. 57–58.

6. But since the resident of the proprietary community must still presumably abide by certain rules and regulations, and since he must still pay for the services he receives, what is the difference to personal freedom between the proprietary community and the political community? The all-important difference is this: in a proprietary community the individual is subject only to those obligations to which he has voluntarily and explicitly contracted himself; the proprietors are not legally empowered to impose new obligations upon him unilaterally. For example, the proprietors of Laguna Niguel could not, through the process of eminent domain, legally condemn, seize and demolish the home of one of the residents. In short, in a proprietary community individual rights are contractually protected; control of the property is in the hands of the owners, rather than city hall.

7. MacCallum, op. cit., p. 9.

8. See Julia Vitullo-Martin, "The Private Sector Shows How to Run a City," *Wall Street Journal*, May 20, 1998, editorial page.

9. MacCallum, op. cit., p. 75.

10. Ibid, p. 85.

Notes to Chapter 21: Protection: Crime; Fire

1. Robert Ravich, "Man Imprisoned on Fake Evidence Gets $750,000," *Los Angeles Times*, August 13, 1975.

2. William C. Rempel, "Scandals Rock Cook County Sheriff Dept.," *Los Angeles Times*, February 19, 1983, p. 14.

3. Jack Nelson and Ronald Ostrow, "Illegal Drug Scene Spurs Rise in Police Corruption," *Los Angeles Times*, June 13, 1998.

4. Narcotics *legislation*, for example, is more damaging to more people than is narcotics itself. The more numerous victims are not the addicts but their prey—those robbed or assaulted and perhaps killed as addicts seek desperately to support a habit made excessively expensive by foolish laws. All narcotics laws should be stricken from the books. The addict is going to get his stuff anyway; better that he get it at free-market rates than be driven into an endless campaign of violent crime against the rest of us.

5. Ed Meagher, "Private Cops—Growing Force of Watchdogs," *Los Angeles Times*, September 15, 1971.

6. Retribution does not seem to be much of a deterrent. In merry olde England, picking pockets was a hanging offense, yet (so the story goes) pickpockets continued to ply their trade even among the crowds gathered to view the hangings.

7. Bernard Wysocki, Jr., "Hired Guns—One Big Risk Is the Security Gurds, Some Companies Find," *Wall Street Journal*, August 30, 1983.

8. Evelyn DeWolfe, "The Good Life with a Lock on It," *Los Angeles Times*, January 2, 1972.

9. John R. Lott, Jr., *More Guns, Less Crime* (Chicago: University of Chicago Press, 1998). See also the book review by James Bovard, *Wall Street Journal*, May 11, 1998.

10. "Fire and Emergency Medical Services Assessment of Scottsdale, Arizona," by University City Science Center, Philadelphia.

11. Monte Williams, "Public Firefighting Goes Private," *New York Times*, January 31, 1996, B:2.

12. A phone conversation with McQueen. He points out, however, that Rural/Metro has cordial relations with the International Association of Fire Fighters elsewhere around the country.

13. William Glaberson, "Experiment in Private Fire Protection Fails for a Westchester Village," *New York Times*, March 13, 1998, B:1.

14. Bill Storm, "Rural Metro Corporation vs. Public Volunteer Furor," http://creager2.chem.clemson.edu/pulse/a1-2-3.htm

15. Glaberson, op. cit. However, an earlier report indicated that the idea originated with the Port Chester fire department itself. Evidently, neither party will own up to the fact that they refused assistance simply out of spite.

16. Ibid.

Notes to Chapter 22: National Defense

1. 1 Samuel 8:11–8:18, a passage remarked upon by Henry Grady Weaver in *The Mainspring of Human Progress* (Irvington-on-Hudson, N.Y.: Foundation for Economic Education, 1953), pp. 82–83.

2. Related by Thomas Costain in *The Last Plantagenets* (Popular Library Edition, 1953), pp. 120–121.

3. An item once related by Ripley. Believe it or not, Ripley's stories were well researched.

4. J. F. Jameson, *The American Revolution Considered as a Social Move-ment*, p. 103; cited by Harold Faulkner, *American Economic History* (New York: Harper, 1924).

5. Ibid, Faulkner, p. 128.

6. C. Northcote Parkinson, *Parkinson's Law* (Cambridge, Mass.: The Riverside Press, 1957), pp. 7–11.

7. Nor should it be. The fact that foreign governments might seize American assets is simply a business risk. The people concerned should handle the problem themselves. Then, if they do it badly, at least it is they alone who suffer the consequences. If the U.S. Government becomes involved, however, the entire nation will be discredited, as in the U.S. backed coups in Chile and in Guatemala, for example.

8. 56th Congress, 1st Session, Vol. 33, p. 704. Cited by John T. Flynn in *As We Go Marching* (New York: Free Life Editions, 1973), p. 217.

9. Spencer Heath MacCallum, *The Art of Community* (Palo Alto, Calif.: Institute for Humane Studies, 1970), p. 206.

10. These insurance fire companies gradually disappeared from the scene. Because the insurance companies were forced to pay for the city fire departments anyway, they could not afford to support their own departments as well. Another example of how government forces private effort from the field.

11. Quoted in "Big Business: New Voices in World Affairs," *Los Angeles Times*, January 17, 1972.

Notes to Chapter 23: The Proper Role of Government

1. Rose Wilder Lane, *The Discovery of Freedom* (1943. Reprint. San Francisco: Fox & Wilkes, 1993).

2. This has been a sound principle of common law for centuries. For example, a New Hampshire Court declared in 1897, "With purely moral obligations the law does not deal. For example, the priest and the Levite who passed by on the other side were not, it is supposed, liable at law for the continued suffering of the man who fell among thieves, which they might and morally ought to have prevented or relieved." The court then suggested the case of the man who sees a two-year-old child standing on a railroad track as a train approaches. He could easily save the child, but "If he does not, he could perhaps justly be styled a ruthless savage and moral monster, but he is not lia-

ble for damages for the child's injury, or indictable under the statute for the child's death."

3. Henry Thomas Buckle, *History of Civilization in England* (D. Appleton & Co., 1893), p. 498. One wonders what Buckle might have to say about the National Endowment for the Arts.

4. David Horowitz, *The Politics of Bad Faith* (New York: The Free Press, 1998), p. 184.

Notes to Chapter 24: The Limits of Political Action

1. Thomas Sowell, *The Economics and Politics of Race* (New York: William Morrow and Company, Inc., 1983), p. 246.

2. Cited in *The Freeman*, date unknown.

Notes to Chapter 25: Twilight of the State

1. But what are the correct values? This is an important question, of course, but not the subject at the moment. We are not trying to prescribe a particular set of values, but rather the kind of society in which the individual is free to choose, promote and defend his own values, whatever they might be.

2. Albert Speer, *Inside the Third Reich* (New York: Macmillan, Collier edition, 1981), p. 548.

3. From the exchange of correspondence between Rose Wilder Lane and businessman Jasper Crane of the the du Pont Corporation in *The Lady and the Tycoon* (Caldwell, Idaho: Caxton Press, 1973), p. 263.

4. "Your Chances of a Tax Audit," *U.S. News and World Report*, May 15, 1972, p. 50.

5. Henry Manne, "Fighting Back Against Controls," *Reason*, April, 1974.

Index

Fox & Wilkes

Charles James Fox (1749–1806) inherited wealth and guidance from his father, who tutored him in gambling and who advised, "Never do today what you can put off 'til tomorrow." In 1768, just nineteen, the roguish Charles Fox took his seat in Parliament and quickly earned the esteem of his colleagues, Edmund Burke among them. The two joined forces on many causes, including that of the American Revolution, until Burke's horror over the French Revolution occasioned a permanent break. Fox fought for religious toleration, called for abolishing the slave trade, and advocated electoral reform. In defending his views he was a powerful orator, acknowledged as the ablest debater of his day. Neither party nor crown could dissuade him from following his own path. Above all things Fox hated oppression and intolerance, and in his passion for liberty transcended the conventional party politics of his day.

Like Fox, **John Wilkes** (1727–1797), too, could be extravagant in his passions. He married into his money and was an active member of the proudly blasphemous Hellfire Club. A few years after joining Parliament in 1757, he began a weekly journal, *The North Briton*, that became notorious for its wit and wickedness. In the famous issue #45 Wilkes assailed a speech given in the King's name; he was jailed for his temerity. His *Essay On Woman*, an obscene parody of Pope's *Essay On Man*, along with a reprinting of #45, led to further imprisonment and expulsion from Parliament. But the public rioted for his release and kept voting him back into office. Wilkes eventually won substantial damages and set important precedents regarding Parliamentary privilege and seizure of personal papers. After finally being allowed to rejoin Parliament in 1774 as Lord Mayor of London, he introduced libel legislation ensuring rights to jury trial, and continued to fight for religious tolerance and judicial and parliamentary reform. The monument on his grave aptly describes him as a friend of liberty.

Both Fox and Wilkes could be self-indulgent, even reckless in pursuit of their own liberty, but they never let personal foibles hinder them in championing the rights of the individual.